D0948281

OUR IRISH THEATRE

The Coole Edition

General Editors:

T. R. Henn, C.B.E., Litt.D.

Colin Smythe, M.A.

1. Lady Gregory: a photograph taken by Katherine E. McClellan at Smith College, Northampton, Mass. when Lady Gregory lectured there in 1911. Courtesy of the Smith College Archives.

OUR IRISH THEATRE
A CHAPTER OF AUTOBIOGRAPHY
BY LADY GREGORY

with a foreword by
Roger McHugh

COLIN SMYTHE
GERRARDS CROSS
1972

Copyright 1913 by Lady Gregory
This edition copyright © 1972 the Lady Gregory Estate
Foreword copyright © 1972 Colin Smythe Ltd.

1st Published (New York and London) 1913
2nd edition (paperback, offset from 1913 edition) 1965
3rd edition (revised and enlarged) published by
Colin Smythe Ltd, Gerrards Cross, Buckinghamshire
in 1972 as the fourth volume of the Coole Edition

For permission to publish the Bernard Shaw material in this volume, acknowledgement is made to the Society of Authors for the Bernard Shaw Estate.
For permission to publish the John Quinn material, acknowledgement is made to the John Quinn Memorial Collection, Manuscript Division, The New York Public Library, Astor, Lenox & Tilden Foundations.

SBN 900675 284

Printed and bound in Great Britain by
The Garden City Press Limited, Letchworth, Hertfordshire
SG6 1JS

FOREWORD

TOWARDS the end of her days Lady Gregory jotted down a note of the different parts she had played in life; a "questor" for the Lane Pictures, a theatre director, a playwright, a Gaelic Leaguer, a rebel "with the Nationalists all through—more than they know or my nearest realised." In literary activities alone, she might have added several more, including those of folklore collector, provider of versions of our heroic tales, narrator of Kiltartan stories of saints, wonders and historical events, and poet. My task is comparatively a light one. It is to introduce a book whose scope in time is roughly from 1896 to 1913; completed in her sixty-first year, it looks back to the time of her middle forties, perhaps to 1896, for, although she gives her starting-point as 1898, external evidence establishes that the conversations which led to the idea of an Irish Literary Theatre occurred during 1897 and possibly stemmed from earlier talks she had with Yeats, and Edward Martyn at the residence of the Count de Basterot at Duras in 1896. Yeats was certainly busy on the project in Dublin in Autumn 1897, although legal and other technicalities caused over eighteen months' delay before the first production could take place. That span of seventeen years saw the launching of a project conceived by writers who were almost untried as playwrights, its junction with a dedicated group of actors led by the Fay brothers, the foundation of the Abbey Theatre through the generosity of an English patron, Miss Horniman, its successful weathering of storms which blew from opposite points of the compass, and its culminating triumph with two successful American tours. In this book Lady Gregory, like the old woman in her poem,[1] lights her candles of remembrance to these events and to some of the people who made them possible.

Our Irish Theatre is a unique personal account of the establishment of an indigenous Irish theatre. Its exceptional quality lies in its immediacy of impact; not in its general style, which is sometimes scrappy, often discursive, but in the way in which personal reminiscence, correspondence and notes written at the

[1] "An Old Woman Remembers."

time of the events described, discussions of principles and description of people are blended. This is particularly effective in the first chapter and in those dealing with the troubles over *The Playboy, Blanco Posnet* and the American tour; occasions when the course of events was alternately hurried and halted at every hand's turn by circumstances which changed from day to day, sometimes from hour to hour. More leisurely is the chapter on some supporters of the Irish Literary Theatre movement: Sir Frederic Burton, John O'Leary, W. H. Lecky and Douglas Hyde. Her description of them is, I think, moving in the way in which it shows how Irishmen of very different backgrounds and political beliefs could be brought together in a common cause by a woman whose capacity for such binding-force is recorded in Yeats's lines:

> They came like swallows and like swallows went.
> And yet a woman's powerful character
> Could keep a swallow to its first intent . . .[2]

Her own first intent was to be of service to her country. George William Russell wrote that he thought of her as one of a group "who thought in the noblest and most disinterested way about their country, going deeper than those who came after them in time."[3] Besides this sense of national perspective, her sense of Ireland's literary perspective is seen in her article "The Irish Theatre and the People," in which she looks back at the nineteenth century; at the *Nation* poets "roughly hammered links on one chain," at the scholars O'Curry, O'Donovan, O'Daly and Standish Hayes O'Grady, whose work in revealing the treasures of ancient Irish manuscript material preceded that of Standish James O'Grady; and she adds perceptively that "the old culture they were bringing to light has never died, but was fresh and living in the country still." Hence she appreciated the significance of the work of Douglas Hyde in restoring the key language. On the novelists of the nineteenth century she is less sound; she diminishes Carleton, perhaps as a counterbalance to Yeats's somewhat sentimental laudation, and cursorily dismisses Lever whose later novels provide a European context to one of the last remarks in her *Journals*; "But the days of landed property have passed. It is better so." Doubtless she was judging Lever on the basis of his early novels as a propagator of what Yeats called "that comic scarecrow, the stage Irishman," whom the Irish Literary Theatre movement wished to abolish. On the other hand her

2 "Coole Park."
3 Letter to W. B. Yeats, May 23, 1932.

translations of Molière, Goldoni and Sudermann helped to repair the broken link between Irish and continental literature and widened the perspective of Irish dramatists to some extent.

Her chapter on play-writing is illuminating on her collaboration with Yeats and with Hyde and on her own beginnings and development as a dramatist. Her account of Hyde's influence on the folk-play does not quite square with that of Synge, who recorded that Hyde's little play *Casadh an tSugáin* (*The Twisting of the Rope*, 1901) awoke him to the possibilities of the material of the peasant play; that, though slight, it had the germ of a new idea, the folk-play, and so gave a direction and impulse to Irish drama towards which Yeats and Lady Gregory were tending.[4] Such contrasting impressions of a time in which many influences were coalescing are inevitable. In Yeats's preface to *Cuchulain of Muirthemne* (1902) he attributed the discovery of the literary use of distinctive Irish-English speech to Lady Gregory, while Synge in reviewing it, contradicted this and pointed out that Hyde had anticipated her, a fact which Lady Gregory admits, with certain qualifications, in this chapter. None of them was strictly correct, since the groundwork of such discovery had been laid by a number of nineteenth-century novelists; but, as Lady Gregory puts it, poetry is "the apex of the flame" and Hyde's translations lit up the contemporary horizon suddenly and effectively for the real dramatists.

In some ways this chapter is less satisfactory than "Lady Gregory on Play-making"[5] which is more coherent and full of the commonsense to be found also in the Abbey Theatre circular, "Advice to Playwrights." Prentice playwrights can still learn a great deal from it, though maturer dramatists may find her generalisations about tragedy rather *simpliste*. True, Yeats echoes her belief, or she echoes his, that little characterisation is needed in tragedy; but hers seems to rest upon a misconception of Greek tragedy, his upon a criterion based upon a selection of the intense moments of classical and Elizabethan tragedy in which character expands into universality.[6] Hamlet, to whom they both refer, is certainly no puppet and could not expand into something universal had he not first been established in depth as a character. It is in relation to this over-simplification of the psychology of character that one may perceive the validity of part of James Joyce's argument in his pamphlet *The Day of the Rabblement*

[4] Unpublished article of 1906 in Berg Collection, New York Public Library.

[5] See The Lectures of Lady Gregory; Volume 15 of the Coole Edition.

[6] *The Tragic Theatre* (1910).

(1901); it was unjust in its sweeping accusation of Yeats and Lady Gregory for "surrendering to the trolls," but made a strong plea for the production of European masterpieces as models for Irish playwrights; what Yeats dismissed as "the modish interest in psychology" had already proved, as Joyce recognised, a potent instrument in the probing of character in the great tragedies of Ibsen and of Strindberg. I do not know whether Lady Gregory shared his view—her exploration of the character of Grania would perhaps indicate otherwise—but her talent lay in short folk-comedies and these certainly did their work in attracting audiences when they were badly needed.

The editors of this series have thought fit to substitute for the original chapter on Synge in *Our Irish Theatre* her article on him which appeared in the *English Review* and which is slightly longer. Its interest lies mainly in the extracts from Synge's letters which it presents, but it is noteworthy that Synge, as she says, originally intended to open *The Playboy* with the quarrel between Christy and his father; in which case the audience presumably would have shared from the beginning the secret that Old Mahon had not really been slain and the comedy would have had a very different tone. Significantly, although she calls *Riders to the Sea* and *In the Shadow of the Glen* masterpieces, she refrains from any such comment upon *The Playboy*; an example of great tact, for when she was in America, battling bravely in defence of it, she wrote to Hugh Lane, "If you knew how I hate the *Playboy* that I go out fighting for!" Miss Coxhead has rightly pointed out that when in 1921 Lady Gregory published her biography of Lane, she included this remark, which therefore represents her real opinion.[7] The reasons for it may be those which Miss Coxhead adduces, that Lady Gregory was fundamentally a moral writer, sharing with most women writers a predisposition "towards benevolent interference, towards teaching and comforting and setting to rights"—women writers on Lady Gregory herself seem to share this tendency—but if these are the right reasons they would help to account for the fading of interest in all but a handful of her thirty-odd plays. I think myself that her dislike of *The Playboy*, as of Denis Johnston's *The Old Lady Says No* (whose title was literally the message scrawled on his rejected manuscript), was partly due to a very limited critical capacity, largely caused by writing for an unsophisticated audience, and partly to a certain prudishness which is reflected in her bowdlerisation of the heroic tales, and

[7] Elizabeth Coxhead, *Lady Gregory* A Literary Portrait (2nd Edition 1966), 6. 117. (Now only available from Colin Smythe Ltd.)

in her attempts to excise from *The Playboy* such passages as "stretched out retching on the holy stones." All the more credit to her then for her courage in the various "fights" with which *Our Irish Theatre* is largely concerned. Like Swift she loved human liberty and it is chiefly as a "bonny fechter" for the theatre as well as an indefatigable worker in it, in a variety of capacities, that she emerges as a person from its pages.

Our Irish Theatre is, as her letter to Mr. Huntington[8] makes clear, "an expression of personality," given intimacy by the use of many letters written to her and by her. It conveys many of the leading facets of the personality made permanent by various artists; the idealism and dignity of Mancini's portrait, the resolute bravery of A.E.'s, the intelligence shown in the eyes and brow of John Butler Yeats's, and the warrior of many campaigns reflected in the worn face and combative upthrust chin of Epstein's bronze.

Of the literary impressions of her during the span of years, George Moore's is perhaps the most graphic. It was written during a visit to Coole to see Yeats:

> "A middle-aged woman, agreeable to look upon, perhaps for her broad, handsome, intellectual brow enframed in iron-grey hair. The brown, wide-open eyes are often lifted in looks of appeal and inquiry, and a natural wish to sympathise softens her voice until it whines. It modulated, however, very pleasantly as she yielded her attention to Yeats."

There had been an exchange of polite scratches on that occasion and a decade had not removed Moore's memory of them in 1911; not hers either, for Moor's part in helping the Irish Literary Theatre, in finance, in directing, in collaboration and in publicity, is decidedly played down in *Our Irish Theatre*. Moore, who had been associated with the Independent Theatre as a writer and a director of plays had announced in 1898 that psychological drama was the only possible literary drama for that time and had dreamed of making Dublin an intellectual centre for world drama, and I think that his estrangement from both Yeats and Lady Gregory was partly due to their feeling that he represented an aim inimical to theirs.

Her book also does scant justice to the Fay brothers. They had started an Irish school of acting several years before the formation of the Irish Literary Theatre. The news of this stirred them but it was not until 1902 when that movement, essentially a writers' movement, had made little progress that contact was established through J. H. Cousins and A.E. The latter agreed to

[8] See page 257.

finish his *Deirdre* for the Fays, and also, as he recorded, "with a good deal of difficulty I induced Yeats to give them Kathleen Ni Houlihan."[9] Both plays were first produced in April 1902 by W. J. Fay's company. It was at the Fays' suggestion that the Irish National Theatre Society was formed. "I drew up the rules for it at Willie Fay's request," continues A.E.,

> "of course they would never have made the society famous but for the writers like Yeats, Synge and Lady Gregory coming along. But they ought to get the credit for founding the Irish School of Acting, as the writers founded the literary drama. I like Lady Gregory, but she does not know the origins of the National Theatre Society because she was not in Dublin. She writes pleasant gossip, but is as inaccurate as George Moore, almost, in parts where I can check it."

The junction of the writers with the actors produced its own difficulties. The Fays' group were dedicated amateurs, organised on a co-operative basis, and many of its members were actively engaged in nationalist activities. When in 1905 the I.N.T.S. became a limited company, with Yeats, Lady Gregory and Synge as directors, the majority of its original members, including A.E., withdrew and formed the Theatre of Ireland group, whose productions vied with those of the Abbey until 1912, when the Irish Volunteer movement absorbed their interest. The Fays had remained on with the Abbey but the next few years saw continual friction; first over Miss Horniman's insistence on the appointment of an English producer-manager, which caused indiscipline among the players and aroused the Fays' resentment; then, when he had departed, W. G. Fay wanted contracts for the players, so that he could have disciplinary powers over them instead of finding them running to the directors and by-passing his authority. With this, according to Fay, was involved a larger question of policy, that of building up a competent and versatile repertory company. "Of course it would be possible to muddle through in the old way," he wrote, "if we were content to potter along with peasant plays, which would mean stagnation and ultimately, when we found no more pots of broth to boil and no more news to spread, death."[10] But the memorandum which Yeats prepared for the meeting of the directors which was to consider the Fays' practical demands, also stressed the limitations of depending on the popularity of the plays of Lady Gregory and William Boyle (by modern standards a very bad

[9] *Letters from A.E.* ed. Denson, pp. 96-7.
[10] W. G. Fay, *The Fays of the Abbey Theatre* (1935).

playwright) and the necessity of performing continental masterpieces; so the real issue was the authority of W. G. Fay, and when his demands on this score were rejected, he and his brother left.

"I did not much care for Lady Gregory's book *Our Irish Theatre*, she centralises herself a great deal too much," wrote Russell to Quinn; but it is difficult to see how she could have written it at all if she had not done so. It is not, nor does it claim to be, a history of the Irish Theatre: but it is much more readable than the official history commissioned by the Abbey Theatre authorities and "compiled" by Lennox Robinson[11] and some day will help to provide the material for a proper history. Meanwhile, in the years since its first appearance, a number of books have helped towards this end; notably Una Ellis-Fermor's *The Irish Dramatic Movement* (1939), Máire Nic Shiubhlaigh's *The Splendid Years* (1955) and Gerard Fay's *The Abbey Theatre, Cradle of Genius* (1958). Interest in Lady Gregory has also been revived by Elizabeth Coxhead's *Lady Gregory* (1961), by Ann Saddlemyer's *In Defence of Lady Gregory, Playwright* (1966), and by many illuminating references to her in B. L. Reid's *The Man from New York* (1968), a biography of John Quinn, who shared her American battles for *The Playboy*. O'Casey's autobiographies describe her in her seventies and, perhaps surprisingly, reveal a rapport with her which he did not feel with Yeats or A.E. He describes her affectionately but exactly, even to the reproduction of her curious lisping speech, which must have played havoc with her lines on the occasion when she stood-in for Máire Nic Shiubhlaigh in the title-rôle of Kathleen ni Houlihan.[12] Her remark on that occasion was typical; "after all, what is wanted but a hag and a voice?"

Yet, when all is said and done, this appearance does not lack its symbolic value. She had helped transform the Irish literary scene by a complete and disinterested "series of enthusiasms," as she called her life. They were linked strongly by the continuing purpose of serving their country without lowering its standards, and it was only fitting that when Yeats accepted the world's highest literary award in 1923, he visualised Synge and Lady Gregory, who were bound to him by that common purpose, standing by his side.

ROGER McHUGH

[11] *Ireland's Abbey Theatre: A History 1899–1951* (Sidgwick & Jackson 1951)

[12] *The Splendid Years*, p. 30.

CONTENTS

APPENDICES

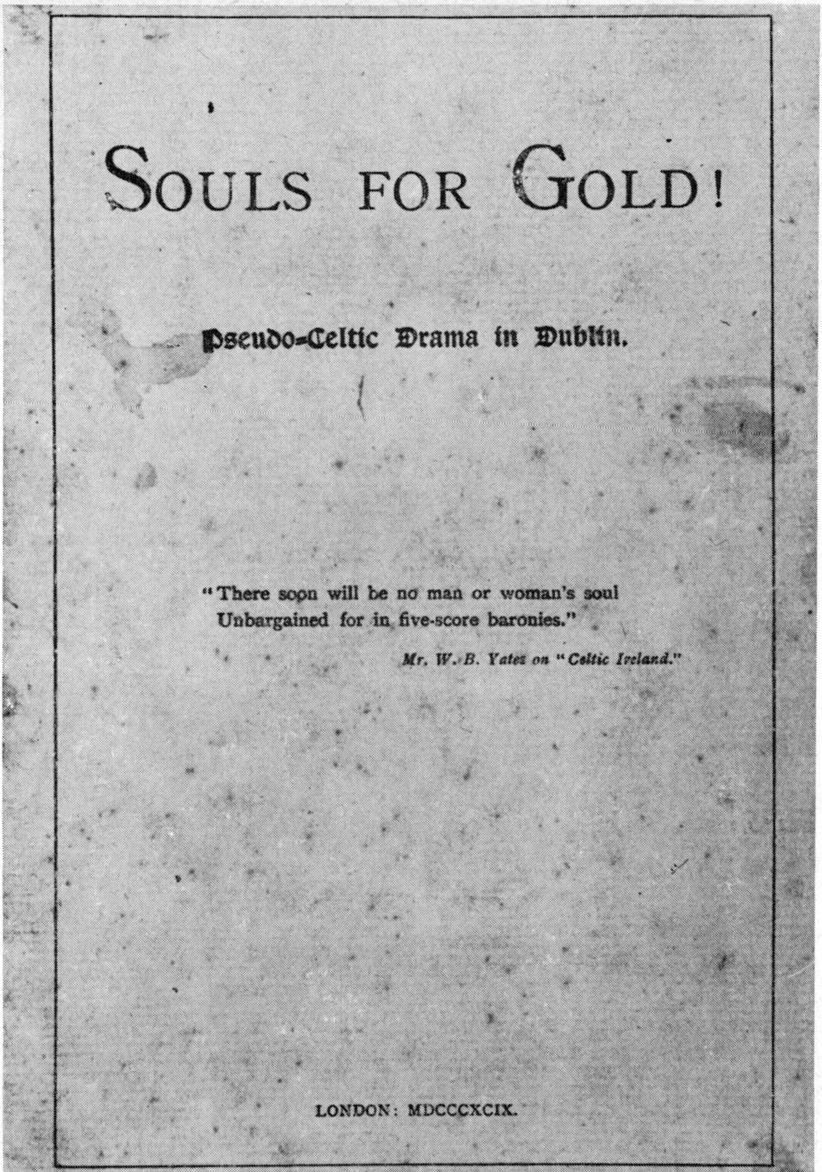

SOULS FOR GOLD!

Pseudo-Celtic Drama in Dublin.

"There soon will be no man or woman's soul
Unbargained for in five-score baronies."

Mr. W. B. Yates on "Celtic Ireland."

LONDON: MDCCCXCIX.

1a. The cover of *Souls for Gold* by Frank Hugh O'Donnell. See Appendix VIII.

1b. W. B. Yeats, J. M. Synge and G. W. Russell (A.E.) fishing on Coole Lake. Drawn by H. Oakley. Courtesy of Major Richard Gregory.

ILLUSTRATIONS

OUR IRISH THEATRE

I

THE THEATRE IN THE MAKING

To Richard Gregory.—Little Grandson: When I go into the garden in the morning to find you a nectarine or tell you the names of flowers, Catalpa, Love-lies-bleeding, Balsam, Phlox, you ask me why I cannot stay but must go back to the house, and when I say it is to write letters, you ask, "What for?" And when winter comes, you will ask me why I must go away over the sea instead of waiting for your Christmas stocking and your tree.

The other day I was sitting outside the door, where the sweet-peas grow, with an old man, and when you came and called me he got up to go away, and as he wished me good-bye, he said: "They were telling me you are going to America, and says I, 'Whatever the Lady does, I am certain she is doing nothing but what she thinks to be right.' And that the Lord may keep you safe and protect you from the power of your enemy."

Some day when I am not here to answer, you will maybe ask, "What were they for, the writing, the journeys, and why did she have an enemy?" So I will put down the story now, that you may know all about it bye and bye.

FOURTEEN or fifteen years ago I still wrote from time to time in a diary I used to keep till the sand in the hour-glass on my table began to run so fast that I had to lay by the book as well as embroidery, and archaeology, and drying lavender, and visits to the houses of friends.

I was in London in the beginning of 1898, and I find written, "Yeats and Sir Alfred Lyall to tea, Yeats stayed on. He is full of playwriting. . . . He with the aid of Miss Florence Farr, an actress who thinks more of a romantic than of a paying play, is very keen about taking or building a little theatre somewhere in the suburbs to produce romantic drama, his own plays, Edward Martyn's, one of Bridges', and he is trying to stir up Standish O'Grady and Fiona Macleod to write some. He believes there will be a reaction after the realism of Ibsen, and romance will have its turn. He has put a 'great deal of himself' into his own play

The Shadowy Waters and rather startled me by saying about half his characters have eagles' faces."

Later in the year I was staying for a few days with the old Count de Basterot, at Duras, that is beyond Kinvara and beside the sea. He had been my husband's warm friend, and always in the summer time we used to go and spend at least one long day with him,—we two at first, and then later I went with my son and the boy and girl friends of his childhood. They liked to go out in a hooker and see the seals showing their heads, or to paddle delicately among the jellyfish on the beach. It was a pleasant place to pass an idle day. The garden was full of flowers. Lavender and carnations grew best, and there were roses also and apple trees, and many plums ripened on the walls. This seemed strange, because outside the sheltered garden there were only stone-strewn fields and rocks and bare rock-built hills in sight, and the bay of Galway, over which fierce storms blow from the Atlantic. The Count remembered when on Garlic Sunday men used to ride races, naked, on unsaddled horses out into the sea; but that wild custom had long been done away with by decree of the priests. Later still, when Harrow and Oxford took my son away and I had long spaces of time alone, I would sometimes go to Duras to spend a few days.

I always liked to talk and listen to the Count. He could tell me about French books and French and Italian history and politics, for he lived but for the summer months in Ireland and for the rest of the year in Paris or in Rome. Mr. Arthur Symons has written of him and his talks of race,—to which he attributed all good or bad habits and politics—as they took long drives on the Campagna. M. Paul Bourget came more than once to stay in this Burren district, upon which he bestowed a witty name, "Le Royaume de Pierre." It was to M. Bourget that, on his way to the modest little house and small estate, the Count's old steward and servant introduced the Atlantic, when on the road from the railway station at Gort its waters first come in sight: *Voila la mer qui baigne l'Amérique et les terres de Monsieur le Comte.* For he—the steward—had been taken by his master on visits to kinsmen in France and Italy—their names are recorded in that sad, pompous, black-bordered document I received one day signed by those who have *l'honneur de vous faire part de la perte douloureuse qu'ils viennent d,éprouver en la personne de Florimond Alfred Jacques, Comte de Basterot, Chevalier de l'ordre du Saint Sépulcre, leur cousin germain et cousin* [who died at Duras (Irland) September 15, 1904]; *la Marquise de la Tour Maubourg, le Vicomte et la Vicomtesse de*

Bussy, la Baronne d'Acker de Montgaston, le Marquis et la Marquise de Courcival, le Comte et la Comtesse Gromis de Trana, la Comtesse Irène d' Entrèves, and so on, and so on. I do not know whether the bearers of these high-sounding names keep him in their memory—it may well be that they do, for he was a friend not easily forgotten—but I know there is many a prayer still said on the roads between Kinvara and Burren and Curranroe and Ballinderreen for him who "never was without a bag of money to give in charity, and always had a heart for the poor."

On one of those days at Duras in 1898,[1] Mr. Edward Martyn, my neighbour, came to see the Count, bringing with him Mr. Yeats, whom I did not then know very well, though I cared for his work very much and had already, through his directions, been gathering folk-lore. They had lunch with us, but it was a wet day, and we could not go out. After a while I thought the Count wanted to talk to Mr. Martyn alone; so I took Mr. Yeats to the office where the steward used to come to talk,—less about business I think than of the Land War or the state of the country, or the last year's deaths and marriages from Kinvara to the headland of Aughanish. We sat there through that wet afternoon, and though I had never been at all interested in theatres, our talk turned on plays. Mr. Martyn had written two, *The Heather Field* and *Maeve*. They had been offered to London managers, and now he thought of trying to have them produced in Germany where there seemed to be more room for new drama than in England. I said it was a pity we had no Irish theatre where such plays could be given. Mr. Yeats said that had always been a dream of his, but he had of late thought it an impossible one, for it could not at first pay its way, and there was no money to be found for such a thing in Ireland.

We went on talking about it, and things seemed to grow possible as we talked, and before the end of the afternoon we had made our plan. We said we would collect money, or rather ask to have a certain sum of money guaranteed. We would then take a Dublin theatre and give a performance of Mr. Martyn's *Heather Field* and one of Mr. Yeats's own plays, *The Countess Cathleen.* I offered the first guarantee of £25.

A few days after that I was back at Coole, and Mr. Yeats came over from Mr. Martyn's home, Tillyra, and we wrote a formal letter to send out. We neither of us write a very clear hand, but a friend had just given me a Remington typewriter and I was learning to use it, and I wrote out the letter with its help. That typewriter has done a great deal of work since that

[1] In fact 1897.

day, making it easy for the printers to read my plays and translations, and Mr. Yeats's plays and essays, and sometimes his poems. I have used it also for many, many hundreds of letters that have had to be written about theatre business in each of these last fifteen years. It has gone with me very often up and down to Dublin and back again, and it went with me even to America last year that I might write my letters home. And while I am writing the leaves are falling, and since I have written those last words on its keys, she who had given it to me has gone. She gave me also the great gift of her friendship through more than half my lifetime, Enid, Lady Layard, Ambassadress at Constantinople and Madrid, helper of the miserable and the wounded in the Turkish-Russian war; helper of the sick in the hospital she founded at Venice, friend and hostess and guest of queens in England and Germany and Rome. She was her husband's good helpmate while he lived—is not the Cyprus treaty set down in that clear handwriting I shall never see coming in here again? And widowed, she kept his name in honour, living after him for fifteen years, and herself leaving a noble memory in all places where she had stayed, and in Venice where her home was and where she died.

Our statement—it seems now a little pompous—began:

"We propose to have performed in Dublin in the spring of every year certain Celtic and Irish plays, which whatever be their degree of excellence will be written with a high ambition, and so to build up a Celtic and Irish school of dramatic literature. We hope to find in Ireland an uncorrupted and imaginative audience trained to listen by its passion for oratory, and believe that our desire to bring upon the stage the deeper thoughts and emotions of Ireland will ensure for us a tolerant welcome, and that freedom to experiment which is not found in theatres of England, and without which no new movement in art or literature can succeed. We will show that Ireland is not the home of buffoonery and of easy sentiment, as it has been represented, but the home of an ancient idealism. We are confident of the support of all Irish people, who are weary of misrepresentation, in carrying out a work that is outside all the political questions that divide us."

I think the word "Celtic" was put in for the sake of Fiona Macleod whose plays however we never acted, though we used to amuse ourselves by thinking of the call for "author" that might follow one, and the possible appearance of William Sharp in place of the beautiful woman he had given her out to be, for even then we had little doubt they were one and the same person.

I myself never quite understood the meaning of the "Celtic Movement," which we were said to belong to. When I was asked about it, I used to say it was a movement meant to persuade the Scotch to begin buying our books, while we continued not to buy theirs.

We asked for a guarantee fund of £300 to make the experiment, which we hoped to carry on during three years. The first person I wrote to was the old poet, Aubrey de Vere. He answered very kindly, saying, "Whatever develops the genius of Ireland, must in the most effectual way benefit her; and in Ireland's genius I have long been a strong believer. Circumstances of very various sorts have hitherto tended much to retard the development of that genius; but it cannot fail to make itself recognised before very long, and Ireland will have cause for gratitude to all those who have hastened the coming of that day."

I am glad we had this letter, carrying as it were the blessing of the generation passing away to that which was taking its place. He was the first poet I had ever met and spoken with; he had come in my girlhood to a neighbour's house. He was so gentle, so fragile, he seemed to have been wafted in by that "wind from the plains of Athenry" of which he wrote in one of his most charming little poems. He was of the Lake School, and talked of Wordsworth, and I think it was a sort of courtesy or deference to him that I determined to finish reading *The Excursion,* which though a reader of poetry it had failed me, as we say, to get through. At last one morning I climbed up to a wide wood, Grobawn, on one of the hillsides of Slieve Echtge, determined not to come down again until I had honestly read every line. I think I saw the sun set behind the far-off Connemara hills before I came home, exhausted but triumphant! I have a charming picture of Aubrey de Vere in my mind as I last saw him, at a garden party in London. He was walking about, having on his arm, in the old-world style, the beautiful Lady Somers, lovely to the last as in Thackeray's day, and as I had heard of her from many of that time, and as she had been painted by Watts.

Some gave us their promise with enthusiasm but some from good will only, without much faith that an Irish Theatre would ever come to success. One friend, a writer of historical romance, wrote: "October 15th. I enclose a cheque for £1, but confess it is more as a proof of regard for *you* than of belief in the drama, for I cannot with the best wish in the world to do so, feel hopeful on that subject. My experience has been that any attempt at treating Irish history is a fatal handicap, not to say absolute *bar,* to anything in the shape of popularity, and I cannot see how any drama can flourish which is not to some degree supported by the public, as it is even more dependent on it than literature is. There *are* popular Irish dramatists, of course, and *very* popular ones, but then unhappily they did not treat of Irish subjects, and *The School for Scandal* and *She Stoops to Conquer* would hardly come under your category. You will think me very discouraging, but I cannot help it, and I am also afraid that putting plays experimentally on the boards is a very costly entertainment. Where will they be acted in the first instance? And has any stage manager undertaken to produce them? Forgive my tiresomeness; it does not come from want of sympathy, only from a little want of hope, the result of experience."

"October 19th: I seize the opportunity of writing again as I am afraid you will have thought I wrote such a unsympathetic letter. It is not, believe me, that I would not give anything to see Irish literature and Irish drama taking a good place, as it ought to do, and several of the authors you name I admire extremely. It is only from the practical and *paying* point of view that I feel it to be rather rash. Plays cost more, I take it, to produce than novels, and one would feel rather rash if one brought out a novel at one's own risk."

I think the only actual refusals I had were from three members of the Upper House. I may give their words as types of the discouragement which we have often met with from friends: "I need not, I am sure, tell you how I gladly would take part in anything for the honour of Old Ireland and especially anything of the kind in which you feel an interest; but I must tell you frankly that I do not much believe in the movement about which you have written to me. I have no sympathy, you will be horrified to hear, with the 'London Independent Theatre', and I am sure that if Ibsen and Co. could know what is in my mind, they would regard me as a 'Philistine' of the coarsest class! Alas! so far from wishing to see the Irish characters of Charles Lever supplanted by more refined types, they have always been the delight of my heart, and there is no author in whose healthy, rollicking company, even nowadays, I spend a spare hour with more thorough enjoyment. I am very sorry that I cannot agree with you in these matters, and I am irreclaimable; but all the same I remain with many pleasant remembrances and good wishes for you and yours, Yours very truly——"

Another, the late Lord Ashbourne, wrote: "I know too little of the matter or the practicability of the idea to be able to give my name to your list, but I shall watch the experiment with interest and be glad to attend. The idea is novel and curious and how far it is capable of realisation I am not at all in a position to judge. Some of the names you mention are well known in literature but not as dramatists or playwriters, and therefore the public will be one to be worked up by enthusiasm and love of country. The existing class of actors will not, of course, be available, and the existing playgoers are satisfied with their present attractions. Whether 'houses' can be got to attend the new plays, founded on new ideas and played by new actors, no one can foretell."

One, who curiously has since then become an almost too zealous supporter of our theatre, says: "I fear I am not too sanguine about the success in a pecuniary way of a 'Celtic Theatre' nor am I familiar with the works, dramatic or otherwise, of Mr. Yeats or of Mr. Martyn. Therefore, at the risk of branding myself in your estimation as a hopeless Saxon and Philistine, I regret I cannot see my way to giving my name to the enterprise or joining in the guarantee." On the other hand, Professor Mahaffy says, rather unexpectedly, writing from Trinity College: "I am ready to risk £5 for your scheme and hope they may yet play their drama in Irish. It will be as intelligible to the nation as Italian, which we so often hear upon our stage."

And many joined who had seemed too far apart to join in any scheme. Mr. William Hartpole Lecky sent a promise of £5 instead of the £1 I had asked. Lord Dufferin, Viceroy of India and Canada, Ambassador at Paris, Constantinople, St. Petersburg, and Rome, not only promised but sent his guarantee in advance. I returned it later, for the sums guaranteed were never called for, Mr. Martyn very generously making up all loss. Miss Jane Barlow, Miss Emily Lawless, the Lord Chancellor of Ireland ("Peter the Packer" as he was called by Nationalists), John O'Leary, Mr. T. M. Healy, Lord and Lady Ardilaun, the Duchess of St. Albans, Doctor Douglas Hyde, the Rt. Hon. Horace Plunkett, Mr. John Dillon, M.P., all joined. Mr. John Redmond supported us, and afterwards wrote me a letter of commendation with leave to use it. Mr. William O'Brien was another supporter. I did not know him personally but I remember one day long ago going to tea at the Speaker's house, after I had heard him in a debate, and saying I thought him the most stirring speaker of all the Irish party, and I was amused when my gentle and dignified hostess, Mrs. Peel, said, "I quite agree with you. When I hear William O'Brien make a speech, I feel that if I were an Irishwoman, I should like to go and break windows."

Then Mr. Yeats and Mr Martyn went to Dublin to make preparations, but the way was unexpectedly blocked by the impossibility of getting a theatre. The only Dublin theatres, the Gaiety, the Royal, and the Queen's, were engaged far ahead, and in any case we could not have given them their price. Then we thought of taking a hall or a concert room, but there again we met with disappointment. We found there was an old Act in existence, passed just before the Union, putting a fine of £300 upon any one who should give a performance for money in any unlicensed building. As the three large theatres were the only buildings licensed, a claim for a special licence would have to be argued by lawyers, charging lawyer's fees, before the Privy Council. We found that even amateurs who acted for charities were forced to take one of the licensed theatres, so leaving but little profit for the charity. There were suggestions made of forming a society like the Stage Society in London, to give performances to its members only, but this would not have been a fit beginning for the National Theatre of our dreams. I wrote in a letter at that time: "I am all for having the Act repealed or a Bill brought in, empowering the Municipality to license halls when desirable." And although this was looked on as a counsel of perfection, it was actually done within the year. I wrote to Mr. Lecky for advice and help, and he told me there was a Bill actually going through the House of Commons, the Local Government (Ireland) Bill, in which he thought it possible a clause might be inserted that would meet our case. Mr John Redmond and Mr. Dillon promised their help; so did Mr. T. M. Healy, who wrote to Mr. Yeats: "I am acquainted with the state of the law in Dublin which I should gladly assist to alter as proposed. Whether the Government are equally well disposed may be doubted, as the subject is a little outside their Bill, and no adequate time exists for discussing it and many other important questions. They will come up about midnight or later and will be yawned out of hearing by our masters."

A Clause was drawn up by a Nationalist member, Mr. Clancy, but in July, 1898, Mr. Lecky writes from the House of Commons: "I have not been forgetting the Celtic Theatre and I think the enclosed Clause, which the Government have brought forward, will practically meet its requirements. The Attorney-General objected to Mr. Clancy's Clause as too wide and as interfering with existing patent rights, but promised a Clause authorising amateur acting. I wrote to him, however, stating the Celtic case, and urging that writers should be able, like those who got up the Ibsen plays in London, to get regular actors to play for them, and I think this Clause will allow it. . . . After Clause 59 insert the following Clause: (1) Notwithstanding anything in the Act of Parliament of Ireland of the twenty-sixth year of King George the Third, Chapter fifty-seven, intituled an Act for regulating the stage in the city and county of Dublin, the Lord Lieutenant may on the application of the council for the county of Dublin or the county borough of Dublin grant an occasional license for the performance of any stage play or other dramatic entertainment in any theatre, room or building where the profits arising therefrom are to be applied for charitable purpose or in aid of funds of any society instituted for the purpose of science, literature, or the fine arts exclusively. (2) The license may contain such conditions and regulations as appear fit to the Lord Lieutenant, and may be revoked by him."

This Clause was passed but we are independent now of it,—the Abbey Theatre holds its own Patent. But the many amateur societies which play so often here and there in Dublin may well call for a blessing sometimes on the names of those by whom their charter was won.

We announced our first performance for May 8, 1899, nearly a year after that talk on the Galway coast, at the Ancient Concert Rooms. Mr. Yeats's *Countess Cathleen* and Mr. Martyn's *Heather Field* were the plays chosen, as we had planned at the first. Mr. George Moore gave excellent help in finding actors, and the plays were rehearsed in London. But then something unexpected happened. A writer who had a political quarrel with Mr. Yeats sent out a pamphlet in which he attacked *The Countess Cathleen*, on the ground of religious unorthodoxy. The plot of the play, taken from an old legend, is this: during a famine in Ireland some starving country people, having been tempted by demons dressed as merchants to sell their souls for money that their bodies may be saved from perishing, the Countess Cathleen sells her own soul to redeem theirs, and dies. The accusation made was that it was a libel on the people of Ireland to say that they could under any circumstances consent to sell their souls and that it was a libel on the demons that they counted the soul of a countess of more worth than those of the poor. At Cathleen's death the play tells us, "God looks on the intention, not the deed," and so she is forgiven at the last and taken into Heaven; and this it was said is against the teaching of the Church.

Mr. Martyn is an orthodox Catholic, and to quiet his mind, the play was submitted to two good Churchmen. Neither found heresy enough in it to call for its withdrawal. One of them, the Rev. Dr. Barry, the author of *The New Antigone*, wrote:

"BRIDGE HOUSE, WALLINGFORD,
"March 26, 1899."

"DEAR MR. YEATS,

"I read your *Countess Cathleen* as soon as possible after seeing you. It is beautiful and touching. I hope you will not be kept back from giving it by foolish talk. Obviously, from the literal point of view theologians, Catholic or other, would object that no one is free to sell his soul in order to buy bread even for the starving. But St. Paul says, 'I wish to be anathema for my brethren'; which is another way of expressing what you have put into a story. I would give the play first and explanations afterwards.

"Sometimes perhaps you will come and spend a night here and I shall be charmed. But don't take a superfluous journey now. It is an awkward place to get at. I could only tell you, as I am doing, that if people will not read or look at a play of this kind in the spirit which dictated it, no change you might make would satisfy them. You have given us what is really an Auto, in the manner of Calderon, with the old Irish folk-lore as a perceptive; and to measure it by the iron rule of experts and schoolmen would be most unfair to it. Some one else will say that you have learned from the Jesuits to make the end justify the means—and much that man will know of you or the Jesuits. With many kind wishes for your success, and fraternal greetings in the name of Ireland,

"Ever yours,
"WILLIAM BARRY."

So our preparations went on. Mr. Yeats wrote a little time before the first performance: "Everybody tells me we are going to have good audiences. My play, too, in acting goes wonderfully well. The actors are all pretty sound. The first Demon is a little over-violent and restless but he will improve. Lionel Johnson has done a prologue which I enclose."

That prologue, written by so Catholic and orthodox a poet, was spoken before the plays at the Ancient Concert Rooms on May 8, 1899:

The May fire once on every dreaming hill
All the fair land with burning bloom would fill;
All the fair land, at visionary night,
Gave loving glory to the Lord of Light.
Have we no leaping flames of Beltaine praise
To kindle in the joyous ancient ways;
No fire of song, of vision, of white dream,
Fit for the Master of the Heavenly Gleam;

For him who first made Ireland move in chime
Musical from the misty dawn of time?

Ah, yes; for sacrifice this night we bring
The passion of a lost soul's triumphing;
All rich with faery airs that, wandering long,
Uncaught, here gather into Irish song;
Sweet as the old remembering winds that wail,
From hill to hill of gracious Inisfail;
Sad as the unforgetting winds that pass
Over her children in her holy grass
At home, and sleeping well upon her breast,
Where snowy Deirdre and her sorrows rest.

Come, then, and keep with us an Irish feast,
Wherein the Lord of Light and Song is priest;
Now, at this opening of the gentle May,
Watch warring passions at their storm and play;
Wrought with the flaming ecstasy of art,
Sprung from the dreaming of an Irish heart.

But alas! His call to "watch warring passions at their storm and play," was no vain one. The pamphlet, *Souls for Gold*, had been sent about, and sentences spoken by the demons in the play and given detached from it were quoted as Mr. Yeats' own unholy beliefs. A Cardinal who confessed he had read none of the play outside these sentences condemned it. Young men from the Catholic University were roused to come and make a protest against this "insult to their faith." There was hooting and booing in the gallery. In the end the gallery was lined with police, for an attack on the actors was feared. They, being English and ignorant of Ireland, found it hard to understand the excitement, but they went through their parts very well. There was enthusiasm for both plays, and after the first night London critics were sent over, Mr. Max Beerbohm among them, and gave a good report. Yet it was a stormy beginning for our enterprise, and a rough reception for a poetic play. The only moment, I think, at which I saw Mr. Yeats really angry was at the last performance. I was sitting next him, and the play had reached the point where the stage direction says, "The Second Merchant goes out through the door and returns with the hen strangled. He flings it on the floor." The merchant came in indeed, but without the strangled hen. Mr. Yeats got up, filled with suspicions that it also might have been objected to on some unknown ground, and went round to the back of the stage. But he was given a simple explanation. The chief Demon said he had been given charge of the hen, and had hung it out of a window every night, "And this morning," he said, "when I pulled up the string, there was nothing on it at all."

But that battle was not a very real one. We have put on *Countess Cathleen* a good many times of late with no one speaking against it at all. And some of those young men who hissed it then are our good supporters now.

The next year English actors were again brought over to play, this time in the Gaiety Theatre. A little play by Miss Milligan, *The Last Feast of the Fianna* was given, and Mr. Martyn's *Maeve*, and on alternate nights *The Bending of the Bough*, founded by Mr. George Moore on Mr. Martyn's *Tale of a Town*. They were produced on the evening of February 20, 1900. "On the evening before the production," I wrote, "Mr. Yeats gave a little address on the play, *Maeve*, in which he said there is a wonderful literary invention, that of Peg Inerny, the old woman in rags in the daytime, but living another and second life, a queen in the ideal world, a symbol of Ireland. The financial question touched in *The Bending of the Bough* was chosen, because on it all parties are united, but it means really the cause nearest to each of our hearts. The materialism of England and its vulgarity are surging up about us. It is not Shakespeare England sends us, but musical farces, not Keats and Shelley, but *Titbits*. A mystic friend of his had a dream in which he saw a candle whose flame was in danger of being extinguished by a rolling sea. The waves sometimes seemed to go over it and quench it, and he knew it to be his own soul and that if it was quenched, he would have lost his soul. And now our ideal life is in danger from the sea of commonness about us."

The Bending of the Bough was the first play dealing with a vital Irish question that had appeared in Ireland. There was a great deal of excitement over it. My diary says: "M. is in great enthusiasm over it, says it will cause a revolution. H. says no young man can see that play and leave the house as he came into it. . . . The Gaelic League in great force sang *Fainne Geal an Lae* between the acts, and *The Wearing of the Green* in Irish! And when 'author' could not appear there were cries of 'An Craoibhin,' and cheers were given for Hyde. The actors say they never played to so appreciative an audience, but were a little puzzled at the applause, not understanding the political allusions. The play hits so impartially all round that no one is really offended, certainly not the Nationalists and we have not heard that Unionists are either. Curiously, *Maeve*, which we didn't think a Nationalist play at all, has turned out to be one, the audience understanding and applauding the allegory. There is such applause at 'I am only an old woman but I tell you that Erin will never be subdued' that Lady ——, who was at a performance, reported to the Castle that they had better boycott it, which they have done. G. M. is, I think a little puzzled by his present political position, but I tell him and E. Martyn we are not working for Home Rule; we are preparing for it."

In our third year, 1901, Mr. F. R. Benson took our burden on his shoulders and gave a fine performance of *Diarmuid and Grania*, an heroic play by Mr. George Moore and Mr. Yeats. I wrote: "I am so glad to hear of Benson's appreciation. Anyhow, he can hardly be supposed to be on the side of incendiarism; he is so very respectable. Trinity College won't know whether to go or to stay away." Mr. Yeats wrote: "Yesterday we were rehearsing at the Gaiety. The kid Benson is to carry in his arms was wandering in and out among the stage properties. I was saying to myself, 'Here are we, a lot of intelligent people who might have been doing some sort of decent work that leaves the soul free; yet here we are, going through all sorts of trouble and annoyance for a mob that knows neither literature nor art. I might have been away, away in the country, in Italy perhaps, writing poems for my equals and my betters. That kid is the only sensible creature on the stage. He knows his business and keeps to it.' At that very moment one of the actors called out, 'Look at the kid, eating the property ivy!' "

This time also we produced Casadh-an-tSugáin, (*The Twisting of the Rope*) by the founder of the Gaelic League, Dr. Douglas Hyde. He himself acted the chief part in it and even to those who had no Irish, the performance was a delight, it was played with so much gaiety, ease, and charm. It was the first time a play written in Irish had ever been seen in a Dublin theatre.

Our three years' experiment had ended, and we hesitated what to do next. But a breaking and rebuilding is often for the best, and so it was now. We had up to this time, as I have said, played only once a year, and had engaged actors from London, some of them Irish certainly, but all London-trained. The time had come to play oftener and to train actors of our own. For Mr. Yeats had never ceased attacking the methods of the ordinary theatre, in gesture, in staging, and in the speaking of verse. It happened there were two brothers living in Dublin, William and Frank Fay, who had been in the habit of playing little farces in coffee palaces and such like in their spare time. William had a genius for comedy, Frank's ambitions were for the production of verse. They, or one of them, had thought of looking for work in America, but had seen our performances, and thought something might be done in the way of creating a school of acting in Ireland. They came to us at this time and talked matters over. They had work to do in the daytime and could only rehearse at night. The result was that Mr. Yeats gave his *Kathleen ni Houlihan* to be produced by Mr. Fay at the same time as a play by Mr. George Russell (A.E.), in St. Theresa's Hall, Clarendon Street. I had written to Mr. Yeats: "If all breaks up, we must try and settle something with Fay, possibly a week of the little play he has been doing through the spring. I have a sketch in my head that might do for Hyde to work on. I will see if it is too slight when I have noted it down, and if not, will send it to you."

Early, in 1902, Mr. Russell wrote to me: "I have finished *Deirdre* at last. Heaven be praised! in the intervals of railway journeys, and the Fays are going to do their best with it. I hope I shall not suffer too much in the process, but I prefer them to English actors as they are in love with their story." A little hall in Camden Street was hired for rehearsal, Mr. Russell writing in the same year: "I will hand cheque to Fay. I know it will be a great assistance to them as the little hall will require alterations and fittings and as none of the Company are in possession of more than artisan's wages. They have elected W.B.Y. as president of the Irish National Dramatic Society, and A.E. as vice-president, and we are the gilding at the prow of the vessel. They have begun work already and are reading and rehearsing drama for the autumn."

Mr. Fay was very hopeful and full of courage. He wrote in December, 1902: "I have received your letter and parcel. I am not doing this show on a large scale as I am leaving *The Hour-glass* off till the middle of January. . . . I am just giving a show of *The Pot of Broth*, *The Foundations*, and *Elis and the Beggarman*, and I'm not making a fuss about it, as I want to try how many people the hall will hold, and what prices suit best, so it is more or less an experimental show and then, about the middle of January, I will do the first real show with *The Hour-glass* as principal feature. The hall took a great deal of work to get right, and as we had to do all the work ourselves, we had very little time to rehearse." And he says later: "I received your kind note, also enclosures, for which we are very much obliged. We are indeed getting into very flourishing conditions, and if things only continue in the present state, I have no doubt we shall be able to show a fairly good balance at the end of the year. I have all but concluded an arrangement with a branch of the Gaelic League to take our hall for three nights a week, and that will leave us under very small rental if it comes off. About the performance and how it worked out. I spent twenty-five shillings on printing, etc., and we took altogether about four pounds fifteen shillings, so I see no reason to complain financially. But I find the stage very small, and the want of dressing-rooms makes it very difficult to manage about the scenery, as all your actors have to stand against the walls while it is being changed. I think, however, we can struggle through if we don't attempt very large pieces. The hall was rather cold, but I think I can manage a stove and get over that."

That show of *The Hour-glass* went well, and in that year—1903—two of Mr. Yeats's verse plays were produced, *The King's Threshold* and *Shadowy Waters*. In that year also, new names came in, my own with *Twenty-five*, Mr. Padraic Colum's with *Broken Soil*, and that of J. M. Synge with *The Shadow of the Glen*. I wrote to Mr. Yeats, who was then in America: "After *Shadow of the Glen* your sisters and Synge came in and had some supper with me. Your sister had asked one of her work girls how she liked Synge's comedy, and she said, 'Oh, very well. I had been thinking of writing a story on that subject myself.' They asked quite a little girl if she thought the girl in Colum's play ought to have stayed with her lover or gone with her father. 'She was right to go with her father.' 'Why?' 'Because her young man had such a big beard.' 'But he might have cut it off.' 'That would be no good. He was so dark he would look blue if he did that.' Saturday night brought a larger audience and all went well. The few I knew, Harvey, etc., were quite astonished at the beauty of *Shadowy Waters*, and some giggling young men behind were hushed almost at once, and I heard them saying afterwards how beautiful it was. I should like to hear it once a week through the whole year. The only vexing part was Aibric's helmet, which has immense horns. A black shadow of these was thrown down, and when Aibric moved, one got the impression there was a he-goat going to butt at him over the side of the ship." And again from Coole: "Synge wrote asking me if I could provide four red petticoats, Aran men's caps, a spinning-wheel, and some Connacht person in Dublin who will teach the players to keen. The last item is the most difficult. All the actors want pampooties (the cowskin shoes worn by the Aran people), though I warned them the smell is rather overpowering. Tell Mr. Quinn what a great comfort his money is for such things as these, upon which the company might think they ought not to spend their little capital, and Synge would have been unhappy without." Through the nuns at Gort I heard of a spinning-wheel in a cottage some way off, which, though it had been in her family over a hundred years, the owner wanted to sell. A cart was sent for this, and we have had it in the theatre ever since. As to the keening I found a Galway woman near Dublin who promised to teach the actors. But when they arrived at her house, she found herself unable to raise the keen in her living room. They had all to go upstairs, and the secretary of the company had to lie under a sheet as the corpse. The lessons were very successful, and at the first performance in London of *Riders to the Sea*, the pit went away keening down the street.

Mr. Yeats said of Mr. Fay and his little company, "They did what amateurs seldom do, worked desperately." This was the beginning of a native school of acting, an Irish dramatic company.

I remember, in 1897, hearing Mr. Bernard Shaw make a speech before the Irish Literary Society in London, following a lecture on "Irish Actors of the Nineteenth Century." He very wittily extinguished the lecturer, who, he said, truly enough had enumerated the best actors and actresses and then had gone on to say they were not Irish. "As to what an Irishman is," he said, "is a complex question, for wherever he may have been born, if he has been brought up in Ireland, that is quite sufficient to make him an Irishman. It is a mistake to think an Irishman has not common sense. It is the Englishman who is devoid of common sense or at least has so small a portion of it that he can only apply it to the work immediately before him. That is why he is obliged to fill the rest of his horizon with the humbugs and hypocrisy that fill so large a part of English life. The Irishman has a better grasp of facts and sees them more clearly; only he fails in putting them into practice, and has a great objection to doing anything that will lead to any practical result. It is a mistake to think the Irishman has feeling; he has not; but the Englishman is full of feeling. What the Irishman has is imagination; he can imagine himself in the situation of others." Then as if afraid of making the Irish members of his audience too well pleased with themselves, he gave his summing up: "But the Irish language is an effete language and the nation is effete, and as to saying there are good Irish actors, there are not, and there won't be until the conditions in Ireland are favourable for the production of drama, and when that day comes, I hope I may be dead."

I am glad we have shown Mr. Shaw that he can be in the wrong, and I am glad he is not dead, for he has been a good friend to us. But our players have proved that even the wise may be deceived. They have won much praise for themselves and have raised the dignity of Ireland, and I for one owe them very grateful thanks for the way they have made the characters in my comedies laugh and live.

In May, 1903, the Irish National Theatre Society went for the first time to London. It was hard for the actors to get away. They had their own work to do. But they asked their employers for a whole Saturday holiday. They left Dublin on Friday night, arrived in London on the Saturday morning, played in the afternoon, and again in the evening at the Queen's Gate Hall, and were back at work in Dublin on Monday morning. The plays taken were: Mr. Fred Ryan's *Laying the Foundations*, Mr. Yeats's *Hour-glass, Pot of Broth*, and *Kathleen ni Houlihan*, and my own *Twenty-five*. I was not able to go but Mr. Yeats wrote to me: "London, May 4, '03. The plays were a great success. I never saw a more enthusiastic audience. I send you some papers, all that I have found notices in. When I remember the notices of literary adventures on the stage, I think them better than we could have hoped.... I have noticed that the young men, the men of my own generation or younger, are the people who like us. It was a very distinguished audience. Blunt was there, but went after your play as he is just recovering from influenza and seems to be really ill. I thought your play went very well. Fay was charming as Christy. The game of cards is still the weak place, but with all defects, the little play has a real charm. If we could amend the cards it would be a strong play too. Lady Aberdeen, Henry James, Michael Field—who has sent me an enthusiastic letter about the acting—Mrs. Wyndham—the Chief Secretary's mother—Lord Monteagle, Mrs. Thackeray Ritchie, and I don't know how many other notables were there, and all I think were moved. The evening audience was the more Irish and *Kathleen* and *The Pot of Broth* got a great reception. *The Foundations* went well, indeed everything went well."

This was but the first of several London visits, and the good audience and good notices were a great encouragement. And this visit led also to the generous help given us by Miss Horniman. She took what had been the old Mechanics' Institute in Abbey Street, Dublin, adding to it a part of the site of the old Morgue, and by rebuilding and reconstructing turned it into what has since been known as the Abbey Theatre, giving us the free use of it together with an annual subsidy for a term of years.

Miss Horniman did all this, as she says in a former[2] letter to

[2] Elizabeth Coxhead in her book *Lady Gregory: A Literary Portrait* suggests that this should be a "formal letter."

Mr. Yeats, because of her "great sympathy with the artistic and dramatic aims of the Irish National Theatre Company as publicly explained by you on various occasions." She also states in that letter: "I can only afford to make a very little theatre, and it must be quite simple. You all must do the rest to make a powerful and prosperous theatre with a high artistic ideal." We have kept through many attacks and misunderstandings the high artistic ideal we set out with. Our prosperity enabled us to take over the Abbey Theatre two years ago when our Patent and subsidy came to an end. I feel sure Miss Horniman is well pleased that we have been able to show our gratitude by thus proving ourselves worthy of her great and generous gift.

But in Dublin a new theatre cannot be opened except under a Patent from the Crown. This costs money even when not opposed, and if it is opposed, the question has to be argued by counsel, and witnesses have to be called in and examined as if some dangerous conspiracy were being plotted. When our Patent was applied for, the other theatres took fright and believed we might interfere with their gains, and they opposed our application, and there was delay after delay. But at last the enquiry was held before the Privy Council, and Mr. Yeats wrote on its eve: "3d August, 1904. The really important things first. This day is so hot that I have been filled with alarm lest the lake may begin to fall again and the boat be stranded high up on the bank and I be unable to try my new bait. I brought the boat up to a very shallow place the day I left. I have been running about all over the place collecting witnesses and have now quite a number. I will wire to-morrow if there is anything definite about decision. In any case I will write full particulars."

"August 4th. Final decision is postponed until Monday but the battle is won to all intents and purposes. There appears to be no difficulty about our getting a Patent for the plays of the Society. I sent you a paper with the report of proceedings, —— and ——, did well for us, but I must say I was rather amused at their anxiety to show that they supported us not out of love for the arts but because of our use as anti-emigration agents and the like. I think I was a bad witness. Counsel did not examine me but asked me to make a statement. The result was, having expected questions and feeling myself left to wander through an immense subject, I said very little. I was disappointed at being hardly cross-examined at all. By that time I had got excited and was thirsting for everybody's blood. One barrister in cross-examining T. P. Gill, who came after me, tried to prove that Ibsen and Maeterlinck were immoral writers. He asked was it not true that a play by Maeterlinck called *The Intruder* had raised an immense outcry in London because of its immorality. Quite involuntarily I cried out, 'My God!' and Edward Martyn burst into a loud fit of laughter. I suppose he must have meant *Monna Vanna.* He also asked if the Irish National Theatre Society had not produced a play which was an attack on marriage. Somebody asked him what was the name of the play. He said it didn't matter and dropped the subject. He had evidently heard some vague rumour about *The Shadow of the Glen.* I forgot to say that William Fay gave his evidence very well, as one would expect. He had the worst task of us all, for O'Shaughnessy, a brow-beating cross-examiner of the usual kind, fastened on to him. Fay, however, had his answer for everything."

The Patent was granted to me, "Dame Augusta Gregory," as Patentee, and in it I was amongst other things "Enjoined and commanded to gather, entertain, govern, privilege, and keep such and so many players," and not to put on the stage any "exhibition of wild beasts or dangerous performances or to allow women or children to be hung from the flies or fixed in positions from which they cannot release themselves." "It being our Royal will and pleasure that for the future our said theatre may be instrumental to the promotion of virtue and instruction of human life."

The building was not ready for us until the end of the year. Mr. Yeats wrote in August: "I have just been down to see the work on the Abbey Theatre. It is all going very quickly and the company should be able to rehearse there in a month. The other day, while digging up some old rubbish in the Morgue, which is being used for dressing-rooms, they found human bones. The workmen thought they had lit on a murder, but the caretaker said, 'Oh, I remember, we lost a body about seven years ago. When the time for the inquest came, it couldn't be found.' "

I remembered this when Mr. Yeats wrote to me lately from the Abbey: "The other day at a performance of *Countess Cathleen* one of the players stopped in the midst of his speech and it was a moment or two before he could go on. He told me afterwards his shoulder had suddenly been grasped by an invisible hand."

When the time for the opening came, I was ill and could not leave home, but had reports from him through the days before the opening. "December 24, 1904. The Company are very disappointed that you will not be up for the first night. Fay says they would all act better if you were here."

"December 20, 1904. I hear from Robert that you may get up for a little to-day. I hope you will take a long rest. I shall see about the awning for the old woman's stall to-night. Synge has a photograph, which will give us a picturesque form. We changed all the lighting on Saturday, and the costumes look much better now. In any case everything looks so much better on the new stage. G. came in last night with a Boer, who went to Trinity, because, so far as I could make out, he thought he would find himself among sympathetic surroundings. He and some other young Boers, including one who is said to have killed more Englishmen at Spion Kop than anybody else, had to go to a university in Europe and chose Ireland. Finding the sort of place it is, they look at the situation with amusement and are trying to get out more men of their own sort to form a rebellious coterie. . . . I mention G., in order to say that he wants to try his hand at translating *Œdipus the King* for us. To-night we go on experimenting in lighting and after that will come the great problem of keeping the bottom of the trews from standing out like frilled paper at the end of a ham bone."

And finally on the very day of the opening: "December 27, '04. I am confident of a fairly good start with the plays,—the stars are quiet and fairly favourable."

Then after the first night, December 27th, I had good telegrams and then a letter: "A great success in every way. The audience seemed 'heavy' through the opening dialogue—Fool and Blind man—and then it woke up, applauding for a long time after the exit of the kings. There was great enthusiasm at the end. *Kathleen* seemed more rebellious than I ever heard it, and —— solemnly begged me to withdraw it for fear it would stir up a conspiracy and get us all into trouble. Then came your play—a success from the first. One could hardly hear for the applause. Fay was magnificent as the melancholy man. The whole play was well played all through. I don't think I really like the stone wall wings. However, I was very near and will know better to-night. I got a beautiful light effect in *Baile's Strand*, and the audience applauded the scene even before the play began. The cottage, too, with the misty blue outside its door is lovely. We never had such an audience or such enthusiasm. The pit clapped when I came in. Our success could not have been greater. Even —— admits that your comedy [*Spreading the News*], 'is undoubtedly to be very popular.' "

We worked for several years with Mr. W. Fay as producer, as manager, as chief actor. In 1903, when all his time was needed for the enterprise, we paid him enough to set him free from other work, a part coming from the earnings of the Company, a part from Mr. Yeats, and a part from myself, for we had little capital at that time, outside £50 given by our good friend Mr. John Quinn, Attorney and Counsellor in New York. But even large sums of money would have been poor payment not only for William Fay's genius and his brother's beautiful speaking of verse, but for their devotion to the aim and work of the theatre, its practical and its artistic side. But they left us early in 1908 at a time of disagreement with other members, and of discouragement. I am very sorry that they, who more than almost any others had laid the foundation of the Irish Theatre, did not wait with us for its success.

But building up an audience is a slow business when there is anything unusual in the methods or the work. Often near midnight, after the theatre had closed, I have gone round to the newspaper offices, asking as a favour that notices might be put in, for we could pay for but few advertisements and it was not always thought worth while to send a critic to our plays. Often I have gone out by the stage door when the curtain was up, and come round into the auditorium by the front hall, hoping that in the dimness I might pass for a new arrival and so encourage the few scattered people in the stalls. One night there were so few in any part of the house that the players were for dismissing them and giving no performance at all. But we played after all and just after the play began, three or four priests from the country came in. A friend of theirs and of the Abbey had gone beyond the truth in telling them it was not a real theatre. They came round afterwards and told us how good they thought the work and asked the Company to come down and play in the West. Very often in the green room I have quoted the homely proverb, heard I know not where, "Grip is a good dog, but Hold Fast a better"! For there is some French blood in me that keeps my spirit up, so that I see in a letter to Mr. Yeats I am indignant at some attributions of melancholy: "I who at church last Sunday, when I heard in the Psalms 'Thou hast anointed me with the joy of gladness above my fellows', thought it must apply to me, and that some oil of the sort must have kept me watertight among seas of trouble." And Mr. Yeats in his turn wrote to encourage me in some time of attacks: "Any fool can fight a winning battle, but it needs character to fight a losing one, and that should inspire us; which reminds me that I dreamed the other night that I was being hanged, but was the life and soul of the party."

For there was not always peace inside the theatre, and there came from time to time that breaking and rebuilding that is in the course of nature, and one must think all for good in the end. And so I answered some one at a time of discord, "I am myself a lover of peace so long as it is not the peace of a dead body." And to Mr. Yeats I wrote: "I am much more angry really than you are with those who have wasted so much of your time. I look on it as child-murder. *Deirdre* might be in existence now but for this." And to one who left us but has since returned: "I want you to sit down and read Mr. Yeats's notes in the last two numbers of *Samhain* and to ask yourself if the work he is doing is best worth helping or hindering. Remember, he has been for the last eight years working with his whole heart and soul for the creation, the furtherance, the perfecting, of what he believes will be a great dramatic movement in Ireland. I have helped him all through, but we have lost many helpers by the way. Mr. Lecky, who served us well in getting the law passed that made these dramatic experiments possible, publicly repudiated us because of Mr. Yeats's letter on the Queen's visit. . . . Others were lost for different reasons ——, ——, all of whom had been helpful in their time. Now others are dropping off. It is always sad to lose fellow-workers, but the work must go on all the same. 'No man putting his hand to the plough and drawing back is fit for the kingdom of God.' He is going on with it. I am going on with it as long as life and strength are left to me. . . . It is hard to hold one's own against those one is living amongst, I have found that; and I have found that peace comes, not from trying to please one's neighbours but in making up one's own mind what is the right path and in then keeping to it. And so God save Ireland, and believe me your sincere friend."

This now, according to my memory, is how I came to work for a National Theatre in Ireland and how that Theatre began.

II

THE BLESSING OF THE GENERATIONS

On the walls of the landing outside your nursery door there are pictures hanging, painted as you paint your own with water-colours, but without any blot or blur. Some are of blue hills and of streams running through brown bogs, but many of them are of young girls and of women, barefooted and wearing home-dyed clothes, knitting or carrying sheaves; or of fishermen dressed in white. All, girls and women and men alike, have gentle faces. There is no sign of the turf-smoke that dries the skin to leather. There are no lines or wrinkles to be seen. It may be faces were like that before the great famine came that changed soft bodies to skin and bone and turned villages to grazing for goats. Your great-grandfather fed his people at that time and took their sickness and died. But perhaps if that painter were living now, he would draw likenesses in the same way, with the furrows and ridges left out. For he could only see gentleness like his own in whatever he had a mind to paint.

A little lower on the staircase there are pictures you do not look at now, likenesses of men not very young, who had done something that made others like to meet them and who dined together at the Grillon Club. Your grandfather is there with many of his friends; some of them became friends of mine. Here is one that wrote books, you will maybe read them bye and bye, about good men that once lived in Ireland, and how Europe learned manners, and about witches that were thrown into ponds.

Near the library door there is a drawing of an old man. He looks very tired and sad. He was shut up in prison for more years than you have lived. He could not see the lime trees blooming out or the chestnuts breaking from their husks.

That is a younger man on the other wall. There is something like a laugh in his eyes. He will live and work a long time, I hope, for the work he has done is very good. He gave you a blessing in Irish one time when I brought him to see you in your cot.

AMONG the names on my first list of guarantors is that of Sir Frederic Burton, painter, and for many years Director of the National Gallery in Trafalgar Square. And this name, like that of

Aubrey de Vere, brings together movements divided by half a century; for Frederic Burton had, through personal friendship with Thomas Davis, come so near to that side of the National movement of 1848 which expressed itself in writing, that he had drawn the design for the title-page of the *Spirit of the Nation*, that book of rebel songs and ballads. And he had known others of that time whose names have been remembered, Ferguson and Stokes and O'Curry. It would make my heart give a quicker beat to hear him say: "When I was in Aran with Petrie," or "my model for the Blind Girl at the Holy Well was Doctor Petrie's daughter," or "Davis was such a dear fellow I could refuse him nothing," or, as an apology for not having read Mitchell's wonderful *Gaol Journal*, "I did not like his appearance when I saw him. Davis took me to see him somewhere. He was a regular Northern and did not make a good impression on me. His skin was blotched and he had ginger-coloured hair." Though he resented the rising fame of Clarence Mangan, because, as he thought, it was at the expense of Thomas Moore, "who had—though no one would class him among the great poets—mellifluous versification, exquisite choice of language, and was endowed at least with a delicate fancy approaching to imagination," the only authentic portrait of Mangan, not taken indeed from life, but after death in an hospital, was drawn by him.

He had wandered and painted in Germany and in the west of Ireland, in Connemara and in his own county of Clare, till his work at the National Gallery forced him to give up his art. But in his last days he would often speak of his early days in the West, and of country people he remembered, a girl near Maam who was a great singer, and a piper, Paddy Conneely, who was the best judge of sheep and cattle in the whole country.

He was during the Land War when I first knew him, a very strong Unionist, for his sensitive nature shrank from its harsh and violent methods, and for a while he felt that he had no longer a country to take pride in. In 1899 he wrote: ". . . I look forward with some uneasiness to the advent of *Patriots* from beyond sea, now American citizens under the Stars and Stripes. With this outlook before it, the Government is reducing the Irish Constabulary, a most extraordinary proceeding and a quite unaccountable one except indeed on the theory that every administration is doomed to fatuity where Irish affairs have to be dealt with. For the police are the appointed guardians of civil order, and however abused or resisted, are recognised as such. But if the military have to be called out, what a handle is given to vapourers on both sides of the Irish sea! And what about the dismissed Constables? Will they not be thrown into the ranks of the Patriots?"

And in 1895 he had written, refusing an invitation to dine with me—I cannot remember who I said was coming, but he expressed this regret: "Especially as I enjoy meeting Sir A. and Lady Clay, and should have liked to see a bird so rare as an *honest* Nationalist." Yet he kept a spirit of independence that was akin to rebellion, even through those years of official position and pleasant London dinners, and friendships, and the Athenæum Club.

During the years after the death in 1892 of my husband, who had been a trustee of the National Gallery, and Sir Frederic's death in 1900, our friendship became a close one. Our talk turned very often from pictures and Italy to Ireland. In 1897 I published *Mr. Gregory's Letter-box*, a political history of the years between 1812 and 1830, taken from letters to and by my husband's grandfather, then Under-Secretary for Ireland. Sir Frederic was much pleased with the book. He came to see me when he had read it and said: "I am glad you have come down on the real culprit, George III," and quoted one or two people who had said his obstinacy was the cause of so many of Ireland's troubles. But after a little he said very gravely: "I see a tendency to Home Rule on your own part." I said, "I defy any one to study Irish History without getting a dislike and distrust of England." He was silent for a time and then said, "That is my feeling," and told me how patriotic he had been as a boy through disliking "O'Connell and his gang." Later he accused me of having become "A red hot Nationalist," and said I had no Irish blood, but I convinced him I had, both Irish and French.

He was as angry at the time of the Boer War as any Mayo ballad-singer or Connacht Ranger's wife. "According to the doctor I am better, but really this war is killing me. It is the worst affair I recollect. It is utterly inglorious . . . I grieve particularly for our brave Irishmen whose lives have been squandered to no purpose." He was to the end a Unionist, so far as his political doctrine went, but I think his rooted passion for Ireland increased, and made, as such strong passions are used to do, all politics seem but accidental, transitory, a business that is outside the heart of life.

The language movement, of which I was able to bring him news, began to excite him. One day I found him "excited and incredulous at Atkinson's evidence against the Irish language, in which he says all Irish books are filthy and all folk-lore is at bottom abominable." And then he got, "on your recommendation and Doctor Hyde's reputation as a scholar" the History of Irish Literature and wrote: "I am reading Dr. Hyde's Literary History with the greatest interest. It is a high pleasure to find the matter he deals with treated by a true scholar and in a reasonable and philosophic spirit. But indeed the advance in this respect since my earlier days is marvellous. At that time the comparative method was hardly, if at all, thought of. Rabid Irishmen, who often didn't know their own language but at second hand, and knew no other tongue at all, spouted the rankest absurdities. Now true light has been let in and Irish history, archæology, literature, and poetry are the gainers. Let us not grudge to the Germans their meed of honour in having led the way." And again: "I should be exceedingly sorry if the Irish language died out of men's mouths altogether. I look upon the loss of a language or even a dialect as equivalent to the extirpation of a species in natural history. . . ." Then, in 1899: "Those addresses of Dr. Hyde and Mr. Yeats are very interesting and, I would fain hope, may find a response in the hearts of the people who heard them. The subject is one full of sadness. Self-respect, a decaying language, a dying music, how shall they be resuscitated! I could weep when I recollect how full Munster, Connacht, and even Ulster were in my earlier days of exquisite native music—when in fact among the peasantry and the Irish of the towns you heard no other; when the man at the plough-tail had his peculiar 'whistle,' strange, wild, and full of melody and rhythm. All this must now have passed away irrevocably. May the language have a better chance! I cannot tell you how much Doctor Hyde's book has moved me. Principally it is a manful effort."

When I was again in London, he showed me the Literary History close at hand and asked me a little nervously what was Douglas Hyde's age. My answer, or surmise, pleased him, and he said: "Then he will be able to work for a long time." Once or twice, when we went on to talk of other things, he came back to this and said, "I am so glad he is a young man."

He was jealous for the honour of Ireland even in lesser things. He was very much interested in the beginning of our theatre. In 1899 he writes: "I am happy to sign the guarantee form for the coming year, and enclose it. You are a dreamy lot in Erin. As you say, I think the quality comes from the atmosphere. Here there is more of the opposite than suits me, but I dream still, as I have done all my lifetime. I trust there will be no shindy at the performance of *Countess Cathleen.* But if not, our compatriots will have been for once untrue to themselves!" And later: "I am sincerely glad the experiment was on the whole successful and that those who intended mischief after all made but a poor effort to inflict it. . . . Altogether it appears as if the old palmy days of Dublin independent appreciation of the drama were about to be revived in our altered times. I congratulate Mr. Yeats on the success of the drama as an acting piece, and in everything except —— ——'s beautiful Irish hyperbole. I recollect an account of a concert given at Clonmel several years ago, in which the eloquent local journalist said of one of the amateur lady singers, after the loftiest eulogy, 'but it was in her last song that Miss —— —— gave the *coup de grace* to her performance.' "

He cared very much for Mr. Yeats's work, but I could never persuade him to come and meet him. He always made some excuse. At last he made a promise for one afternoon, but, in place of coming, he wrote, saying he was half ashamed to confess to so much enthusiasm, but he was so much under the spell of the poems that he was afraid that, in meeting the writer, the spell might be broken. He told me when next I saw him that of the poets he had known the only ones that did not disappoint him were William Morris and Rossetti. "Swinburne was excitable; Tennyson was grumpy and posing; Browning was charming as a friend, but not fulfilling my idea of what a poet should be." But I did bring them together in the end, and he thanked me later and confessed my faith had been justified.

In 1900, during his last illness, I was often with him. I had been away in Dublin for our plays and I find a note written after my return to London: "Went to see Sir F. He is in bed, and I fear, or indeed must hope, the end is very near. . . . I went up to see him. He was clear but drowsy, at first a little inarticulate, but when I got up to go, he held my hand a long time, speaking with great kindness . . . asked for Robert, and how the plays had gone. I told him of them, and of the *Times* notice of *Maeve*, saying its idealism had been so well received by an Irish audience, and of the notice on the same page telling that *Tess* in London had been jeered at by an audience who found it too serious. He said: 'That is just what one would expect.' He asked if Robert had been abroad yet, and I said no, he was so fond of Ireland he had not cared to go until now, and that I myself found every year an increased delight and happiness in Ireland. He said, 'It is so with me. My best joys have been connected with Ireland.' Then he spoke of Celtic influence in English literature and said, 'There will some day be a great Pan-Celtic Empire.' And so we parted."

I am glad that he who had been even a little moved by that stir in the mind, that rush of revolutionary energy that moved the poets and patriots and rebels of '48, should after half a hundred years have been stirred by the intellectual energy that came with a new generation, as its imagination turned for a while from the Parliament where all was to have been set right, after the break in the Irish party and after Parnell's death.

"I enclose you a guarantee paper filled up for such a sum as I can afford (or perhaps more) to lose, but I hope there will be no loss for anybody in the matter, while there will certainly be some gain to Ireland! I'd have answered sooner but that I am suffering from a horrible form of dyspepsia, with exceptional langour." It is no wonder if the old man who sent with this his promise for twenty shillings was somewhat broken in health. He was the last of the Fenian triumvirate,—Kickham, Luby, O'Leary,—and he had come back to Dublin after fifteen years of banishment and five of penal servitude at Portland. John O'Leary had been turning over books on the stalls by the Seine in Paris, when one day somebody had come to him and asked him to come back to Ireland where a rising was being planned, and he had come.

A part of the romance of my early days had been the whispered rumours of servants, and the overheard talk of my elders, of the threatened rising of the Fenians:

"An army of Papists grim
"With a green flag o'er them.
"Red coats and black police
"Flying before them."

The house of Roxborough, my old home, had once been attacked by Whiteboys. My father had defended it, firing from the windows, and it was not hard to believe that another attack might be made. It seemed a good occasion for being allowed to learn to shoot with my brothers, but that was in those days not thought fitting, even in self-defence, for a girl, and my gun was never loaded with anything more weighty than a coppercap. So when this new business of the theatre brought me to meet, amongst many others till then unknown, John O'Leary, I remembered those old days and the excitement of a Fenian's escape—might he not be in hiding in our own woods or haylofts? And I wondered to find that not only Nationalists admired and respected so wild and dangerous a rebel. So I asked Mr. Yeats to tell me the reason, for he had known him well and had even shared a lodging with him for a while; so that his friends would say: "You have the advantage over us. O'Leary takes so long to convert to any new thing, and you can begin with him at breakfast." And he wrote to me: "When John O'Leary returned from exile, he found himself in the midst of a movement which inherited the methods of O'Connell and a measure of his success. Journalists and politicians were alike in his eyes untruthful men, thinking that any means that brought the end were justified, and for that reason certain, as he thought, to miss the end desired. The root of all was, though I doubt if he put the thought into words, that journalists and politicians looked for their judges among their inferiors, and assumed those opinions and passions that moved the largest number of men. Their school is still dominant, and John O'Leary had seen through half his life, as we have seen, men coarsening their thought and their manners, and exaggerating their emotions in a daily and weekly press that was like the reverie of an hysterical woman. He was not of O'Connell's household. His master had been Davis, and he was quick to discover and condemn the man who sought for judgment not among his equals or in himself. He saw, as no one else in modern Ireland has seen, that men who make this choice are long unpopular, all through their lives it may be, but grow in sense and courage with their years, and have the most gazers even in the end.

"Yet he was not unjust to those who went the other way. He imputed to them no bad motives, for I have heard him say of a man that he distrusted, 'He would not sacrifice himself but he would risk himself,' and of a man who seemed to him to appeal always to low motives, the chief mischief-maker of his kind, 'He would sacrifice himself.' Yet, what he himself commended with his favourite word '*morale*' was the opposite of that sudden emotional self-sacrifice, the spurious heroism of popular movements, being life-long hardness and serenity, a choice made every day anew. He thought but little of opinions, even those he had sacrificed so much for, and I have heard him say, 'There was never cause so bad that it has not been defended by good men for good reasons.' And of Samuel Ferguson, poet and antiquarian, who was not of his party or any Nationalist party, 'He has been a better patriot than I.' He knew that in the end, whatever else had temporary use, it was simple things that mattered, the things a child can understand, a man's courage and his generosity.

"I do not doubt that his prison life had been hard enough, but he would not complain, having been in 'the hands of his enemies'; and he would often tell one of that life, but not of its hardships. A famous popular leader of that time, who made a great noise because he was in prison as a common felon for a political offence, made him very angry. I said 'It is well known that he has done this, not because he shrinks from hardship but because there is a danger in a popular movement that the obscure men who can alone carry it to success, may say, "our leaders are treated differently." ' He answered, 'There are things a man must not do, even to save a nation.' And when I asked 'What things?' he said, 'He must not weep in public.' He knew that a doctrine expediency cries out on would have but few to follow, and he would say, 'Michael Davitt wants his converts by the thousand. I shall be satisfied with half a dozen.' Most complained of his impracticability, and there was a saying that an angel could not find a course of action he would not discover a moral flaw in, and it is probable that his long imprisonment and exile, while heightening his sense of ideal law, had deprived him of initiative by taking away its opportunities. He would often complain that the young men would not follow him, and I once said, 'Your power is that they do not. We can do nothing till we have converted you; you are our conscience.' Yet he lived long enough to see the young men grow to middle life and assume like their fathers before them that a good Irishman is he who agreed with the people. Yet we, when we withstand the people, owe it to him that we can feel we have behind us an Irish tradition. 'My religion,' he would say, 'is the old Persian one, "To pull the bow and speak the truth." '

"I do not know whether he would have liked our unpopular plays, but I cannot imagine him growing excited because he thought them slanders upon Ireland. O'Connell had called the Irish peasantry the finest peasantry upon earth, and his heirs found it impossible to separate patriotism and flattery. Again and again John O'Leary would return to this, and I have heard him say, 'I think it probable that the English national character is finer than ours, but that does not make me want to be an Englishman.' I have often heard him defend Ireland against one charge or another, and he was full of knowledge, but the patriotism he had sacrificed so much for marred neither his justice nor his scholarship.

"He disapproved of much of Parnell's policy, but Parnell was the only man in Irish public life of his day who had his sympathy, and I remember hearing some one say in those days before the split that are growing vague to me, that Parnell never came to Dublin without seeing him. They were perhaps alike in some hidden root of character though the one had lived a life of power and excitement, while the other had been driven into contemplation by circumstance and as I think by nature. Certainly they were both proud men."

He was, when I knew him, living in a little room, books all around him and books in heaps upon the floor. I would send him sometimes snipe or golden plover from Kiltartan bog or woodcock from the hazel woods at Coole, hoping to tempt him with something that might better nourish the worn body than the little custard pudding that was used to serve him for his two days' dinner, because of that "horrible dyspepsia" that often makes those who have been long in prison live starving after their release, mocked with the sight of food.

It was through reading Davis's poems he had become a Nationalist, and his own influence had helped to shape this other poet in the same fashion, for from the time of Yeats's boyhood there had been a close friendship between them, the old man admiring the young man's genius, and taking his side in the quarrels that arose about patriotism in poetry and the like. I remember their both dining with me one evening in London and coming on to see a very poor play, very badly acted by some Irish society. At its end Yeats was asked to say some words of gratitude for the performance, during which we had all felt impatient and vexed. He did speak at some length, and held his audience, and without telling any untruth left them feeling that all had gone well. John O'Leary turned to me and said fervently, "I don't think there is anything on God's earth that Willie Yeats could not make a speech about!"

There is a bust of John O'Leary in the Municipal Gallery. The grand lines of the massive head, the eyes full of smouldering fire, might be those of some ancient prophet understanding his people's doom.

There is nothing of storm or unrest about that other Dublin monument, that bronze figure sitting tranquilly within the gates of Trinity College and within its quadrangle. Lecky was the reasoner, the philosopher, the looker-on writing his histories, even of Ireland, through the uproar of the Land War with the same detachment as did the Four Masters, writing their older history amongst the wars and burnings of the seventeenth century that were so terrible in Ireland.

He had been a debater while an undergraduate of Trinity, and it was fitting that he should have represented it in Parliament during his last years.

Trinity, where Wolfe Tone had been an undergraduate a

hundred years earlier had changed in that hundred years. I was in Paris in 1900 and went to see an old acquaintance, that most imaginative archæologist, Salomon Reinach. He told me he had been lately to Ireland and he had been astonished by two things, the ignorance of the Irish language—it was not known even by the head of the Dublin Museum or the head of its archæological side—and by the hostility of Trinity College to all things Irish. "It is an English fort, nothing else." "Its garrison," the students, had gone out and broken the windows of a newspaper office while he was there, and he had spent an evening with Doctor Mahaffy, who was "much astonished that I was no longer taken up with Greek things, and that I found Irish antiquity so much more interesting."

I have already told of Lecky's help to our theatre. He had a real affection for his country, but was not prone to join societies or leagues. He had given us his name as one of our first guarantors, offering £5 instead of the £1 I had asked. But he publicly withdrew his name later, without his usual reasonableness, because of letters written by Mr. Yeats and Mr. George Moore at the time of Queen Victoria's visit to Dublin. This had been announced as a private visit, and Nationalists had promised a welcome. Then it was turned into a public one, and there was a good deal of angry feeling, and it seemed as if the theatre—although quite outside politics—would suffer for a while. Though Mr. Yeats wrote: "I don't think you need be anxious about next year's theatre. Clever Unionists will take us on our merits, and the rest would never like us at any time. I have found a greatly increased friendliness on the part of some of the younger men here. In a battle like Ireland's which is one of poverty against wealth, one must prove one's sincerity by making oneself unpopular to wealth. One must accept the baptism of the gutter. Have not all teachers done the like?" I answered that I preferred the baptism of clean water. I was troubled by the misunderstanding of friends.

Trinity College is not keeping aloof now, and as to Mr. Lecky himself, the House of Commons took away some prejudices. He spoke to me of Mr. John Redmond and his leadership with great admiration and esteem. I find a note written after a pleasant dinner with him and Mrs. Lecky in Onslow Gardens: "He grieved over the exaggerated statements of the financial reformers. I pressed Land Purchase as the solution of our trouble, but he says what is true, 'It means changing every hundred pounds into seventy.' Talking of Robert's future, he said, 'It is a great thing to have a competence behind one.' He said he had been brought up for the Church, but found he could not enter it, and went abroad and drifted, never thinking he would marry, and leading a solitary life, and so took to letters and succeeded. He thinks Parliament lessens one's interest in political questions,—so much connected with them is of no value, and there is so much empty noise."

I often heard of his speaking well and even boasting of our Theatre and its work, but though he often came to see me, he would not quite give up fault-finding. "Dined at Lecky's; he rather cross. He took me down to dinner and said first thing, 'What silly speeches your Celtic people have been making.' 'Moore?' I asked. 'Yes, and Yeats. Oh, very silly!' He is in bad humour because Blackrock, which he has known, and known to speak English all his life, has sent him a copy of resolutions in favour of the revival of Irish. In revenge I told him how a Deputy Lieutenant (Edward Martyn) was proclaiming himself a convert to Nationalism through reading his *Leaders of Public Opinion in Ireland*. But that book, he used to say, had been a long time in influencing anybody, for of its first edition only thirty copies had been sold."

He forgave us all after a while, used to come and ask for news whenever I had come to London from home, and told me quite proudly after a visit to Oxford that the undergraduates there accepted no living poet but Keats. But to the last he would say to me plaintively on parting, "Do not do anything incendiary when you go back to Ireland."

My first meeting with Douglas Hyde had been when he came in one day with a broken bicycle during lunch at my neighbour Mr. Martyn's house where I was staying. He had been coming by train, but had got out at a village, Craughwell (as I myself did a good while afterwards on the same errand), in search of Raftery, the Connacht poet. I had my own pony carriage with me, and that afternoon I drove to the Round Tower and the seven churches of Kilmacduagh, taking with me Douglas Hyde and Mr. William Sharp, whom I even then suspected of being "Fiona Macleod." Mr. Sharp—not by my invitation—took the place beside me, and left the back seat for the poet-dramatist, the founder of the Gaelic League of Ireland.

He often came to stay with me and my son at Coole after that. The first time was in winter, for a shooting party. Some old ladies—our neighbours—asked our keeper who our party was, and on hearing that one was a gentleman who spoke to the beaters in Irish, they said, "he can not be a gentleman if he speaks Irish." With all his culture and learning, his delight was in talking with the people and hearing their poems and fragments of the legends. I remember one day, he went into a thatched cottage to change his boots after shooting snipe on Kilmacduagh bog, and talked with an old woman who had not much English and who welcomed him when he spoke in her own tongue. But when she heard he was from Mayo, looked down on by dwellers in Galway, she laughed very much and repeated a line of a song in Irish which runs:

"There'll be boots on me yet, says the man from the county Mayo!"

Near Kilmacduagh also he was told a long story, having Aristotle for its hero. Sometimes he was less lucky. I brought an old man to see him, I was sure could give him stories. But he only told one of a beggar who went to Castle ——, a neighbouring house, the master of which had given him a half-penny, saying, "that is for my father's and mother's soul." "And the beggar added another half-penny to it, and laid it down on the step, and, 'There's a half-penny for my father's soul and and a half-penny for my mother's, and I wouldn't go to the meanness of putting them both in one.' "

He has done his work by methods of peace, by keeping quarrels out of his life, with all but entire success. I find in a letter to Mr. Yeats: "I will send you Claideam that you may see some of the attacks by recalcitrant Gaelic Leaguers on the Craoibhin. Well, I am sorry, but if he can't keep from making enemies, what chance is there for the like of us?"

He was one of the vice-presidents of our Society for a while and we are always grateful to him for that *Twisting of the Rope* in which he played with so much gaiety, ease, and charm. But in founding the Gaelic League, he had done far more than that for our work. It was a movement for keeping the Irish language a spoken one, with, as a chief end, the preserving of our own nationality. That does not sound like the beginning of a revolution, yet it was one. It was the discovery, the disclosure of the folk-learning, the folk-poetry, the folk-tradition. Our Theatre was caught into that current, and it is that current, as I believe, that has brought it on its triumphant way. It is chiefly known now as a folk-theatre. It has not only the great mass of primitive material and legend to draw on, but it has been made a living thing by the excitement of that discovery. All our writers, Mr. Yeats himself, were influenced by it. Mr. Synge found what he had lacked before—fable, emotion, style. Writing of him I have said "He tells what he owes to that collaboration with the people, and for all the attacks, he has given back to them what they will one day thank him for. . . . The return to the people, the reunion after separation, the taking and giving, is it not the perfect circle, the way of nature, the eternal wedding-ring?"

III

PLAY-WRITING

When we first planned our Theatre, there were very few plays to choose from, but our faith had no bounds and as the Irish proverb says, "When the time comes, the child comes."

The plays that I have cared for most all through, and for love of which I took up this work, are those verse ones by Mr. Yeats *The Countess Cathleen* with which we began, *The Shadowy Waters, The King's Threshold,* and the rest. They have sometimes seemed to go out of sight because the prose plays are easier to put on and to take from place to place; yet they will always be, if I have my way, a part of our year's work. I feel verse is more than any prose can be, the apex of the flame, the point of the diamond. The well-to-do people in our stalls sometimes say, "We have had enough of verse plays, give us comedy." But the people in the sixpenny places do not say they get too much of them, and the players themselves work in them with delight. I wrote to Mr. Yeats when *On Baile's Strand* was being rehearsed: "Just back from rehearsal, and cheered up on the whole. The Molière goes very well, and will be quite safe when the two servants have been given a little business. Synge says it was quite different to-night. They all waked up in honour of me. As to *Baile's Strand*, it will be splendid. . . . The only real blot at present is the song, and it is very bad. The three women repeat it together. Their voices don't go together. One gets nervous listening for the separate ones. No one knows how you wish it done. Every one thinks the words ought to be heard. I got Miss Allgood to speak it alone, and that was beautiful, and we thought if it didn't delay the action too long, she might speak it, and at the end she and the others might sing or hum some lines of it to a definite tune. If you can quite decide what should be done, you can send directions, but if you are doubtful, I almost think you must come over. You mustn't risk spoiling the piece. It is quite beautiful. W. Fay most enthusiastic, says you are a wonderful man, and keeps repeating lines. He says, 'There is nothing like that being written in London.' "

But the listeners, and this especially when they are lovers of verse, have to give so close an attention to the lines, even when given their proper value and rhythm as by our players, that ear and mind crave ease and unbending, and so comedies were needed to give this rest. That is why I began writing them, and it is still my pride when one is thought worthy to be given in the one evening with the poetic work.

I began by writing bits of dialogue, when wanted. Mr. Yeats used to dictate parts of *Diarmuid and Grania* to me, and I would suggest a sentence here and there. Then I, as well as another, helped to fill spaces in *Where There is Nothing*. Mr. Yeats says in dedicating it to me: "I offer you a book which is in part your own. Some months ago, when our Irish dramatic movement took its present form, I saw somebody must write a number of plays in prose if it was to have a good start. I did not know what to do, although I had my dramatic fables ready and a pretty full sketch of one play, for my eyes were troubling me, and I thought I could do nothing but verse, which one can carry about in one's head for a long time, and write down, as De Musset put it, with a burnt match. You said I might dictate to you, and we worked in the mornings at Coole, and I never did anything that went so easily and quickly; for when I hesitated you had the right thought ready and it was almost always you who gave the right turn to the phrase and gave it the ring of daily life. We finished several plays, of which this is the longest, in so few weeks that if I were to say how few, I do not think anybody would believe me."

Where There is Nothing was given by the Stage Society in London, but Mr. Yeats was not satisfied with it, and we have since re-written it as *The Unicorn from the Stars*. Yet it went well and was vital. It led to an unexpected result: "I hear that some man of a fairly respectable class was taken up with a lot of tinkers somewhere in Munster, and that the Magistrate compared him to 'Paul Ruttledge.' The next night one of the tinkers seems to have said something to the others about their being in a book. The others resented this in some way, and there was a fight, which brought them all into Court again. I am trying to get the papers."

Later in the year we wrote together *Kathleen ni Houlihan* and to that he wrote an introductory letter addressed to me: "One night I had a dream almost as distinct as a vision, of a cottage where there was well-being and firelight and talk of a marriage, and into the midst of that cottage there came an old woman in a long cloak. She was Ireland herself, that Kathleen ni Houlihan for whom so many songs have been sung and for whose sake so many have gone to their death. I thought if I could write this out as a little play, I could make others see my dream as I had seen it, but I could not get down from that high window of dramatic verse, and in spite of all you had done for me, I had not the country speech. One has to live among the people, like you, of whom an old man said in my hearing, 'She has been a serving maid among us,' before one can think the thoughts of the people and speak with their tongue. We turned my dream into the little play, *Kathleen ni Houlihan*, and when we gave it to the little theatre in Dublin and found that working people liked it, you helped me to put my other dramatic fables into speech."

For *The Pot of Broth* also I wrote dialogue and I worked as well at the plot and the construction of some of the poetic plays, especially *The King's Threshold* and *Deirdre*; for I had learned by this time a good deal about play-writing to which I had never given thought before. I had never cared much for the stage, although when living a good deal in London, my husband and I went, as others do, to see some of each season's plays. I find, in looking over an old diary, that many of these have quite passed from my mind, although books I read ever so long ago, novels and the like, have left at least some faint trace by which I may recognise them.

We thought at our first start it would make the whole movement more living and bring it closer to the people if the Gaelic League would put on some plays written in Irish. Dr. Hyde thought well of the idea, and while staying here at Coole, as he did from time to time, he wrote *The Twisting of the Rope*, based on one of Mr. Yeats's Hanrahan stories; *The Lost Saint* on a legend given its shape by Mr. Yeats, and *The Nativity* on a scenario we wrote together for him. Afterwards he wrote *The Marriage* and *The Poorhouse,* upon in each case a scenario written by me. I betray no secret in telling this, for Dr. Hyde has made none of the collaboration, giving perhaps too generous acknowledgment, as in Galway, where he said, when called before the curtain after *The Marriage*, that the play was not his but that Lady Gregory had written it and brought it to him, saying "*Cur Gaedilge air,*" "Put Irish on it." I find in a letter of mine to Mr. Yeats: "Thanks for sending back Raftery. I haven't sent it to Hyde yet. The real story was that Raftery by chance went into a house where such a wedding was taking place 'that was only a marriage and not a wedding' and where there was 'nothing but a herring for the dinner,' and he made a song about it and about all the imaginary grand doings at it that has been remembered ever since. But it didn't bring any practical good to the young people, for Raftery himself 'had to go to bed in the end without as much as a drop to drink, but he didn't mind that, where they hadn't it to give.' "

But it went through some changes after that: "I have a letter from the Craoibhin. He has lost his Trinity College play and must re-write it from my translation. He is not quite satisfied with Raftery (*The Marriage*). 'I don't think Maire's uncertainty if it be a ghost or not is effective on the stage. I would rather have the ghost "out and out" as early as possible, and make it clear to the audience.' I rather agree with him. I think I will restore the voice at the door in my published version."

And again I wrote from Galway: "I came here yesterday for a few days' change, but the journey, or the little extra trouble at leaving, set my head aching, and I had to spend all yesterday in a dark room. In the evening, when the pain began to go, I began to think of the Raftery play, and I want to know if this end would do. After the miser goes out, Raftery stands up and says, 'I won't be the only one in the house to give no present to the woman of the house,' and hands her the plate of money, telling them to count it. While they are all gathered round counting it, he slips quietly from the door. As he goes out, wheels or horse steps are heard, and a farmer comes in and says, 'What is going on? All the carts of the country gathered at the door, and Seaghan, the Miser, going swearing down the road?' They say it is a wedding party called in by Raftery. But where is Raftery? Is he gone? They ask the farmer if he met him outside —the poet Raftery—and he says, 'I did not, but I stood by his grave at Killeenin yesterday.' Do you think that better? It gets rid of the good-byes and the storm, and I don't think any amount of hints convey the ghostly idea strongly enough. Let me know at once; just a word will do."

As to *The Poorhouse*, the idea came from a visit to Gort Workhouse one day when I heard that the wife of an old man, who had been long there, maimed by something, a knife I think, that she had thrown at him in a quarrel, had herself now been brought into the hospital. I wondered how they would meet, as enemies or as friends, and I thought it likely they would be glad to end their days together for old sake's sake. This is how I wrote down my fable: "Scene, ward of a workhouse; two beds containing the old men; they are quarrelling. Occupants of other invisible beds are heard saying, 'There they are at it again; they are always quarrelling.' They say the matron will be coming to call for order, but another says the matron has been sent for to see somebody who wants to remove one of the paupers. Both old men wish they could be removed from each other and have the whole ridge of the world between them. The fight goes on. One old man tells the other that he remembers the time he used to be stealing ducks, and he a boy at school. The other old man remembers the time his neighbour was suspected of going to Souper's school, etc., etc. They remember the crimes of each other's lives. They fight like two young whelps that go on fighting till they are two old dogs. At last they take their pillows and throw them at each other. Other paupers (invisible) cheer and applaud. Then they take their porringers, pipes, prayer-books, or whatever is in reach, to hurl at each other. They lament the hard fate that has put them in the same ward for five years and in beds next to each other for the last three months, and they after being enemies the whole of their lives. Suddenly a cry that the matron is coming. They settle themselves hurriedly. Each puts his enemy's pillow under his head and lies down. The matron comes in with a countrywoman comfortably dressed. She embraces one old man. She is his sister. Her husband died from her lately and she is lonesome and doesn't like to think of her brother being in the workhouse. If he is bedridden itself, he would be company for her. He is delighted, asks what sort of house she has. She says, a good one, a nice kitchen, and he can be doing little jobs for her. He can be sitting in a chair beside the fire and stirring the stirabout for her and throwing a bit of food to the chickens when she is out in the field. He asks when he can go. She says she has the chance of a lift for him on a neighbour's cart. He can come at once. He says he will make no delay. A loud sob from the old man in the other bed. He says, 'Is it going away you are, you that I knew through all my lifetime, and leaving me among strangers?' The first old man asks his sister if she will bring him too. She is indignant, says she won't. First old man says maybe he'd be foolish to go at all. How does he know if he'd like it. She says, he is to please himself; if he doesn't come, she can easily get a husband, having, as she has, a nice way of living, and three lambs going to the next market. The first man says, well, he won't go; if she would bring the other old man, he would go. She turns her back angrily. Paupers in other beds call out she'll find a good husband amongst them. She pulls on her shawl scornfully to go away. She gives her brother one more chance; he says he won't go. She says good-bye and bad luck to him. She leaves. He says that man beyond would be lonesome with no one to contradict him. The other man says he would not. The first man says, 'You want some one to be arguing with you always.' The second man, 'I do not.' The first man says. 'You are at your lies again.' The second takes up his pillow to heave at him again. Curtain falls on two men arming themselves with pillows."

I intended to write the full dialogue myself, but Mr. Yeats thought a new Gaelic play more useful for the moment, and rather sadly I laid that part of the work upon Dr. Hyde. It was all for the best in the end, for the little play, when we put it on at the Abbey, did not go very well. It seemed to ravel out into loose ends, and we did not repeat it; nor did the Gaelic players like it as well as *The Marriage* and *The Lost Saint*. After a while, when the Fays had left us, I wanted a play that would be useful to them, and with Dr. Hyde's full leave I re-wrote the *Poorhouse* as *The Workhouse Ward*. I had more skill by that time, and it was a complete re-writing, for the two old men in the first play had been talking at an imaginary audience of other old men in the ward. When this was done away with the dialogue became of necessity more closely knit, more direct and personal, to the great advantage of the play, although it was rejected as "too local" by the players for whom I had written it. The success of this set me to cutting down the number of parts in later plays until I wrote *Grania* with only three persons in it, and *The Bogie Men* with only two. I may have gone too far, and have, I think, given up an intention I at one time had of writing a play for a man and a scarecrow only, but one has to go on with experiment or interest in creation fades, at least so it is with me.

In 1902, my *Twenty-five* was staged; a rather sentimental comedy, not very amusing. It was useful at the time when we had so few, but it was weak, ending, as did for the most part the Gaelic plays that began to be written, in a piper and a dance. I tried to get rid of it afterwards by writing *The Jackdaw* on the same idea, but in which I make humour lay the ghost of sentiment. But *Twenty-five* may yet be rewritten and come to a little life of its own. *Spreading the News* was played at the opening of the Abbey Theatre, December 27, 1904. I heard it attacked at that time on the ground that Irish people never were gossips to such an extent, but it has held its own, and our audiences have had their education as well as writers and players, and know now that a play is a selection not a photograph and that the much misquoted "mirror to nature" was not used by its author or any good play-writer at all.

Perhaps I ought to have written nothing but these short comedies, but desire for experiment is like fire in the blood, and I had had from the beginning a vision of historical plays being sent by us through all the counties of Ireland. For to have a real success and to come into the life of the country, one must touch a real and eternal emotion, and history comes only next to religion in our country. And although the realism of our young writers is taking the place of fantasy and romance in the cities, I still hope to see a little season given up every year to plays on history and in sequence at the Abbey, and I think schools and colleges may ask to have them sent and played in their halls, as a part of the day's lesson. I began with the daring and light-heartedness of a schoolboy to write a tragedy in three acts upon a great personality, Brian the High King. I made many bad beginnings, and if I had listened to Mr. Yeats's advice I should have given it up, but I began again and again till it was at last moulded in at least a possible shape. It went well with our audience. There was some enthusiasm for it, being the first historical play we had produced. An old farmer came up all the way from Kincora, the present Killaloe, to see it, and I heard he went away sad at the tragic ending. He said, "Brian ought not to have married that woman. He should have been content with a nice, quiet girl from his own district." For stormy treacherous Gormleith of many husbands had stirred up the battle that brought him to his death. *Dervorgilla* I wrote at a time when circumstances had forced us to accept an English stage-manager for the Abbey. I was very strongly against this. I felt as if I should be spoken of some day as one who had betrayed her country's trust. I wrote so vehemently and sadly to Mr. Yeats about it that he might have been moved from the path of expediency, which I now think was the wise one, had the letter reached him in time, but it lay with others in the Kiltartan letter-box during a couple of weeks, Christmas time or the wintry weather giving an excuse to the mail-car driver whose duty it is to clear the box as he nightly passed it by. So he wrote: "I think we should take Vedrenne's recommendation unless we have some strong reason to the contrary. If the man is not Irish, we cannot help it. If the choice is between filling our country's stomach or enlarging its brains by importing precise knowlege, I am for scorning its stomach for the present.... I should have said that I told Vedrenne that good temper is essential, and he said the man he has recommended is a vegetarian and that Bernard Shaw says that vegetarians are wonderful for the temper."

Mr. Synge had something of my feeling about alien management. He wrote later: "The first show of —— was deplorable. It came out as a bastard literary pantomime, put on with many of the worst tricks of the English stage. That is the end of all the Samhain principles and this new tradition that we were to lay down! I felt inclined to walk out of the Abbey and go back no more. The second Saturday was much less offensive. —— is doing his best obviously and he may perhaps in time come to understand our methods."

To come back to play-writing, I find in a letter to Mr. Yeats. "You will be amused to hear that although, or perhaps because, I had evolved out of myself 'Mr. Quirke' as a conscious philanthropist, an old man from the workhouse told me two days ago that he had been a butcher of Quirke's sort and was quite vainglorious about it, telling me how many staggery sheep and the like he had killed, that would, if left to die, have been useless or harmful. 'But I often stuck a beast and it kicking yet and life in it, so that it could do no harm to a Christian or a dog or an animal.' " And later: "Yet another 'Mr. Quirke' has been to see me. He says there are no sick pigs now, because they are all sent off to . . . no, I mustn't give the address. Has not a purgatory been imagined where writers find themselves surrounded by the characters they have created?"

The Canavans, as I say in a note to it, was "written I think less by logical plan than in one of those moments of lightheartedness that, as I think, is an inheritance from my great-grandmother Frances Algoin, a moment of that 'sudden Glory, the Passion which maketh those Grimaces called Laughter.' Some call it farce, some like it the best of my comedies. This very day, October 16th, I have been sent a leaf from the examination papers of the new University, in which the passage chosen from literature to 'put Irish on' is that speech of Peter Canavan's beginning: 'Would any one now think it a thing to hang a man for, that he had striven to keep himself safe?"

But we never realise our dreams. I think it was *The Full Moon* that was in the making when I wrote: "I am really getting to work on a little comedy, of which I think at present that if its feet are of clay, its high head will be of rubbed gold, and that people will stop and dance when they hear it and not know for a while the piping was from beyond the world! But no doubt if it ever gets acted, it will be 'what Lady Gregory calls a comedy and everybody else, a farce!' "

The Deliverer is a crystallising of the story, as the people tell it, of Parnell's betrayal. Only yesterday some beggar from Crow Lane, the approach to Gort, told me he heard one who had been Parnell's friend speak against him at the time of the split: "He brought down O'Shea's wife on him and said he was not fit to be left at large. The people didn't like that and they hooted him and he was vexed and said he could buy up the whole of them for half a glass of porter!" I may look on *The Rising of the Moon* as an historical play, as my history goes, for the scene is laid in the historical time of the rising of the Fenians in the sixties. But the real fight in the play goes on in the sergeant's own mind, and so its human side makes it go as well in Oxford or London or Chicago as in Ireland itself. But Dublin Castle finds in it some smell of rebellion and has put us under punishment for its sins. When we came back from America last March, we had promised to give a performance on our first day in Dublin and *The Rising of the Moon* was one of the plays announced. But the stage costumes had not yet arrived, and we sent out to hire some from a depot from which the cast uniforms of the Constabulary may be lent out to the companies performing at the theatres—the Royal, the Gaiety, and the Queens. But our messenger came back empty-handed. An order had been issued by the authorities that "no clothes were to be lent to the Abbey because *The Rising of the Moon* was derogatory to His Majesty's forces." So we changed the bill and put on the *Workhouse Ward*, in which happily a quilt and blanket cover any deficiency of clothes.

We wanted to put on some of Molière's plays. They seemed akin to our own. But when one translation after another was tried, it did not seem to carry, to "go across the footlights." So I tried putting one into our own Kiltartan dialect, *The Doctor in Spite of Himself*, and it went very well. I went on, therefore, and translated *Scapin* and *The Miser*. Our players give them with great spirit; the chief parts—Scapin, Harpagon, and Frosine—could hardly be bettered in any theatre. I confess their genius does not suit so well the sentimental and artificial young lovers.

Mr. Yeats wrote from Paris: "Dec. 19, '08, I saw two days ago a performance of *Scapin* at the Odeon. I really like our own better. It seemed to me that a representation so traditional in its type as that at the Odeon has got too far from life, as we see it, to give the full natural pleasure of comedy. It was much more farcical than anything we have ever done. I have recorded several pieces of new business and noted costumes which were sometimes amusing. The acting was amazingly skilful and everything was expressive in the extreme. I noticed one difference between this production and ours which almost shocked me, so used am I to our own ways. There were cries of pain and real tears. Scapin cried when his master threatened him in the first act, and the old man, beaten by the supposed bully, was obviously very sore. I have always noticed that with our people there is never real suffering even in tragedy. One felt in the French comedians an undercurrent of passion—passion which our people never have. I think we give in comedy a kind of fancifulness and purity."

It is the existence of the Theatre that has created play-writing among us. Mr. Boyle had written stories, and only turned to plays when he had seen our performances in London. Mr. Colum claimed to have turned to drama for our sake, and Mr. Fitzmaurice, Mr. Ray, and Mr. Murray—a National schoolmaster—would certainly not have written but for that chance of having their work acted. A.E. wrote to me: "I think the Celtic Theatre will emerge all right, for if it is not a manifest intention of the gods that there should be such a thing, why the mania for writing drama which is furiously absorbing our Irish writers?" And again almost sadly: "Would it be inconvenient for me to go to Coole on Monday next . . . ? I am laying in a stock of colours and boards for painting and hope the weather will keep up. I hear Synge is at Coole, and as an astronomer of human nature, calculating the probable effect of one heavenly body on another which is invisible, I suppose W.B.Y. is at drama again and that the summer of verse is given over."

I asked Mr. Lennox Robinson how he had begun, and he said he had seen our players in Cork, and had gone away thinking of nothing else than to write a play for us to produce. He wrote and sent us *The Clancy Name*. We knew nothing of him, but saw there was good stuff in the play, and sent it back with suggestions for strengthening it and getting rid of some unnecessary characters. He altered it and we put it on. Then he wrote a three-act play *The Cross Roads*, but after he had seen it played he took away the first act, making it a far better play, for it is by seeing one's work on the stage that one learns best. Then he wrote *Harvest* with three strong acts, and this year *Patriots*, which has gone best of all.

One of the heaviest tasks had been reading the plays sent in. For some years Mr. Yeats and I read every one of these; but now a committee reports on them first and sends back those that are quite impossible with a short printed notice:

"The Reading Committee of the National Theatre Society regret to say that the enclosed play, which you kindly submitted to them, is, for various reasons, not suitable for production by the Abbey Company."

If a play is not good enough to produce, but yet shows some

skill in construction or dialogue, we send another printed form written by Mr Yeats:

"ADVICE TO PLAYWRIGHTS WHO ARE SENDING PLAYS TO THE ABBEY, DUBLIN

"The Abbey Theatre is a subsidised theatre with an educational object. It will, therefore, be useless as a rule to send it plays intended as popular entertainments and that alone, or originally written for performance by some popular actor at the popular theatres. A play to be suitable for performance at the Abbey should contain some criticism of life, founded on the experience or personal observation of the writer, or some vision of life, of Irish life by preference, important from its beauty or from some excellence of style; and this intellectual quality is not more necessary to tragedy than to the gayest comedy.

"We do not desire propagandist plays, nor plays written mainly to serve some obvious moral purpose; for art seldom concerns itself with those interests or opinions that can be defended by argument, but with realities of emotion and character that become self-evident when made vivid to the imagination.

"The dramatist should also banish from his mind the thought that there are some ingredients, the love-making of the popular stage for instance, especially fitted to give dramatic pleasure; for any knot of events, where there is passionate emotion and clash of will, can be made the subject matter of a play, and the less like a play it is at the first sight the better play may come of it in the end. Young writers should remember that they must get all their effects from the logical expression of their subject, and not by the addition of extraneous incidents; and that a work of art can have but one subject. A work of art, though it must have the effect of nature, is art because it is not nature, as Goethe said: and it must possess a unity unlike the accidental profusion of nature.

"The Abbey Theatre is continually sent plays which show that their writers have not understood that the attainment of this unity by what is usually a long shaping and reshaping of the plot, is the principal labour of the dramatist, and not the writing of the dialogue.

"Before sending plays of any length, writers would often save themselves some trouble by sending a 'Scenario,' or scheme of the plot, together with one completely written act and getting the opinion of the Reading Committee as to its suitability before writing the whole play."

I find a note from Mr. Yeats: "Some writer offers us a play which 'unlike those at the Abbey,' he says, is so constructed as to admit any topic or a scene laid in any country. It will under the circumstances, he says, 'do good to all.' I am sending him 'Advice to Playwrights.' "

The advice was not always gratefully received. I wrote to Mr. Yeats: "Such an absurd letter in the *Cork Sportsman*, suggesting that you make all other dramatists rewrite their plays to hide your own idiosyncrasy!"

If a play shows real promise and a mind behind it, we write personally to the author, making criticisms and suggestions. We were accused for a while of smothering the work of young writers in order that we might produce our own, but time has done away with that libel, and we are very proud of the school of drama that has come into being through the creation of our Theatre. We were advised also to put on more popular work, work that would draw an audience for the moment from being topical, or because the author had friends in some league. But we went on giving what we thought good until it became popular. I wrote once, thinking we had yielded over much: "I am sorry ——'s play has been so coldly received (a play that has since become a favourite one), but I think it is partly our own fault. It would have got a better welcome a year ago. We have been humouring our audience instead of educating it, which is the work we ought to do. It is not only giving so much —— and ——, it is the want of good work pressed on, and I believe the want of verse, which they respect anyhow. . . . I think the pressing on of Synge's two plays the best thing we can do for this season. We have a great backing now in his reputation. In the last battle, when we cried up his genius, we were supposed to do it for our own interest. . . . I only read Gerothwohl's speech after you left, and thought that sentence most excellent about the theatre he was connected with being intended 'for art and a thinking Democracy.' It is just what we set out to do, and now we are giving in to stupidity in a Democracy. I think the sentence should be used when we can."

One at least of the many gloomy prophecies written to Mr. Yeats at some time of trouble has not come true: "I am giving you the situation as it appears to me. Remember there is —— and —— and ——. An amalgamation of all the dissentients with a Gaelic dramatic society would leave Synge, Lady Gregory, and Boyle with yourself, and none of these have drawing power in Dublin. . . . You who initiated the theatre movement in Ireland, will be out of it."

Neither Mr. Yeats nor I take the writing of our plays lightly. We work hard to get clearly both fable and idea. *The Travelling Man* was first my idea and then we wrote it together. Then Mr. Yeats wrote a variant of it as a Pagan play, *The Black Horse*, and to this we owe the song, "There's many a strong farmer whose heart would break in two." It did not please him however, and then I worked it out in my own way. I wrote to him: "I am not sure about your idea, for if the Stranger wanted the child to be content with the things near him, why did he make the image of the Garden of Paradise and ride to it? I am more inclined to think the idea is the soul having once seen the Christ, the Divine Essence, must always turn back to it again. One feels sure the child will through all its life. And the mother, with all her comforts, has never been quite satisfied, because she wants to see the Christ again. But the earthly side of her built up the dresser, and the child will build up other earthly veils; yet never be quite satisfied. What do you think?"

And again: "I am trying so hard to get to work on a play and first excuses came—Thursday headache; now I feel myself longing to take over the saw-mill, which has stopped with the head sawyer's departure and only wants a steady superintendent; or to translate *L'Avare* or the Irish fairy tales, or anything rather than creative work! You feel just the same with the Theatre; anything that is more or less external administration is so easy! Why were we not born to be curators of museums?"

At another time he writes: "Every day up to this I have worked at my play in the greatest gloom and this morning half the time was the worst yet—all done against the grain. I had half decided to throw it aside, till I had got back my belief in myself with some sheer poetry. When I began, I got some philosophy and my mind became abundant and therefore cheerful. If I can make it obey my own definition of tragedy, passion defined by motives, I shall be all right. I was trying for too much character. If, as I think you said, farce is comedy with character left out, melodrama is, I believe, tragedy with passion left out."

As to our staging of plays, in 1903, the costumes for *The Hour-Glass* were designed by my son, and from that time a great deal of the work was done by him. *The Hour-Glass* dresses were purple played against a green curtain. It was our first attempt at the decorative staging long demanded by Mr. Yeats. Mr. Yeats says, in *Samhain*, 1905, "Our staging of *Kincora*, the work of Mr. Robert Gregory, was beautiful, with a high grave dignity and that strangeness which Ben Jonson thought to be a part of all excellent beauty."

The first acts of the play are laid in King Brian's great hall at Kincora. It was hung with green curtains, there were shields embossed with designs in gold upon the walls, and heavy mouldings over the doors. The last act showed Brian's tent at Clontarf; a great orange curtain filled the background, and it is hard to forget the effect at the end of three figures standing against it, in green, in red, in grey. For a front scene there was a curtain—we use it still in its dimness and age—with a pattern of tree stems interlaced and of leaves edged with gold. This was the most costly staging we had yet attempted: it came with costumes to £30. A great deal of unpaid labour went into it. Mr. Fay discovered a method of making papier mâché, a chief part of which seemed to be the boiling down of large quantities of our old programmes, for the mouldings and for the shields. I have often seen the designer himself on his knees by a great iron pot—one we use in cottage scenes—dying pieces of sacking, or up high on a ladder painting his forests or leaves. His staging of *The Shadowy Waters* was almost more beautiful; the whole stage is the sloping deck of a galley, blue and dim, the sails and dresses are green, the ornaments all of copper. He staged for us also, for love of his art and of the work, my own plays, *The White Cockade, The Image, Dervorgilla*, and Mr. Yeats's *On Baile's Strand* with the great bronze gates used in other plays as well, in Lord Dunsany's *Glittering Gate* and in *The Countess Cathleen*. It was by him the scenery for Mr. Yeats's *Deirdre* was designed and painted, and for Synge's *Deirdre of the Sorrows*. I am proud to think how much "excellent beauty" he has brought to the help of our work.

IV

THE FIGHT OVER "THE PLAYBOY"

WHEN Synge's *Shadow of the Glen* was first played in the Molesworth Hall in 1903, some attacks were made on it by the *Sinn Fein* weekly newspaper. In the play the old husband pretends to be dead, the young wife listens to the offers of a young farmer, who asks her to marry him in the chapel of Rathvanna when "Himself will be quiet a while in the Seven Churches." The old man jumps up, drives her out of the house, refusing to make peace, and she goes away with a tramp, a stranger from the roads. Synge was accused of having borrowed the story from another country, from "a decadent Roman source," the story of the widow of Ephesus, and given it an Irish dress. He declared he had been told this story in the West of Ireland. It had already been given in Curtin's tales. Yet the same cry has been made from time to time. But it happened last winter I was at New Haven, Connecticut, with the Company, and we were asked to tea at the house of a Yale professor. There were a good many people there, and I had a few words with each, and as they spoke of the interest taken in the plays, a lady said: "My old nurse has been reading *The Shadow of the Glen*, but she says it is but a hearth tale; she had heard it long ago in Ireland." Then others came to talk to me, and next day I went on to speak at Smith College. It was not till later I remembered the refusal to take Synge's word, and that now *Shadow of the Glen* had been called a "hearth tale." I was sorry I had not asked for the old woman's words to be put down, but I could not remember among so many strangers who it was that had told me of them. But a little later, in New York, one of the younger Yale professors came round during the plays to the little sitting-room at the side of the stage at the Maxine Elliott Theatre where I received friends. I asked him to find out what I wanted to know, and after a while I was sent the words of the old woman who is a nurse in a well-known philanthropic family: "Indeed, Miss, I've heard that story many's the time. It's what in the old country we call a fireside story. In the evening the neighbours would be coming in and sitting about the big fire, in a great stone chimney like you know, and the big long hearthstone in front, and the men would be stretching out on their backs on the stones and telling stories just the like of that; how that an old man had a young wife, and he began to fear she wasn't true to him, and he got himself into the bed and a big thorn stick with him, and made out to be dead, and when his wife was watching beside him in the night and thinking him safe dead, the other man came in and began talking to her to make her marry him; and himself jumped up out of the bed and gave them the great beating, just the same as in the book, Miss, only it reads more nice and refined like. Oh, there were many of those fireside stories they'd tell!"

But the grumbling against this play was only in the papers and in letters, and it soon died out, although I find in a letter from Mr. Yeats before the opening of the Abbey: "The *Independent* has waked up and attacked us again with a note and a letter of a threatening nature warning us not to perform Synge again." *The Well of the Saints* was let pass without much comment, though we had very small audiences for it, for those were early days at the Abbey. It was another story when in 1907 *The Playboy of the Western World* was put on. There was a very large audience on the first night, a Saturday, January 26th. Synge was there, but Mr. Yeats was giving a lecture in Scotland. The first act got its applause and the second, though one felt the audience were a little puzzled, a little shocked at the wild language. Near the end of the third act there was some hissing. We had sent a telegram to Mr. Yeats after the first act—"Play great success"; but at the end we sent another—"Audience broke up in disorder at the word shift." For that plain English word was one of those objected to, and even the papers, in commenting, followed the example of some lady from the country, who wrote saying "the word omitted but understood was one she would blush to use even when she was alone."

On the Monday night *Riders to the Sea*, which was the first piece, went very well indeed. But in the interval after it, I noticed on one side of the pit a large group of men sitting together, not a woman among them. I told Synge I thought it a sign of some organised disturbance and he telephoned to have the police at hand. The first part of the first act went undisturbed. Then suddenly an uproar began. The group of men I had noticed booed, hooted, blew tin trumpets. The editor of one of the Dublin weekly papers was sitting next to me, and I asked him to count them. He did so and said there were forty making the disturbance. It was impossible to hear a word of the play. The curtain came down for a minute, but I went round and told the actors to go on playing to the end, even if not a word could be heard. The police, hearing the uproar, began to file in, but I thought the disturbers might tire themselves out if left alone, or be satisfied with having made their protest, and I asked them to go outside but stay within call in case of any attempt being made to injure the players or the stage. There were very few people in the stalls, but among them was Lord Walter Fitzgerald, grand-nephew of the patriot, the adored Lord Edward. He stood up and asked that he and others in the audience might be allowed to hear the play, but this leave was refused. The disturbance lasted to the end of the evening, not one word had been heard after the first ten minutes.

Next day Mr. Yeats arrived and took over the management of affairs. Meanwhile I had asked a nephew at Trinity College to come and bring a few fellow athletes, that we might be sure of some able-bodied helpers in case of an attack on the stage. But, alas! the very sight of them was as a match to the resin of the pit, and a roar of defiance was flung back,—townsman against gownsman, hereditary enemies challenging each other as they are used to do when party or political processions march before the railings on College Green. But no iron railings divided pit and stalls, some scuffles added to the excitement, and it was one of our defenders at the last who was carried out bodily by the big actor who was playing Christy Mahon's slain father, and by Synge himself.

I had better help from another nephew. A caricature of the time shows him in evening dress with unruffled shirt cuffs, leading out disturbers of the peace. For Hugh Lane would never have worked the miracle of creating that wonderful gallery at sight of which Dublin is still rubbing its eyes, if he had not known that in matters of art the many count less than the few. I am not sure that in the building of our nation he may not have laid the most lasting stone; no fear of a charge of nepotism will scare me from "the noble pleasure of praising," and so I claim a place for his name above the thirty, among the chief, of our own mighty men.

There was a battle of a week. Every night protestors with their trumpets came and raised a din. Every night the police carried some of them off to the police courts. Every afternoon the papers gave reports of the trial before a magistrate who had not heard or read the play and who insisted on being given details of its incidents by the accused and by the police.

We held on, as we had determined, for the week during which we had announced the play would be acted. It was a definite fight for freedom from mob censorship. A part of the new

National movement had been, and rightly, an attack on the stage Irishman, the vulgar and unnatural butt given on the English stage. We had the destroying of that scarecrow in mind among other things in setting up our Theatre. But the societies were impatient. They began to dictate here and there what should or should not be played. Mr. Colum's plays and Mr. Boyle's were found too harsh in their presentment of life. I see in a letter about a tour we were arranging: "Limerick has not yet come to terms. They have asked for copies of proposed plays that they may 'place same before the branch of the Gaelic League there.' "

At Liverpool a priest had arranged an entertainment. The audience did not like one of the plays and hooted. The priest thereupon appeared and apologised, saying he would take the play off. In Dublin, Mr. Martin Harvey, an old favourite, had been forced to take off after the first night a little play because its subject was Irish belief in witchcraft. The widow of a writer of Irish plays that had been fairly popular was picketed through Ireland with her company and was nearly ruined, no one being allowed to enter the doors. Finally, at, I think, Athlone, she was only allowed to produce a play after it had been cut and re-arranged by a local committee, made up of the shopkeepers of the town. We would not submit Mr. Synge's work or any of the work we put on to such a test, nor would we allow any part of our audience to make itself final judge through preventing others from hearing and judging for themselves. We have been justified, for Synge's name has gone round the world, and we should have been ashamed for ever if we had not insisted on a hearing for his most important work. But, had it been a far inferior play and written by some young writer who had never been heard of, we should have had to do the same thing. If we had been obliged to give in to such organised dictation, we should of necessity have closed the Theatre. I respected the opinion of those among that group who were sincere. They, not used to works of imagination and wild fantasy, thought the play a libel on the Irish countryman, who has not put parricide upon his list of virtues; they thought the language too violent or it might be profane. The methods were another thing; when the tin trumpets were blown and brandished, we had to use the same loud methods and call the police. We lost some of our audience by the fight; the pit was weak for a while, but one after another said, "There is no other theatre to go to," and came back. The stalls, curiously, who appeared to approve of our stand, were shy of us for a long time. They got an idea we were fond of noise and quarrels. That was our second battle, and even at the end of the week, we had won it.

An organiser of agriculture, sent to County Clare, reported that the District Councils there were engaged in passing resolutions, "Against the French Government and *The Playboy*." Mrs. Coppinger in *The Image* says, on some such occasion, "Believe me there is not a Board or a Board Room west of the Shannon but will have a comrade cry put out between this and the Feast of Pentecost." And anyhow in our case some such thing happened.

But Synge's fantasy is better understood now even by those "who have never walked in Apollo's garden," and *The Playboy* holds its place in the repertory of the Abbey from year to year.

EDITOR'S NOTE

The following chapter was originally written in Autumn 1912, if we date it from the two italicised introductory paragraphs. A later version of this chapter, without these paragraphs, appeared in the March 1913 issue of *The English Review.*

The text given here is that of the later version. The only changes between the first and second versions which have been noted are those where material has been inserted, deleted or changed. New material which appeared in the later version for the first time is enclosed by square brackets; deletions are noted at the bottom of the page, where the original is given. The paragraph symbol, ¶, is used to show where the paragraphs started in the Autumn 1912 version. Mistakes in the setting have been corrected, as it is obvious that Lady Gregory did not see proofs before the article was published, and it is possible that a number of the changes in grammar were made by the *Review's* editor, Mr. Austin Harrison.

V

SYNGE

It is October now and leaves have fallen from the branches of the big copper-beech in the garden; I saw the stars shining through them last night. You were asleep then, but in the day-time you can see the sky all blue through their bareness. And the dry red heaps under them are noisy when pheasants, looking for mast, hurry away as you come calling, running, down the hill. The smooth trunk of the tree that was in shadow all through the summer shines out now like silver. You stop to look at letters cut in the bark. You can read most of them yourself. You came under the wide boughs a few weeks ago, when a soldier who has gone now to set in order all the British dominions over sea carved that "Ian H." far out of your reach, as high as his own head. There is another name higher again, for the painter who cut that "A" and that "J" climbed up to write it again where we could not follow him, higher than the birds make their nests. There are letters of other names, "G.B.S." and "W.B.Y." Strangers know the names they stand for; they are easily known. But there to the north those letters, "J.M.S.," stand for a name that was not known at all at the time it was cut there, a few years before you were born.

The days are getting short and in the evening, when you ask me for something to paint or to scribble on, I sometimes give you one from a bundle of old sheets of paper, with three names printed at the head of it, with the picture of a woman and a dog. The names are those of three friends who worked together for a while: Yeats's name and my own and the name of John Millington Synge.

¶ I first saw J. M. Synge in the North Island of Aran.[1] I was staying there gathering folk-lore, talking to the people, and felt quite angry when I passed another outsider walking here and there, talking also to the people. I was jealous of not being alone on the island among the fishers and seaweed gatherers. I did not speak to the stranger, nor was he inclined to speak to me; he also looked on me as an intruder, I only heard his name. But

[1] "I first saw Synge in the north island of Arran."

a little later in the summer Mr. Yeats, who was staying with me at Coole, had a note from Synge saying he was in Aran. They had met in Paris. Yeats had written[2] of him there: "He is really a most excellent man. He lives in a little room which he has furnished himself; he is his own servant. He works very hard and is learning Breton; he will be a very useful scholar."

¶ I asked him here and we became friends at once. I said of him in a letter: "One never has to arrange one's mind to talk to him." He was quite direct, sincere and simple, not only a good listener, but too good a one, not speaking much in general society. His fellow guests at Coole always liked him, and he was pleasant and genial with them, though once, when he had come straight from life on a wild coast, he confessed that a somewhat warlike English lady in the house was "Civilisation in its most violent form." For there could be a sharp edge to his wit, as when he said of a certain actress (not Mrs. Campbell) whose modern methods he disliked, she had turned Yeats's *Deirdre* into "the Second Mrs. Conchubar," and once, when awaking from the anaesthetic after one of those hopeless operations, the first words that could be understood were, "Those damned English can't even swear without vulgarity." ¶ He sent me later, when we had been long working at the theatre, some review of his work from a German newspaper: "What gives me a sympathy with this new man is that he does not go off into sentimentality. Behind this legend I see a laughing face, then he raises his eyebrows in irony and laughs again. Herr Synge may not be a dramatist, he may not be a great poet, but he has something that I like in him,[3] a thing that for many good Germans is a book with seven seals, that is, Humour."

He writes a note with this: "I'd like to quote about 'Humour,' but I don't want to tell Dublin I'm maybe no dramatist, that wouldn't do." ¶ Of his other side, Mr. J. B. Yeats wrote to me: "Coleridge said that all Shakespeare's characters, from Macbeth to Dogberry, were 'ideal realities.' His comedies 'poetry as an unlimited jest,' and his tragedies 'poetry in deepest earnest.'[4] Had he seen Synge's plays he would have called them 'poetry in unlimited sadness.' "

¶ While staying with us he hardly looked at a newspaper. He seemed to look on politics and reforms with a sort of tolerant indifference, though he spoke once of something that had

2 "Yeats wrote of him from there:"

3 ". . . something in him that I like,"

4 "Coleridge said that all Shakespeare's characters from Macbeth to Dogberry are ideal realities, his comedies are poetry as an unlimited jest, and his tragedies 'poetry in deepest earnest.' "

happened as "the greatest tragedy since Parnell's death." He told me that the people of the plays he was writing often seemed the real people among whom he was living, and I think his dreamy look came from this. [When here] he spent a good deal of time wandering in our woods, where many shy creatures still find their homes,[5] marten cats and squirrels and otters and badgers, and by the lake where wild swans come and go. He said he had given up[6] wearing the black clothes he had worn for a while, when they were a fashion with writers, thinking they were not in harmony with Nature, which is so sparing in the use of the harsh colour of the raven. ¶ Simple things always pleased him. In his long illness, at a Dublin hospital where I went to see him every day, he would ask for every detail of a search I was making for a couple of Irish terrier puppies to bring home, and laugh at my adventures again and again. And when I described to him the place where I had found the puppies at last, a little house in a suburb, with a long garden stretching into wild[7] fields with a view of the hills beyond, he was excited, and said that it was just such a Dublin home as he had wanted, and had been sure was somewhere to be found. He asked me at this time about a village on the Atlantic coast where I had stayed for a while in rooms over a post office, and where he had hoped he might go for his convalescence instead of to Germany, which had been arranged for him. I said in talking of it that I felt more and more the time wasted that was not spent in Ireland, and he said: "That is just my feeling."

¶[8] When my *Cuchulain of Muirthemne* came out he said to Mr. Yeats he had been amazed to find in it the dialect he had been trying to master. He wrote to me: "Your *Cuchulain* is a part of my daily bread"; I say this with a little pride, for I was the first to use the Irish idiom as it is spoken, with intention and with belief in it. Dr. Hyde has used it[9] with fine effect in his *Love Songs of Connacht*, but alas! gave it up afterwards in deference to some Dublin editor.

[Also I must be proud of any word of praise from Synge, for he did not use many. Mr. Yeats writes, and expects me to feel personally flattered: "By the way, Synge is becoming quite complimentary. He says your Mancini portrait is the greatest

5 "homes"

6 "He told Mr. Yeats he had given up"

7 "wide"

8 "The rich, abundant speech of the people was a delight to him. When ..." In the second version this sentence was moved to the beginning of the next paragraph but one.

9 "Dr. Hyde indeed has used it"

since Rembrandt." And he writes in his diary a few days after Synge's death: "He had that egotism of the man of genius which Nietzsche compares to the egotism of a woman with child. I never knew what he thought of my work . . . After the first performance of *Hyacinth Halvey*, Lady Gregory went the very moment the play was over to get supper for him, for he was ailing at the time, not waiting for the congratulation of friends. All he said of the triumphant *Hyacinth* was: 'I expected to like it better.' He had under charming and modest manners in all things in life complete absorption in his own dream. I have never heard him praise any writer, living or dead, but some old French farce writers, for here nothing existed but his thought. He claimed nothing for it aloud, he never said any of these confident things I say too often when angry, but one knew that he valued nothing else. He was too confident for self-assertion. I once said to George Moore: 'Synge has always the better of you for you have brief but ghastly moments in which you admit the existence of other writers, Synge never has.' I do not think he disliked other writers, they did not exist. One did not think him an egotist, he was too sympathetic in the ordinary affairs of life and too simple. In the arts he knew no language but his own.

"The rich abundant speech of the people was a delight to him.] He wrote to me after his first visit: I had a very prosperous journey up from Gort. At Athenry an old Irish-speaking wanderer made my acquaintance. He claims[10] to be the best singer in England, Ireland and America. One night he says he sang a song at Moate, and a friend of his heard the words in Athenry. He was so much struck by the event that he had himself examined by one who knew, and found that his singing did not come out of his lungs, but out of his heart, which is a 'winged heart!' "

¶ At the time of his first visit to Coole he had written some poems, not very good for the most part, and a play which was not good at all. I read it again after his death when, according to his written wish, helping Mr. Yeats and[11] sorting out the work to be published or set aside, and again it seemed but of slight merit. But a year later he brought us his two plays, *The Shadow of the Glen*, and the *Riders to the Sea*, both masterpieces, both perfect in their way. He had gathered emotion, the driving force he needed from his life among the people, and it was the working in dialect that had set free his style.

¶ He was anxious to publish his book on Aran and these two

10 "He claimed"
11 "helping Mr. Yeats in sorting"

plays, and so having[12] something to add to that "Forty pounds a year and a new suit when I am too shabby," he used with a laugh to put down as his income. He wrote to me from Paris in February, 1902: "I don't know what part of Europe you may be in now, but I suppose this will reach you if I send it to Coole. I want to tell you the evil fate of my Aran book and ask your advice. It has been to two publishers, to Grant Richards, who was sympathetic, though he refused it as he said it could not be a commercial success, and to Fisher Unwin, who was inclined to be scornful.

¶ "Now that you have seen the book, do you think there would be any chance of Alfred Nutt[13] taking it up? I am afraid he is my only chance, but I don't know whether there is any possibility of getting him to bring out a book of the kind at his own expense, as, after all, there is very little folk-lore in it."

¶ I took the book to London and had it re-typed, for he, like myself, typed his own manuscript,[14] and this was very faint and rubbed, and both Mr. Yeats and I took it to publishers, but they would not take it. Writing in March, '03, he says: ¶ "My play came back from the *Fortnightly* as not suitable for their purposes. And I don't think that Brinsley Johnson intends[15] to bring out the Aran book. I saw him on my way home, but he seemed hopelessly undecided, saying one minute he liked it very much, and that it might be a great success, and that he wanted to be in touch with the Irish movement, and then going off in the other direction and fearing that it might fall perfectly flat! Finally he asked me to let him consider it a little longer."

¶ I was no more successful. I wrote to Mr. Yeats, who was in America: "I went to Bullen[16] about the music for your book . . . I think I told you he had never opened the Synge MS. and said he would rather have nothing to do with it. Masefield has it now." ¶ Then I had a note: "Dear Lady Gregory, I saw Newbolt[17] yesterday and spoke to him about Synge's new play (*Riders to the Sea*), which struck me as being in some ways even better than the other. He has promised to read it if it is sent to him, though he does not much care for plays. Will you post it to the Editor, *Monthly Review* . . . Yours very truly, Arthur Symons." ¶ Nothing came of that, and in December Synge writes: ¶ "I am delighted to find that there is a prospect

12 "and so have something"
13 "Mr. N——"
14 "manuscripts,"
15 "Mr. J. —— intends"
16 "I went to Mr. B."
17 "I saw Mr. N."

of getting the book out at last, and equally grateful for the trouble you have taken with it. I am writing to Masefield to-day to thank him, and ask him by all means to get Mathews to do as he proposes. Do you think if he brings out the plays in the Spring I should add *The Tinker*?[18] I was getting on well with the blind people (in *The Well of the Saints*) till about a month ago, when I suddenly got ill with influenza and a nasty attack on my lung. I am getting better now, but I cannot work yet satisfactorily, so I hardly know when the play is likely to be finished. There is no use trying to hurry on with a thing of that sort when one is not in the mood."

¶ Yet the Aran book was not published, after all, till 1907, when his name had already gone up.[19] *The Shadow of the Glen* and [the] *Riders to the Sea* were published by Mr. Elkin Mathews in 1905. *Riders to the Sea* had already been published in *Samhain*, the little annual of our theatre, edited by Mr. Yeats. And in America a friend of ours and of the Theatre had printed some of the plays in a little edition of fifty copies, thus saving the copyright. It was of Synge and of others as well as myself I thought when, in dedicating a book to John Quinn when I was in America last winter,[20] I wrote: "Best friend, best helper these half score years on this side of the sea."

¶When Synge had joined us in the management of the Theatre he took his share of the work, and though we were amateurs then, we got on somehow or other. He writes about a secretary we had sent for him to report on: "He seems very willing, and I think may do very well if he does not take fright at us. He still thinks it was a terrible thing for Yeats to suggest that Irish people should sell their souls and for you to put His Sacred Majesty James II into a barrel. He should be very useful in working up an audience; an important part of our work which we have rather neglected. By the way, the annual meeting of our company must be held, I suppose, before the year is up. It would be well to have it before we pay off Ryan, as otherwise we shall be sitting about looking with curiosity and awe at the balance sheet."

¶ He went on bravely with his work, always fighting against ill-health.

"Feb. 15, '06. Many thanks for the MS. of *Le Médicin*. I think he is entirely admirable and is certain to go well. This is

[18] "the *Tinkers*?"

[19] "Yet, after all, the Aran book was not published till 1907, when Synge's name had already gone up."

[20] "John Quinn during my first winter in America,"

just a line to acknowledge the MS. as I suppose I shall see you in a day or two.

¶ "My play has made practically no way[21] since, as I have been down for ten days with bronchitis. My lung is not touched, however, and I have got off well considering. I hope I shall be all right by next week."

¶ (About the same date): "I am pleased with the way my play is going, but I find it quite impossible to rush through with it now, so I rather think I shall take it and the typewriter to some place in Kerry where I could work. By doing so I would get some sort of holiday and still avoid dropping the play again—which is a rather dangerous process. If I do this I will be beyond posts. . . . If I do not get a good summer, I generally pay for it in the winter in extra bouts of influenza and all its miseries."

¶ "August 12, '06. I shall be very glad, thanks, to go down and read you my play (*The Playboy*) if it is finished in time, but there is still a great deal to do. I have had a very steady week's work since last Sunday and have made good way, but my head is getting very tired. Working in hot weather takes a lot out of me."

¶ "November 25, '06. I have had rather a worse attack than I expected when I wrote my last note, but I am much better now, and out as usual. One of my lungs, however, has been a little touched, so I shall have to be careful for a while. Would it be possible to put off *The Playboy* for a couple of weeks? I am afraid if I went to work at him again now, and then rehearsed all December, I would be very likely to knock up badly before I was done with him. My doctor says I may do so if it is *necessary*, but he advises me to take a couple of weeks' rest if it can be managed. That cousin of mine who etches is over here now and he wants me to stay with him for a fortnight in a sort of country house he has in Surrey, so if you think *The Playboy* can be put off, I will go across on Thursday or Friday and get back in time to see *The Shadowy Waters* and get *The Playboy* under way for January. What do you think? If so, I would like to read the third act of *Playboy* to you before I go, and then make final changes, while I am away, as I shall have a quiet time."

¶ He worked very hard at *The Playboy*, altering it a good deal as he went on. He had first planned the opening act in the ploughed field, where the quarrel between Christy and his father took place. But when he thought of the actual stage he could not seen any possible side wings for that "wide, windy corner of high, distant hills." He had also talked of the return of the

21 "no headway"

father being at the very door[22] of the chapel where Christy was to wed Pegeen; but in the end all took place within the one cottage room. We all tried at that time to write for as little scene-shifting as might be, for economy of scenery and of stage-hands.[23]

¶ In October, 1906, he writes to Mr. Yeats:[24] "My play, though in its last agony, is not finished, and I cannot promise it for any definite day. It is more than likely that when I read it to you and Fay there will be little things to alter that have escaped me, and with my stuff it takes time to get even half a page of new dialogue fully into key with what goes before it. The play, I think, will be one of the longest we have done, and in places extremely difficult. If we said the 19th, I could only have six or seven full rehearsals, which would not, I am quite sure, be enough . . . I am very sorry, but what is to be done?" ¶Then to me[25] in November: "May I read *The Playboy* to you and Yeats and Fay some time to-morrow, Saturday or Monday according as it suits you all? A little verbal correction is still necessary, and one or two structural points may need—I fancy do need—revision, but I would like to have your opinions on it before I go further."

¶ I remember his bringing the play to us in Dublin, but he was too hoarse to read it, and it was read by Mr. Fay. We were almost bewildered by its abundance and fantasy, but we felt—and Mr. Yeats said very plainly—that there was far too much "bad language," there were too many violent oaths, and the play itself was marred by this. I did not think it was fit to be put on the stage without cutting. It was agreed that it should be cut in rehearsal. A fortnight before its production Mr. Yeats, thinking I had seen a rehearsal, writes:[26] "I should like to know how you thought *The Playboy* acted. . . . Have they cleared many of the objectionable sentences out of it?"

I did not, however, see a rehearsal and did not hear the play again until the night of its production, and then I told Synge that the cuts were not enough, that many more should be made. He gave me leave to do this, and in consultation with the players I took out many phrases which, though in the printed book, have never since that first production been spoken on our stage. I am

22 "He had also thought that the scene of the return of the father should be at the very door"

23 "We all tried at that time to write our plays so as to require as little scene shifting as possible for the sake of economy and of stage-hands."

24 In October, 1906, Synge wrote to Mr. Yeats:"

25 "Then he wrote to me"

26 "wrote:"

sorry that they were not taken out[27] before it had been played at all, but that is just what happened.

¶ On Saturday, January 26, 1907, I found a note from Synge on my arrival in Dublin: "I do not know how things will go to-night. The day company are all very steady, but some of the outsiders in a most deplorable state of uncertainty . . . I have a sort of second edition of influenza and I am looking gloomily at everything. Fay has worked very hard all through, and everything has gone smoothly."

¶ I think the week's rioting helped to break down his health. He was always nervous at a first production, and the unusual excitement of this one upset him and he took[28] a chill and was kept to his bed for a while. Yet he got away to wild places while he could. He wrote to me from the Kerry coast:

"My journey went off all right, and though I had a terrible wet night in Tralee I was able to ride on here next day. When I came up to the house I found, to my horror, a large green tent pitched in the haggard and thought I had run my head into a Gaelic League settlement at last. However, it turned out to be a band of sappers only, who have since moved on." And again: "The day after to-morrow I move on, bag and baggage, to the Great Blasket Island. It is probably even more primitive than Aran, and I am wild with joy at the prospect. I will tell you of my new abode. I am to go out in a curragh on Sunday, when the people are going back from Mass on the mainland, and I am to lodge with the King!"

¶ It was only in the country places he was shy of the Gaelic League. In August, '06, he says: "I went to the Oireactas on Thursday to see their plays. The propagandist play done by the Ballaghadereen Company was clever with some excellent dialogue, and the peasants who acted it were quite admirable. I felt really enthusiastic about the whole show, although the definitely propagandist fragments were, of course, very crude. The play was called, I think, *an T-Atruighe mor* (the big change). I think I have spelled it wrong. It would probably read badly."

¶ The last year was still a struggle against failing strength: –

"April, '08.—I have been waiting from day to day to write, so that I might say something definite about my 'tin-tacks' (an allusion to the old man in *Workhouse Ward* who has pains like tin-tacks in his inside) and possible plans. I was with the doctor again to-day, and he thinks I may have to go into hospital again, and perhaps have an operation, but things are uncertain for a

27 "I am sorry they were not taken out"
28 "upset him. He took"

day or two . . . I fear there is little possibility of my being able to go to the shows this week, so I do not know if you ought to come up, if you can without inconvenience. I am rather afraid of slovenly shows if there are poor houses and no one there to supervise. It is very trying having to drop my rehearsals of *Well of the Saints*—in fact, this unlooked-for complication is a terrible upset every way—I have so much to do."

¶ "August 28th '08.—I have just been with Sir E. Ball. He seems to think I am going on very well, and says I may ride and bicycle and do what I like! All the same, I am not good for much yet. I get tired out very easily. I am half inclined to go to the British Association *matinee* on Friday. I would like to hear Yeats's speech, and I don't think it could do me any harm. In any case, I will go in and see you when you are up: I think of going away to Germany or somewhere before very long. I am not quite well enough for the West of Ireland in this broken weather, and I think the complete change would do me most good. I have old friends on the Rhine I could stay with if I decide to go there. I hear great accounts of the Abbey this week, it almost looks as if Dublin was beginning to know we are there. I have been fiddling with my *Deirdre* a little. I think I'll have to cut it down to two longish acts. The middle act in Scotland is impossible . . . They have been playing *The Well of the Saints* in Munich; I have just got £3.10s. royalties. It was a one-act version I have just heard this minute compressed from my text!"

¶ "January 3rd, '09.—I have done a great deal to *Deirdre* since I saw you, chiefly in the way of strengthening motives and re-casting the general scenario, but there is still a good deal to be done with the dialogue, and some scenes in the first act must be re-written to make them fit in with the new parts I have added. I only work a little every day, and I suffer more than I like with indigestion and general uneasiness inside . . . The doctors are vague and don't say much that is definite . . .

¶ "They are working at *The Miser* now, and are all very pleased with it and themselves. I have not been in to see a rehearsal yet, as I keep out in the country as much as I can."

¶ But his strength did not last long enough to enable him to finish *Deirdre of the Sorrows*, his last play. After he had gone, we took infinite trouble to bring the versions together, and we produced it early in the next year, but it needed the writer's hand. I did my best for it, working at its production through snowy days and into winter nights, until rheumatism seized me with a grip I have never shaken off. I wrote to Mr. Yeats: "I still hope we can start with *Deirdre* . . . I will be in Dublin for rehearsals in Christmas week, though I still hope to get to Paris for Christmas with Robert, but it may not be worth while. I will spend all January at the Theatre, but I must be back on the first of February to do some planting; that cannot be put off." And again, "I am more hopeful of *Deirdre* now. I have got Conchubar and Fergus off at the last in Deirdre's long speech, and that makes an immense improvement; she looks lonely and pathetic with the other two women crouching and rocking themselves on the floor."

¶For we have done our utmost[29] for his work since we lost him, as we did while he was with us here. ¶ He had written a poem, it was in the [Dun Emer] Press[30] at the time of his death:

"With fifteen-ninety or Sixteen-sixteen
We end Cervantes, Marot, Nashe, or Green;
Then Sixteen-thirteen till two score and nine
Is Crashaw's niche, that honey-lipped divine.
And so when all my little work is done,
They'll say I came in Eighteen seventy-one,
And died in Dublin—What year will they write
For my poor passage to the stall of Night?"

¶ Early in 1909 he was sent again into a private hospital in Dublin. A letter came to me from Mr. Yeats dated March 24th: "In the early morning Synge said to the nurse, 'It is no use fighting death any longer,' and turned over and died."

29 "For we have done our best"

30 "the press" [*The English Review* actually prints "Scon Eper Press." These may be simple errors in setting up the type, but it is not improbable that Mr. Austin Harrison, its editor, mis-remembering the name of the press, inserted it himself.]

VI

THE FIGHT WITH THE CASTLE

IN the summer of 1909 I went one day from London to Ayot St. Lawrence, a Hertfordshire village, to consult Mr. Bernard Shaw on some matters connected with our Theatre. When I was leaving, he gave me a little book, *The Shewing-up of Blanco Posnet,* which had just been printed, although not published. It had, however, been already rejected by the Censor, as all readers of the newspapers know; and from that quiet cottage the fiery challenge-giving answers had been sent out. I read the play as I went back in the train, and when at St. Pancras Mr. Yeats met me to talk over the business that had taken me away, I showed him the little book that had been given the black ball, and I said, "Hypocrites."

A little time afterwards Mr. Shaw offered us the play for the Abbey, for the Censor has no jurisdiction in Ireland—an accidental freedom. We accepted it and put it in rehearsal that we might produce it in Horse Show week. We were without a regular stage manager at that time, and thought to have it produced by one of the members of the Company. But very soon the player who had taken it in charge found the work too heavy and troublesome, and withdrew from the stage management, though not from taking a part. I had a letter one morning telling me this, and I left by the next train for Dublin. As I left, I sent a wire to a London actor—a friend—asking if he could come over and help us out of this knot. Meanwhile, that evening, and before his answer came, I held a rehearsal, the first I had ever taken quite alone. I thought out positions during the night, and next morning, when I had another rehearsal, I began to find an extraordinary interest and excitement in the work. I saw that Blanco's sermon, coming as it did after bustling action, was in danger of seeming monotonous. I broke it up by making him deliver the first part standing up on the Sheriff's bench, then bringing him down to sit on the table and speak some of the words into the face of Elder Posnet. After that I sent him with a leap on to the table for the last phrases. I was very much pleased with the effect of this action, and by the time a telegram told me my London friend could come, I was confident enough to do without him.

We were very proud and pleased when the whole production was taken to London later by the Stage Society. I have produced plays since then, my own and a few others. It is tiring work; one spends so much of one's own vitality.

That is what took me away from home to Dublin in that summer time, when cities are out of season. Mr. Yeats had stayed on at Coole at his work, and my letters to him, and letters after that to my son and to Mr. Shaw, will tell what happened through those hot days, and of the battle with Dublin Castle, which had taken upon itself to make the writ of the London Censor run at the Abbey.

I received while in Dublin, the following letter from a permanent official in Dublin Castle:

" Dear Lady Gregory:

" I am directed by the Lord Lieutenant to state that His Excellency's attention has been called to an announcement in the Public Press that a play entitled *The Shewing-up of Blanco Posnet* is about to be performed in the Abbey Theatre.

"This play was written for production in a London theatre, and its performance was disallowed by the Authority which in England is charged with the Censorship of stage plays. The play does not deal with an Irish subject, and it is not an Irish play in any other sense than that its author was born in Ireland. It is now proposed to produce this play in the Abbey Theatre, which was founded for the express purpose of encouraging dramatic art in Ireland, and of fostering a dramatic school growing out of the life of the country.

"The play in question does not seem well adapted to promote these laudable objects or to belong to the class of plays originally intended to be performed in the Abbey Theatre, as described in the evidence on the hearing of the application for the Patent.

"However this may be, the fact of the proposed performance having been brought to the notice of the Lord Lieutenant, His Excellency cannot evade the responsibility cast upon him of considering whether the play conforms in other respects to the conditions of the Patent.

"His Excellency, after the most careful consideration, has arrived at the conclusion that in its original form the play is not in accordance either with the assurances given by those interested when the Patent was applied for, or with the conditions and restrictions contained in the Patent as granted by the Crown.

"As you are the holder of the Patent in trust for the generous founder of the Theatre, His Excellency feels bound to call your attention, and also the attention of those with whom you are associated, to the terms of the Patent and to the serious consequences which the production of the play in its original form might entail . . ."

I tell what followed in letters written to Coole.

"Thursday, August 12th. At the Theatre this morning the Secretary told me Whitney & Moore (our solicitors) had telephoned that they had a hint there would be interference with the production of *Blanco Posnet* by the Castle, and would like to see me.

"I went to see Dr. Moore. He said a Castle Official, whose name he would not give, had called the day before yesterday and said, 'As a friend of Sir Benjamin Whitney, I have come to tell you that if this play is produced it will be a very expensive thing for Miss Horniman.' Dr. Moore took this to mean the Patent would be forfeited. I talked the matter over with him and asked if he would get further information from his friend as to what method they meant to adopt, for I would not risk the immediate forfeiture of the Patent, but would not mind a threat of refusal to give a new Patent, as by that time—1910—perhaps neither the present Lord Lieutenant nor the present Censor would be in office.

"Dr. Moore said he would go and see his friend, and at a quarter past two I had a message on the telephone from him that I had better see the Castle Official or that he wished to see me (I didn't hear very well) before 3 o'clock. I went to the Castle and saw the Official. He said, 'Well.' I said, 'Are you going to cut off our heads?' He said, 'This is a very serious business; I think you are very ill-advised to think of putting on this play. May I ask how it came about?' I said, 'Mr. Shaw offered it and we accepted it.' He said, 'You have put us in a most difficult and disagreeable position by putting on a play to which the English Censor objected.' I answered, 'We do not take his view of it, and we think it hypocrisy objecting to a fallen woman in homespun on the stage, when a fallen woman in satin has been the theme of such a great number of plays that have been passed.' He said, 'It is not that the Censor objected to; it is the use of certain expressions which may be considered blasphemous. Could not they be left out?' 'Then there would be no play. The subject of the play is a man, a horse-thief, shaking his fist at Heaven, and finding afterwards that Heaven is too strong for him. If there were no defiance, there could be no victory. It is the same theme that Milton has taken in Satan's defiance in *Paradise Lost*. I consider it a deeply religious play, and one that could hurt no man, woman or child. If it had been written by some religious leader, or even by a dramatist considered "safe," nonconformists would admire and approve of it.' He said, 'We have nothing to do with that, the fact for us is that the Censor has banned it.' I said, 'Yes, and passed *The Merry Widow*, which is to be performed here the same week, and which I have heard is objectionable, and *The Devil*, which I saw in London.' He said, 'We would not have interfered, but what can we do when we see such paragraphs as these?' handing me a cutting from the *Irish Times* headed, 'Have we a Censor?' I replied, 'We have not written or authorised it, as you might see by its being incorrect. I am sole Patentee of the Theatre.' He said, 'Dublin society will call out against us if we let it go on.' 'Lord Iveagh has taken six places.' 'For that play?' 'Yes, for that play, and I believe Dublin society is likely to follow Lord Iveagh.' He went on 'Archbishop Walsh may object.' I was silent. He said, 'It is very hard on the Lord Lieutenant. You should have had more consideration for him.' I replied. 'We did not know or remember that the power rested with him, but it *is* hard on him, for he can't please everybody.' He said, 'Will you not give it up?' 'What will you do if we go on?' 'Either take no notice or take the Patent from you at once.' I said, 'If you decide to forfeit our Patent, we will not give a public performance; but if we give no performance to be judged by, we shall rest under the slur of having tried to produce something bad and injurious.' 'We must not provoke Public opinion.' 'We provoked Nationalist public opinion in *The Playboy*, and you did not interfere.' 'Aye,' said he, 'exactly so, that was quite different; that had not been banned by the Censor.' I said, 'Time has justified us, for we have since produced *The Playboy* in Dublin and on tour with success, and it will justify us in the case of this play.' 'But *Blanco Posnet* is very inferior to *The Playboy*.' I said, 'Even so, Bernard Shaw has an intellectual position above that of Mr. Synge, though he is not above him in imaginative power. He is recognised as an intellectual force, and his work cannot be despised.' 'Lord Aberdeen will have to decide.' 'I should like him to know,' I said, 'that from a business point of view the refusal to allow this play, already announced, to be given would do us a serious injury.' He said, 'No advertisements have been published.' 'Yes,' I said, 'the posters have been out some days, and there is a good deal of booking already from England as well as here. We are just beginning to pay our way as a Theatre. We should be able to do so if we get about a dozen more stalls regularly. The people who would take our stalls will be frightened off by your action. The continuance of our Theatre at all may depend on what you do now. We are giving a great deal of employment, spending in Dublin over £1500 a year, and our Company bears the highest possible character.' He said, 'I know that well.' I said, 'I know Lord Aberdeen is friendly to our Theatre, though he does not come to it, not liking the colour of our carpets.' He said 'He is a supporter of the drama. He was one of Sir Henry Irving's pall-bearers.' 'When shall we know the decision?' 'In a day or two, perhaps to-morrow. You can produce it in Cork, Galway, or Waterford. It is only in Dublin the Lord Lieutenant has power.' He read from time to time a few lines from the Patent or Act of Parliament before him, 'just to get them into your head.' The last words he read were, 'There must be no profane representation of sacred personages'; 'and that,' he said 'applies to Blanco Posnet's representations of the Deity.' I told him of the Censor's note on *The Playboy*, 'The expression "Khaki cut-throats" must be cut out, together with any others that may be considered derogatory to His Majesty's Forces,' and he laughed. Then I said, 'How can we think much of the opinion of a man like that?' He said, 'I believe he was a bank manager.' We then said good-bye."

"Friday, 5 o'c. Dr. Moore sent for me at 4 o'clock. I went with W. B. Yeats, who had arrived. The Crown Solicitor at the Castle, Sir B. Whitney's 'friend,' had called and told him the Lord Lieutenant was 'entirely opposed to the play being proceeded with and would use every power the law gave him to stop it,' and that, 'it would be much better for us to lay the play aside.'

"We decided to go on with the performance and let the Patent be forfeited, and if we must die, die gloriously. Yeats was for this course, and I agreed. Then I thought it right to let the Permanent Official know my change of intention, and, after some unsuccessful attempts on the telephone, W.B.Y. and I went to see him at the Castle. He was very smiling and amiable this time, and implored us, as we had understood him to do through the telephone, to save the Lord Lieutenant from his delicate position. 'You defy us, you advertise it under our very nose, at the time everyone is making a fight with the Censor.' He threatened to take away our Patent before the play came on at all, if we persisted in the intention. I said that would give us a fine case. Yeats said we intended to do *Œdipus*, that this also was a censored play, although so unobjectionable to religious minds that it had been performed in the Catholic University of Nôtre Dame, and that we should be prevented if we announced it now. He replied, 'Leave that till the time comes, and you needn't draw our attention to it.' We said the *Irish Times* might again draw his attention to it. He proposed our having a private performance only. I said, 'I had a letter from Mr Shaw objecting to that course.' He moaned, and said, 'It is very hard upon us. Can you suggest no way out of it?' We answered, 'None, except our being left alone.' 'Oh, Lady Gregory,' he said, 'appeal to your own common sense.' When I mentioned Shaw's letter, he said, "All Shaw wants is to use the Lord Lieutenant as a whip to lay upon the Censor.' Yeats said, 'Shaw would use him in that way whatever happens.' 'I know he will,' said the Official. At last he asked if we could get Mr. Shaw to take out the passages he had already offered to take out for the Censor. We agreed to ask him to do this, as we felt the Castle was beaten, as the play even then would still be the one forbidden in England."

This is the letter I had received from Mr. Shaw:

"10 Adelphi Terrace, W.C. 12th August, 1909.

Your news is almost too good to be true. If the Lord Lieutenant would only forbid an Irish play without reading it, and after it had been declared entirely guiltless and admirable by the leading high class journal on the side of his own party [*The Nation*], forbid it at the command of an official of the King's household in London, then the green flag would indeed wave over Abbey Street, and we should have questions in Parliament and all manner of reverberating advertisement and nationalist sympathy for the Theatre.

"I gather from your second telegram that the play has, perhaps been submitted for approval. If so, that will be the worse for us, as the Castle can then say they forbade it on its demerits without the slightest reference to the Lord Chamberlain.

"In any case, do not threaten them with a contraband performance. Threaten that we shall be suppressed; that we shall be made martyrs of; that we shall suffer as much and as publicly as possible. Tell them that they can depend on me to burn with a brighter blaze and louder yells than all Foxe's martyrs."

Mr. Shaw telegraphed his answer to the demand for cuts:

"The *Nation* article gives particulars of cuts demanded, which I refused as they would have destroyed the religious significance of the play. The line about moral relations is dispensable as they are mentioned in several other places; so it can be cut if the Castle is silly enough to object to such relations being called immoral, but I will cut nothing else. It is an insult to the Lord Lieutenant to ignore him and refer me to the requirements of a subordinate English Official. I will be no party to any such indelicacy. Please say I said so, if necessary."

I give in the Appendix the *Nation* article to which he refers. My next letter home says: "August 14. Having received the telegram from Shaw and the *Nation* article, we went to the Castle to see the Official, but only found his secretary, who offered to speak to him through a telephone, but the telephone was wheezy, and after long trying, all we could arrive at was that he wanted to know if we had seen Sir H. Beerbohm Tree's evidence, in which he said there were passages in *Blanco* that would be better out. Then he proposed our going to see him at his house, as he has gout and rheumatism and couldn't come to us.

"We drove to his house. He began on Tree, but Yeats told him Tree was the chief representative of the commercial theatre we are opposed to. He then proposed our giving a private performance, and we again told him Shaw had forbidden that. I read him the telegram refusing cuts, but he seemed to have forgotten that he had asked for cuts, and repeated his appeal to spare the Lord Lieutenant. I showed him the *Nation* article, and he read it and said 'But the *Book of Job* is not by the same author as *Blanco Posnet*.' Yeats said, 'Then if you could, you would censor the Deity?' 'Just so,' said he. He asked if we could make no concession. We said, 'no,' but that if they decided to take away the Patent, we should put off the production till the beginning of our season, end of September, and produce it with *Œdipus*; then they would have to suppress both together. He brightened up and said, if we could put it off, things would be much easier, as the Commission would not be sitting then or the Public be so much interested in the question. I said 'Of course we should have to announce at once that it was in consequence of the threatened action of the Castle we had postponed it.' 'Oh, you really don't mean that! You would let all the bulls loose. It would be much better not to say anything at all, or to say the rehearsals took longer than you expected.' 'The public announcement will be more to our own advantage.' 'Oh, that is dreadful!' I said, 'We did not give in one quarter of an inch to Nationalist Ireland at *The Playboy* time, and we certainly cannot give in one quarter of an inch to the Castle.'

" 'We must think of Archbishop Walsh!' I said, 'The Archbishop would be slow to move, for if he orders his flock to keep away from our play, he can't let them attend many of the Censor's plays, and the same thing applies to the Lord Lieutenant.' The Official said, 'I know that.' We said, 'We did not give in to the Church when Cardinal Logue denounced the *Countess Cathleen*. We played it under police protection.' 'I never heard of that. Why did he object?' Yeats said, 'For exactly the same objection as is made to the present one, speeches made by demons in the play.'

"Yeats spoke very seriously then about the principle involved; pointing out that we were trying to create a model on which a great national theatre may be founded in the future, that if we accepted the English Censor's ruling in Ireland, he might forbid a play like Wills' *Robert Emmet,* which Irving was about to act, and was made to give up for political reasons. He said, 'You want, in fact, to have liberty to produce all plays refused by the Censor.' I said, 'We have produced none in the past and not only that, we have refused plays that we thought would hurt Catholic religious feeling. We refused, for instance, to produce Synge's *Tinker's Wedding,* much as we uphold his work, because a drunken priest made ridiculous appears in it. That very play was directly after Synge's death asked for by Tree, whom you have been holding up to us, for production in London.' He said, 'I am very sorry attention was drawn to the play. If no attention had been drawn to it by the papers, we should be all right. It is so wrong to produce it while the Commission is actually sitting and the whole question *sub judice*. We are in close official relation with the English officials of whom the Lord Chamberlain is one; that is the whole question.' We said, 'We see no way out of it. We are determined to produce the play. We cannot accept the Censor's decision as applying to Ireland and you must make up your mind what course to take, but we ask to be let known as soon as possible because if we are to be suppressed, we must find places for our players, who will be thrown out of work.' He threw up his hands and exclaimed, 'Oh, my dear lady, but do not speak of such a thing as possible!' 'Why,' I asked, 'what else have you been threatening all the time?' He said, 'Well, the Lord Lieutenant will be here on Tuesday and will decide. He has not given his attention to the matter up to this' (this does not bear out the Crown Solicitor's story); 'Perhaps you had better stay to see him.' I told him that I wanted to get home, but would stay if absolutely necessary. He said, 'Oh, yes, stay and you will probably see Lady Aberdeen also.' "

Mr. Shaw's next letter was from Kerry where he was motoring. In it he said: "I saw an *Irish Times* to-day with *Blanco* announced for production; so I presume the Castle has not put its foot down. The officials made an appalling technical blunder in acting as agents of the Lord Chamberlain in Ireland; and I worded my telegram in such a way as to make it clear that I knew the value of that indiscretion.

"I daresay the telegram reached the Castle before it reached you."

Meanwhile on August 15th I had written to the Castle:

"I am obliged to go home to-morrow, so if you have any news for us, will you very kindly let us have it at Coole.

"We are, as you know, arranging to produce *Blanco* on Wednesday, 25th, as advertised and booked for, unless you serve us with a 'Threatening notice,' in which case we shall probably postpone it till September 30th and produce it with the already promised *Œdipus*.

"I am very sorry to have given you so much trouble and worry, and, as we told you, we had no idea the responsibility would fall on any shoulders but our own; but I think we have fully explained to you the reasons that make it necessary for us now to carry the matter through."

I received the following answer:

"I am sorry you have been obliged to return to Galway. His Excellency, who arrived this morning, regrets that he has missed you and desires me to say that if you wished an interview with him on Thursday, he would be glad to receive you at the Viceregal Lodge.

"He will give the subject which has been discussed between us his earliest attention."

I received by the same post a long and very kind letter from the Lord Lieutenant, written with his own hand. I am sorry that it was marked "Private," and so I cannot give it here. I may, however, quote the words that brought us back to Dublin. "It would seem that some further personal conference might be very desirable and therefore I hope that it may be possible for you to revisit Dublin on the earliest available day. I shall, of course, be most happy to have an opportunity for a talk with Mr. Yeats."

So my next letter home says: "Friday, 20th. We arrived at the Broadstone yesterday at 2.15, and were met by the Official's secretary, who asked us to go to the Viceregal Lodge. Arrived there, another secretary came and asked me to go and see the Lord Lieutenant alone, saying Mr. Yeats could go in later."

Alas! I must be discreet and that conversation with the King's representative must not be given to the world, at least by me. I can only mention external things: Mr. Yeats, until he joined the conference, being kept by the secretary, whether from poetical or political reasons, to the non-committal subject of Spring flowers; my grieved but necessary contumacy; our joint and immovable contumacy; the courtesy shown to us and, I think, also by us; the kindly offers of a cup of tea; the consuming desire for that tea after the dust of the railway journey all across Ireland; our heroic refusal, lest its acceptance should in any way, even if it did not weaken our resolve, compromise our principles. . . . His Excellency's gracious nature has kept no malice and he has since then publicly taken occasion to show friendship for our Theatre. I felt it was a business forced upon him, who had used his high office above all for reconcilement, as it was upon me, who lived under a peaceful star for some half a hundred years. I think it was a relief to both of us when at last he asked us to go on to the Castle and see again "a very experienced Official."

I may now quote again from my letters: "We found the Official rather in a temper. He had been trying to hear Lord Aberdeen's account of the interview through the telephone and could not. We gave our account, he rather threatening in tone, repeating a good deal of what he had said before. He said we should be as much attacked as they, whatever happened, and that men connected with two newspapers had told him they were only waiting for an opportunity of attacking not only the Lord Lieutenant but the Abbey, if the play is allowed; so we should also catch it. I said, '*Après vous.*' He said Mr. Yeats had stated in the Patent Enquiry, the Abbey was for the production of romantic work. I quoted Parnell, 'Who shall set bounds to the march of a Nation?' We told him our Secretary reported, 'Very heavy booking, first class people, *a great many from the Castle.*'

"He said he would see the Lord Lieutenant on his way home. We went to Dame Street Post Office and wired to Mr. Shaw: 'Have seen Viceroy. Deleted immoral relations, refused other cuts. He is writing to King, who supports Censor.' "

Then, as holder of the Patent, I took counsel's opinion on certain legal points, of which the most vital was this:

"Should counsel be of opinion that the Crown will serve notice requiring the play to be discontinued, then counsel will please say what penalty he thinks querist would expose herself to by disregarding the notice of the Crown and continuing the representation?"

The answer to this question was:

"If the theatre ceases to be licensed, as pointed out above, and any performance for gain takes place there, the penalty under the 26. Geo. III. cap 57, sec. (2) *is £300 for each offence*, to be recovered in a '*qui tam*' action; one half of the £300 going to the Rotunda Hospital, the other half to the informer who sues."

Mr. Yeats and I were just going to a rehearsal at the Abbey on the evening of August 21st when we received a letter from the Castle, telling us that a formal legal document, forbidding the performance of the play, would reach us immediately. The matter had now become a very grave one. We knew that we should, if we went on and this threat were carried out, lose not only the Patent but that the few hundred pounds that we had been able to save and with which we could have supported our players till they found other work, would be forfeited. This thought of the players made us waver, and very sadly we agreed that we must give up the fight. We did not say a word of this at the Abbey but went on rehearsing as usual. When we had left the Theatre and were walking through the lamp-lighted streets, we found that during those two or three hours our minds had come to the same decision, that we had given our word, that at all risks we must keep it or it would never be trusted again; that we must in no case go back, but must go on at any cost.

We wrote a statement in which we told of the pressure put upon us and the objections made, but of these last we said: "there is nothing to change our conviction that so far from containing offence for any sincere and honest mind, Mr. Shaw's play is a high and weighty argument upon the working of the Spirit of God in man's heart, or to show that it is not a befitting thing for us to set upon our stage the work of an Irishman, who is also the most famous of living dramatists, after that work has been silenced in London by what we believe an unjust decision.

"One thing" we continued, "is plain enough, an issue that swallows up all else and makes the merit of Mr. Shaw's play a secondary thing. If our Patent is in danger, it is because the decisions of the English Censor are being brought into Ireland, and because the Lord Lieutenant is about to revive, on what we consider a frivolous pretext, a right not exercised for a hundred and fifty years to forbid at the Lord Chamberlain's pleasure, any play produced in any Dublin theatre, all these theatres holding their Patents from him.

"We are not concerned with the question of the English Censorship now being fought out in London, but we are very certain that the conditions of the two countries are different, and that we must not, by accepting the English Censor's ruling, give away anything of the liberty of the Irish Theatre of the future. Neither can we accept without protest the revival of the Lord Lieutenant's claim at the bidding of the Censor or otherwise. The Lord Lieutenant is definitely a political personage, holding office from the party in power, and what would sooner or later grow into a political Censorship cannot be lightly accepted."

Having sent this out for publication, we went on with our rehearsals.

In rehearsal I came to think that there was a passage that would really seem irreverent and give offence to the genuinely religious minds we respect. It was where Blanco said: "Yah! What about the croup? I guess He made the croup when He was thinking of one thing; and then He made the child when He was thinking of something else; and the croup got past Him and killed the child. Some of us will have to find out how to kill the croup, I guess. I think I'll turn doctor just on the chance of getting back on Him by doing something He couldn't do."

I wrote to Mr. Shaw about this, and he answered in this very interesting letter:

"Parknasilla, 19 August, 1909.

"I have just arrived and found all your letters waiting for me. I am naturally much entertained by your encounters and Yeats' with the Castle. I leave that building cheerfully in your hands.

"But observe the final irony of the situation. The English Censorship being too stupid to see the real blasphemy, makes a fool of itself. But you, being clever enough to put your finger on it at once, immediately proceed to delete what Redford's blunders spared.

"To me, of course, the whole purpose of the play lies in the problem, 'What about the croup?' When Lady ——, in her most superior manner, told me, 'He is the God of Love,' I said, 'He is also the God of Cancer and Epilepsy.' That does not present any difficulty to me. All this problem of the origin of evil, the mystery of pain, and so forth, does not puzzle me. My doctrine is that God proceeds by the method of 'Trial and error,' just like a workman perfecting an aeroplane; he has to make hands for himself and brains for himself in order that his will may be done. He has tried lots of machines—the diphtheria bacillus, the tiger, the cockroach; and he cannot extirpate them, except by making something that can shoot them, or walk on them, or, cleverer still, devise vaccines and anti-toxins to prey on them. To me the sole hope of human salvation lies in teaching Man to regard himself as an experiment in the realisation of God, to regard his hands as God's hands, his brain as God's brain, his purpose as God's purpose. He must regard God as a helpless longing, which *longed* him into existence by its desperate need for an executive organ. You will find it all in *Man and Super Man*, as you will find it all behind *Blanco Posnet*. Take it out of my play, and the play becomes nothing but the old cry of despair—Shakespeare's, 'As flies to wanton boys, so we are to the Gods; they kill us for their sport'—the most frightful blasphemy ever uttered." Mr. Shaw enclosed with this the passage rewritten, as it now appears in the published play.

We put on *Blanco* on the date announced, the 25th August. We were anxious to the last, for counsel were of the opinion that if we were stopped, it would be on the Clause in the Patent against "Any representation which should be deemed or construed immoral," and that if Archbishop Walsh or Archbishop Peacocke or especially the Head of the Lord Lieutenant's own Church, the Moderator of the Presbyterian Assembly, should say anything which might be "deemed and construed" to condemn the play, the threats made would be carried out. There were fears of a riot also, for newspapers and their posters had kept up the excitement, and there was an immense audience. It is a pity we had not thought in time of putting up our prices. Guineas were offered even for standing room in the wings.

The play began, and till near the end it was received in perfect silence. Perhaps the audience were waiting for the wicked bits to begin. Then, at the end, there was a tremendous burst of cheering, and we knew we had won. Some stranger outside asked what was going on in the Theatre. "They are defying the Lord Lieutenant" was the answer; and when the crowd heard the cheering, they took it up and it went far out through the streets.

There were no protests made on any side. And the play, though still forbidden in England, is still played by us, and always with success. And even if the protests hoped for had been made and we had suffered, does not Nietzsche say "A good battle justifies every cause"?

VII

"THE PLAYBOY" IN AMERICA

ON September 7, 1911, I received a letter from Mr. Yeats: "I am trying possible substitutes for Miss O'Neill and some will not do. As a last resource I have told Miss Magee to understudy the part of 'Pegeen Mike.' She was entirely natural and delightful in that small part in *The Mineral Workers* the day before yesterday. I said to someone that she had the sweet of the apple, and would be a Pegeen Mike if she could get the sour of the apple too. Now the serious difficulty of the moment is that there is nobody in the theatre capable of teaching a folk part to an inexperienced person. If there was, I would at once put Miss Magee into Pegeen Mike; by the time she had played it through the States she could come back Miss O'Neill's successor. Now I am going to ask you if you feel well enough for a desperate measure. Can you, if it seem necessary to-morrow, take my place in the steamboat on Tuesday evening? Allowing eight days for the passage—for the boat is slow—you would arrive in Boston on the 20th. *The Playboy* cannot come till about the 28th; you would be able to train Miss Magee for the part, or, of course, another if you prefer her. . . . I can wire to-morrow and get the necessary papers made out (you have to swear you are not an Anarchist). If they want me I can follow next boat and possibly arrive before you. I will go steerage if necessary; that will be quite an amusing adventure, and I shall escape all interviewers. One thing I am entirely sure of, that there is no one but you with enough knowledge of folk to work a miracle."

I could not set out on the same day as the Company. I was needed at home. But I promised to follow in the *Cymric*, sailing from Queenstown a week later.

I think from the very first day Mr. Yeats and I had talked at Duras of an Irish Theatre, and certainly ever since there had been a company of Irish players, we had hoped and perhaps determined to go to *An t-Oilean ur* "the New Island," the greater Ireland beyond the Atlantic. But though, as some Connacht girls said to me at Buffalo, "Since ever we were the height of the table, America it was always our dream," and though we had planned that if for any cause our Theatre should seem to be nearing its end we would take our reserve fund and spend it mainly on that voyage and that venture, we did not ourselves make the opportunity at the last. After we had played in the summer of 1911 at the Court Theatre, as ever for a longer period and to a larger audience, we were made an offer by the theatrical managers, Liebler & Co., to play for three or four months in the United States, and the offer had been accepted. They had mentioned certain plays as essential, among them *The Playboy of the Western World*. Miss O'Neill, who had played its heroine, had married and left us; that is how the difficulty had arisen.

On September 19th I said good-bye to home, where I had meant to spend a quiet winter, writing and planting trees, and to the little granddaughter for whose first appearance in the world I had waited. There had not been many days for preparation, but it was just as well I did not require large trunks, for on the eve of my journey a railway strike was declared in Ireland and there were no trains to take any one to Queenstown. Motors are still few in the country. We wired to Limerick but all were engaged already; to Galway which did not answer at all; and to Loughrea, where the only one had already been engaged by my neighbour, Lord Gough, who had friends with him who also wanted means to travel. I could but send over a message to his home, Lough Cutra Castle, in the dark of night; and a kindly answer came that he would yield his claim to mine. So at midday on September 19, I set out with such luggage as I could take, to cross the five counties that lay between me and Queenstown harbour. One of the tyres broke at intervals, once on the top of a wild mountain in, I think, the County Limerick, and people came out from a lonely cottage to say how far we were from any town or help; and these delays kept us from reaching Cork till after dark. Then we went on towards Queenstown in a fine rain which had begun, and after a while when we stopped to ask the way we were told we had gone eight miles beyond it. But I was in time after all, went out in the tender and joined the *Cymric* next morning, and so made my first voyage across the ocean. The weather was rather cold and rough and I was glad of a rest, and stayed a good deal in my cabin. I knew no one on board and I had leisure to write a little play, *MacDonough's Wife*, which had been forming itself in my mind for a while past.

I had always had a passion for the sea, as I saw it from our coasts and in our bays and invers, and when going through the Mediterranean and the Indian Ocean. But the great Atlantic seemed dark and dead and monotonous, and it was a relief when on the last day or two one could see whales spouting, and a sparrow came and perched on the ship; and then fishing boats, looking strange in shape and rigging, came in sight, and I felt like Christopher Columbus.

Mr. Yeats, who had gone on with the Company, came to meet me on board ship as we arrived at Boston on September 29, St. Michael's Day, and told me of the success of the first performances there; and that evening I went to the Plymouth Theatre and found a large audience, and a very enthusiastic one, listening to the plays. I could not but feel moved when I saw this, and remembered our small beginnings and the years of effort and of discouragement.

The interviewers saved me the trouble of writing letters these first days. I sent papers home instead. It was my first experience of this way of giving news, and I was amused by it. One always, I suppose, likes talking about oneself and what one is interested in, and that is what they asked me to do. I found them everywhere courteous, mannerly, perhaps a little over-insistent. I think I only offended one, a lady in a provincial town. She wanted to talk about *The Playboy*, and for reasons of policy I didn't. She avenged herself by saying I had no sense of humour and that my dress (Paris!) "had no relation to the prevailing modes."

I had plenty to do at first. I had not much time to go about, for I rehearsed all the mornings and could not leave the theatre in the evenings, but when I got free of constant rehearsal I was taken by friends to see, as I longed to see, something of the country. I wanted especially to know what the coast here was like—whether it was very different from our own of Galway and of Clare; and I had a wonderful Sunday at a fine country house on the North Shore, and saw the islands and the reddish rocks, not like our grey ones opposite; and the lovely tints of the autumn leaves, a red and yellow undergrowth among the dark green trees. My hostess's grandchildren were playing about. One said, "I am going to be a bear," and grunted. It made me so glad to think the little grandson at home has a playfellow in the making—in the cradle!

Boston is a very friendly place. There are so many Irish there that I had been told at home there is a part of it called Galway, and I met many old friends. Some I had known as children, sons of tenants and daughters, now comfortably settled in their own houses. I had known of the nearness of America before I came, for I remember asking an old woman at Kiltartan why her daughter who had been home on a visit had left her again, and she had said, "Ah, her teeth were troubling her and her dentist lives at Boston." England, on the other hand, seems a long way off, and there are many tears shed if a child goes even to a good post over the Channel. Two dear old ladies came to see me, daughters of an old steward of my father's. One of them said she used to "braid my hair" as a child that I might be in time for family prayers, and had wept when she saw the snapshots in the papers after I landed, and found I was so changed. She said, weeping, "I hope the people of America know you are a real lady; if not, I could testify to it!" And I was able to write to my son of the well-being of tenants' children: "T. C. and his wife came to the theatre and brought me a beautiful bouquet of pink carnations. I had a visit from M. R., such a handsome smart girl, and from N. H., sending up her visiting card, very pleased with herself. Many of the ladies I meet tell me the cook or laundress or manservant are so excited at their meeting me and know all about me." And the son of a Welsh carpenter who had lived at Roxborough in my childhood met me at the theatre door after *Spreading the News* and said, "I never thought, when you used to teach us in Sunday School, you would ever write such merry comedies." This reminded me of the tailor from Gort who wrote home after a visit to the Abbey, "No one who knows Lady Gregory would ever think she had so much fun in her."

On October 18 I wrote home: "I send a paper with opinions for and against the plays. I am afraid there may be demonstrations against *Harvest* and *The Playboy*. The Liebler people don't mind, think it will be an advertisement. I was cheered by a visit from some members of the Gaelic League, saying they were on our side and asking me to an entertainment next Sunday, and from D. K., who is very religious and wants to go into a convent. She says the attacks on the plays are by very few and don't mean anything. Most of the society people are in the country, but they motor in sixty or eighty miles for the plays. Last night we had a little party on the stage: some Gaelic Leaguers, who brought me a bouquet; some people from the Aran colony—including Synge's friend, McDonough, whom I had also known in Aran; and from Kiltartan Mary R. and a cousin and Mrs. Hession's daughters, with the husband of one. They were very smart, one in a white blouse, another in a blue one with pearl necklace. You must tell Mrs. Hession they are looking so well. The management gave us sandwiches on the stage, and punchbowls of claret cup, and we had Irish songs and I called for a cheer for Ireland in Boston. I enjoyed very much watching the Hession women at the play. They nearly got hysterics in *Workhouse Ward*, and when the old woman comes on, they did not laugh but bent forward and took it quite seriously. It shows the plays would have a great success in the country. The County Galway Woman's League have asked me to be their president. . . . Members of the Gaelic League are working a banner for me. They showed me the painted design at a party given in our honour. Yeats leaves for New York to-day, but comes back for first night of *The Playboy* next Monday and sails Tuesday. They are rather afraid of trouble, but I think the less controversy the better now. It should be left between the management and the audience.

"The manager says we may stay longer in Boston, we are doing so well. I should like to stay on. It is a homey sort of place. I am sent quantities of flowers, my room is full of roses and carnations."

Now as to the trouble over *The Playboy*. We were told, when we arrived, that opposition was being organised from Dublin, and I was told there had already been some attacks in a Jesuit paper, *America*. But the first I saw was a letter in the *Boston Post* of October 4, the writer of which did not wait for *The Playboy* to appear but attacked plays already given, *Birthright* and *Hyacinth Halvey*. The letter was headed in large type, "Dr. J. T. Gallagher denounces the Irish Plays, says they are Vulgar, Unnatural, Anti-National, and Anti-Christian." The writer declared himself astonished at "the parrot-like praise of the dramatic critics." He himself had seen these two plays and "my soul cried out for a thousand tongues to voice my unutterable horror and disgust. . . . I never saw anything so vulgar, vile, beastly, and unnatural, so calculated to calumniate, degrade, and defame a people and all they hold sacred and dear."

Birthright, written by a young National schoolmaster in County Cork, had not been attacked in Ireland; both it and my own *Hyacinth* have been played not only at the Abbey but in the country towns and villages with the approval of the priests and of the Gaelic League. *Birthright* is founded on some of the most ancient of stories, Cain and Abel, Joseph and the pit, jealousy of the favoured younger by the elder, a sudden anger, and "the voice of thy brother's blood crieth to me from the ground." In a photograph of the last scene a Boston photographer had, to fill his picture, brought on the father and mother looking at the struggle between the brothers, instead of coming in, as in the play, to find but a lifeless body before them. This heartlessness was often brought up against us by some who had seen the picture but not the play, and sometimes by those who had seen both.

The Playboy was announced for October 16, and on the 14th the *Gaelic American* printed a resolution of the United Irish Societies of New York, in which they pledged themselves to "drive the vile thing from the stage."

There was, however, very little opposition in the Plymouth Theatre. There was a little booing and hissing, but there were a great many Harvard boys among the audience and whenever there was a sign of coming disapproval they cheered enough to drown it. Then they took to cheering if any sentence or scene was coming that had been objected to in the newspaper attacks, so, I am afraid, giving the impression that they had a particular liking for strong expressions. We had, as I have already told, cut out many of these long ago in Dublin, and had never put them back when we played in England or elsewhere; and so the enemy's paper confessed almost sadly, "it was a revised and amended edition that they saw . . . the most offensive parts were eliminated. It was this that prevented a riot. . . . But most of those present and all the newspaper men had read the excised portions in the *Gaelic American* and were able to fill the gaps."

Because of the attacks in some papers, the Mayor of Boston sent his secretary, Mr. William A. Leahy, to report upon *The Playboy*, and the Police Commissioners also sent their censor. Both reports agreed that the performance was not such as to "justify the elimination of any portion of the play." Mr. Leahy had already written of the other plays: "I have seen the plays and admire them immensely. They are most artistic, wonderfully acted, and to my mind absolutely inoffensive to the patriotic Irishman. I regret the sensitiveness that makes certain men censure them. Knowing what Mr. Yeats and Lady Gregory want to do, I cannot but hope that they succeed and that they are loyally supported in America. My commendation cannot be expressed too forcibly." And after he had seen *The Playboy*, he wrote: "If obscenity is to be found on the stage in Boston, it must be sought elsewhere and not at the Plymouth Theatre." After speaking with some sympathy of the objections made to the plays, he says: "The mistake, however, lies in taking the pictures literally. Some of these playwrights, of course, are realists or copyists of life and like others of their kind they happen to prefer strong brine to rosewater and see truth chiefly in the ugliness of things. But as it happens the two remarkable men among the Irish playwrights are not realists at all. Yeats and Synge are symbolists, and their plays are as fantastic and fabulous as the Tales of the Round Table."

There was no further trouble at Boston. There was nothing but a welcome for all the plays, many of them already so well known, especially through Professor Baker's dramatic classes at Harvard, that we were now and again reproved by some one in the audience if a line or passage were left out, by design or forgetfulness. I wrote home on October 22: "Gaston Mayer came yesterday, representing Liebler. They are delighted with our success, and want us, urged us, to stay till May. We refused this, but will certainly stay January, possibly a little longer. It is rather a question for the Company. They want me to stay all the time. I said I would stay for the present. If I get tired, Yeats will come back.... We had the sad news last night that we are only to have one more week here, and are to do some three night places, opening at Providence on the 30th. Mrs. Gardner came to the theatre this morning, furious at our going so soon."

We said farewell to Boston October 30. Yet it was not quite farewell, for on our last day in America—March 5—we stopped there on the way from Chicago to New York and gave a "flying matinée"; and I brought home the impression of that kind, crowded audience, and the knowledge that having come among strangers, we left real friends.

On October 13 I had written from Boston: "I am sorry to say Flynn (Liebler's special agent), who has been to Providence, announces strong opposition to *The Playboy*. A delegation came to demand its withdrawal, but he refused. I had also a letter saying the Clan-na-Gael was very strong there, and advising that we have police at hand. Of course, had we known this, we should not have put on *The Playboy*, but we must fight it out now. The danger is in not knowing whether we shall get my strong support there. A Harvard lad has interviewed me for a magazine. He promised to try and make up a party to go to Providence Tuesday night, and also to stir up Brown University."

Though we all grieved at leaving friendly Boston, we found friends also in Providence, with its pleasant name and hilly streets and stately old dwelling houses. But a protest had been made before we arrived, and a committee had waited on the Police Commissioners and presented a petition asking them to forbid the performance of *The Playboy*.

"I had to appear before the Police Commissioners this morning. The accusations were absurd and easy to answer; most of them founded upon passages which have never been said upon the stage. I wish I had been allowed to take a copy. There was one clause which accused us of 'giving the world to understand a barbarous marriage custom was in ordinary use in Ireland.' This alluded to the 'drift of chosen females from the Eastern World,' one of those flights of Christy Mahon's fancy which have given so much offence. I showed them the prompt copy with the acting version we have always used. Unluckily the enemy didn't turn up. Of course the play is to be let go on, and there are to be plenty of policemen present in case of disturbance. The police people said they had had the same trouble about a negro play said to misrepresent people of colour.

"The Police Commissioners themselves attended and have published a report, saying they not only found nothing to object to in the play but enjoyed every minute of it. Nevertheless, the protesting committee published its statement: 'How well our objections were founded may be judged from the fact that the Company acting this play has agreed to eliminate from it each and every scene, situation, and word to which we objected, and it is on the basis of this elimination that the play has been permitted to go on.' And I gave my answer: 'I think it may be as well to state that we gave the play to-night exactly as it has been given in London, Oxford, Cambridge, Manchester, and many cities in Ireland and the other night in Boston. The players have never at any time anywhere spoken all the lines in the published book.' " And after its production I wrote home: "Nov. 1st. *The Playboy* went very well last night, not an attempt to hiss."

From another town—Lowell—I wrote: "A newspaper man from Tyrone lamented last night the *Playboy* fight. He said all nationalities here are very sensitive. The Swedes had a play taken off that represented some Swedish women drinking. The French Canadians, he says, are as touchy as the Irish. He said that in consequence of this sensitiveness, in the police reports the nationality of those brought up before the court is not given. I looked in the Lowell newspaper next day, and I saw that this was true. One José Viatchka was brought up charged with the theft of two yards of cloth. She was found guilty and her nationality was not given. Allan Carter made his second appearance for drunkenness. Being an American citizen, even his dwelling place, Canaan, N. H., was not kept secret. Thomas Kilkelly and Daniel O'Leary were fined for drunkenness. I felt very glad that their nationality was not given!"

Yale like Harvard demanded *The Playboy*, and we put it on for one night at New Haven. Synge's plays and others on our list are being used in the course of English literature there, and professors and students wanted to see them. We were there for Monday and Tuesday, the 6th and 7th of November. On the first night we put on other plays. Next day there was a matinée and we gave Mr. Bernard Shaw's *Blanco Posnet* and my own *Image*. I left before the matinée was over for Northampton, as I was to lecture that night at Smith College. Next day I was astonished to see a paragraph in a New Haven paper, saying that the Mayor having been asked to forbid the performance of *The Playboy*, had sent his censor, the Chief of Police, Mr. Cowles, to attend a rehearsal of it; that several passages had been objected to by him and that the manager had in consequence suppressed them, and it had been given at the evening performance without the offending passages. I was astounded. I knew the report could not be correct, must be wholly incorrect, and yet one knows there is never smoke without even a sod of turf. The players, who arrived at Northampton that morning, were equally puzzled. There had been no rehearsal, and the play had been given as ever before. I wired to a friend, the head of the University Press at Yale, to investigate the matter. The explanation came: "Chief Cowles," as the papers called him, had attended, not a rehearsal but the matinée. He was said to have objected to certain passages, though he had not sent word of this to any of our people. The passages he objected to were not spoken at the evening performance of *The Playboy*, because the play in which they are spoken was *Blanco Posnet*. Yale laughed over this till we could almost hear the echoes, indeed the echoes appeared in the next day's papers. *The Gaelic American*, however, announced that in New Haven one of our plays "was allowed to be presented only after careful excision of obscene passages."

Washington was the next place where *The Playboy* was to appear. I wrote home from there on November 12: "Liebler's Manager wired for me to come on here and skip Albany. To-day two or three priests preached against us, and a pamphlet has been given away at the chapel doors denouncing us. I think it would be a good thing to put it up in the Hall of the Abbey framed for Dublin people to see. The worst news is that the players have arrived without Sinclair. He had a fall down six steps when coming down to the stage at Albany and hurt his back. The doctor said it was only the muscles that were hurt and that he would be all right to-day, but he has wired to-day that he cannot move. A bad performance would worry me more than the pamphlet.

"These are some of its paragraphs:

" 'The attention of fair-minded Washingtonians is called to a most malignant travesty of Irish life and religion about to be presented upon the stage of a local theatre by the "Irish Players." This travelling Company is advertised as "coming from the Abbey Theatre, Dublin." True, but they came from Dublin, followed by the hisses and indignation of an outraged populace!

" 'A storm of bitter protest has been raised in every city in which they have presented their false and revolting pictures of Irish life. Dublin people never accepted the plays. They virtually kicked them from the stage. England gave them no reception.'

"Then they quote 'a Boston critic' (this is Dr. Gallagher, who wrote that letter to the Boston papers):

" ' "Nothing but hell-inspired ingenuity and a satanic hatred of the Irish people and their religion could suggest, construct, and influence the production of such plays. On God's earth the beastly creatures of the plays never existed."

" 'Such are the productions which, hissed from Dublin, hawked around England by the "Irish Players" for the delectation of those who wished to see Irishmen shown unfit for self-government, are now offered to the people of Washington. Will Washington tolerate the lie?

" 'THE ALOYSIUS TRUTH SOCIETY.'

"This is the first time any section of the Catholic Church has come into the fight. It is a good thing they denounce all the plays, not only *The Playboy*. On the other hand, the Gaelic Association, of which Monsignor Shahan, President of the Catholic University, is head, has asked me to address its meeting next Thursday, and, of course, I shall do so.

"This invitation was incorrectly reported in the papers, and Monsignor Shahan, who is just leaving for Rome, has denied having 'invited the Irish Players to speak.' The invitations sent out, printed cards with his printed signature, had asked people to come and hear me speak, and I did so and had a good audience; and a resolution was proposed, praising all I had done for literature and the theatre, and making me the first Honorary Member of the Association, and this was agreed to by the whole meeting with applause."

For among the surprises of the autumn I had suddenly found that I could speak. I was quite miserable when, on arriving in Boston, I found it had been arranged for me to "say a few words" at various clubs or gatherings. I thought a regular lecture would be better. If it failed, I would not be asked again or I would have an excuse for silence. It would be easier, too, in a way than the "few words," for I should know how long the lecture ought to be and what people wanted to hear about, and I would have the assurance that they knew what they were coming for instead of having a stranger let loose on them just as they were finishing their lunch. It was at one of these lunches that that wonderful woman who has in Boston, as the Medici in Florence, spent wealth and vitality and knowledge in making such a collection of noble pictures as proves once more that it is the individual, the despot, who is necessary for such a task—bringing the clear conception, the decision of one mind in place of the confusion of many—liked what I said and offered me for my first trial the spacious music room of Fenway Court.

I spoke on playwriting, for I had begun that art so late in life that its rules, those I had worked out for myself or learned from others, were still fresh in my mind; and I wrote home with more cheerfulness than I had felt during the days of preparation, that I thought and was assured my address had gone well; "what I was most proud of was keeping it exactly to the hour. I was glad to find I could fill up so much time. I had notes on the table and just glanced at them now and again but didn't hesitate for a word or miss my points. It is a great relief to me and the discovery of a new faculty. I shan't feel nervous again; that is a great thing."

I had boasted of this a little too soon, for the next letter says: "I had a nice drive yesterday, twenty-five miles to B. A lady called for me in her motor, and we passed through several pretty little New England villages and through woods. Then a wait of an hour before lecture, keeping up small talk and feeling nervous all the time, then the lecture. I forgot to bring my watch and gave them twenty minutes over the hour! It was a difficult place to speak in, a private house,—a room to the right, a room to the left, and a room behind. However they seemed to hear all right. . . . I had a nice run home alone in the dark."

I gave my ideas on "playwriting" again at Philadelphia, and was told just before I began that there were several dramatists in the room, including the author of *Madame Butterfly*. So I had to apologise on the ground of an inferior cook being flattered at being asked to give recipes, whereas a real *chef* keeps the secrets to himself. And sometimes at the end of all my instruction on the rules I gave the hearers as a benediction,

"And may you better reck the rede
Than ever did the adviser!"

Mr. Yeats, when lecturing in America, had written to me from Bryn Mawr: "I have just given my second lecture. . . . They are getting all our books here now. Do you know I have not met a single woman here who puts 'tin-tacks in the soup,' and I find that the woman who does, is recognised as an English type. One teacher explained to me the difference in this way: 'We prepare the girls to live their lives, but in England they are making them all teachers.' "

And I also was delighted with the girls' colleges and wrote home:

"At Vassar the girls were playing a football game in sympathy with the Harvard and Yale match going on. They were all dressed as boys, had made up trousers, or knickers, and some were playing on combs to represent a band, and singing the Yale song, though the sham Harvard had beaten the sham Yale by 25 to 5. They are nice, merry girls, I think as nice as at Smith's where I promised to suggest my granddaughter should be educated. I had an audience of about six hundred, a very good and pleasant one, nearly all girls and a few men. The President was sitting close to the door, and I asked him to call out to me to speak up if he didn't hear, as I was young as a lecturer and always afraid my voice might not reach. He said he would not like to do that, but would hold up a handkerchief if I was to speak louder. About the middle of the lecture I saw him very slowly raise a handkerchief to the level of his face, but I could not catch his eye, so I stopped and asked if that was the signal. He was quite confused and said, No, he wanted to blow his nose, and the girls shrieked with delight. He told me afterwards he had held out as long as he could. The girls had acted some of my plays. *The Jackdaw* is a great favourite there as well as at Smith's, where they have conjugated a verb 'to Jackdaw.' One of the 'Faculty' said she doubted if our players could do *Gaol Gate* as well as Mr. Kennedy, the author of *The Servant in the House*, reads it. . . ."

These lectures gave me opportunity of seeing many places where our plays did not go, and I have delighted memories of rushing waters in Detroit, and of little girls dancing in cruciform Columbus, and of the roar of Niagara Falls, and the stillness of the power house that sends that great energy to create light and motion a hundred or two hundred miles away, and of many another wide-spreading, kindly city where strangers welcomed me, and I seemed to say good-bye to friends. Dozing in midnight trains, I would remember, as in a dream, "the flight of a bird through a lighted hall," the old parable of human life.

To return to the meeting at Washington:

"I had to get away early because Mrs. Taft had asked me

to the White House to hear the Mormon choir. I arrived there rather late but the music was going on. It was a very pretty sight, the long white room with fine old glass chandeliers, and two hundred Mormons—the men in black, the women in white—and about fifty guests. I heard one chorus, and they sang 'The Star-Spangled Banner,' and everyone stood up. Then we moved about and chatted, and I was presented to the President—pleasant enough, but one doesn't feel him on the stage like Roosevelt.

"To-day I had a very scattered rehearsal of *Spreading the News*. The players kept slipping out by a back door, and I found the negroes were dancing and singing out there, it being their dinner hour. It was, of course, irresistible."

One day when we went to rehearsal, the sun was shining and I offered the players a holiday and picnic to Mount Vernon, and we crossed the river and spent the day there very pleasantly. Donovan said, "No wonder a man should fight for such a home as this." I told them the holiday was not a precedent, for we might go to a great many countries before finding so great a man to honour. Washington had been a friend of my grandfather's,[1] who had been in America with his regiment. There was a case of stuffed birds at Roxborough which was said to have been a present from Washington, and there was a field there called Mount Vernon. My grandfather had built a little sea lodge on the Burren coast and had called that also Mount Vernon, so I was specially interested in seeing the house. It is beautifully kept and filled with memorials of its owner and with furniture that belonged to him. The Americans keep their sacred places well. A school at which I lectured wanted to give me a fee; but I did not wish to take one, and I said when they pressed it, that I had seen in a shop window an old jug with portraits of Washington and of Lafayette on it, and had wished for it, but it was nine dollars and I was refraining from luxuries, and that I would accept that if they liked. So it was sent to me, and I brought it safely home to add to my collection of historic delft. It has the date 1824. It was made to commemorate Lafayette's visit at that time, and the words on it are, "A Republic is not always ungrateful." It now stands near another jug of about

[1] In fact Washington had been a friend of Lady Gregory's *great* grandfather. The Persse who had been in America with his regiment was that gentleman's brother. For fuller information regarding this see the Rev. Dr. Jones Mitchell's article called "Colonel William Persse" in Vol. 30 Nos. 3-4, 1963 of the *Galway Archaeological Journal*. William Persse sent Washington a present of some gooseberry bushes.

the same date, on which there is the portrait of that patriot beloved by his people, O'Connell.

On November 18 I arrived at New York. All my work was easier from that time through the help of my friend of some ten years, Mr John Quinn. I had a pleasant little set of rooms at the Algonquin Hotel. I said to Mr. Flynn, Liebler's manager, when I arrived there, "It is near the theatre? Shall I be able to walk there?" "Walk there," he said, "why you could throw a cricket ball to it." I did walk there and back many times a day during my stay, and grew fond of the little corner of the city I got to know so well; but I sometimes envied the cricket ball that would have escaped the dangerous excitement of the five crossings, one of them across 6th Avenue, with motors dashing in all directions, and railway trains thundering overhead. The theatre was charming, I wish we could carry it about on all our tours, and I was given a little room off the stage, which had been Maxine Elliott's own room, and where players and guests often had tea with me.

"Hotel Algonquin, New York, Monday, 20th November. We opened very well last night. A crowded house and very enthusiastic, *Rising of the Moon, Birthright*, and *Spreading the News* were given. All got five or more curtains. One man made rather a disturbance at the fight in *Birthright*, saying it was 'not Irish,' but his voice was drowned and he left. I was told that —— one of the enemy who was there, said, 'Such things do not happen in Ireland; they may happen in Lady Gregory's own family.' *The Playboy* is to be put on next week. J. Q. seems a bit anxious about *The Playboy*; says they may 'throw things,' and that seems what the *Gaelic American* is inviting them to do when it says *The Playboy* 'must be squelched' and a lesson taught to Mr. Yeats and his fellow-agents of England, and that I have no right to appeal for respect for my sex.

"Last night as I went into the theatre I heard my name spoken, and a girl told me she was the daughter of old Matt Cahel, the blacksmith who had lived at Roxborough, and she had come to see the plays and said her father would have been so proud, if he had lived, to know I was here. I am glad of this, for I hear the plays were preached against by some priests last Sunday. Father Flanagan thinks the attacks all come from Dublin. The players are convinced they are from some of our non-paying guests. . . . I think we must revise that list. *The Playboy* is to be put on next Monday. I am glad they are not putting off the fight any longer. It tries the players' nerves. It will be on for four nights and a matinée. By going behind myself and gathering a party and cheering with what voice I had left, I at last got the shouts for Hughie in *Birthright* to be less of a mournful wail."

"Friday, November 24th. I have been to-day to lunch with Mrs. ——, a Catholic lady I had met in London, who gave a lunch to me to show she was on our side. There was a Father X. there, who is not in this diocese and is very much shocked at the action of the priests. One told his congregation on Sunday from the altar, it would be a mortal sin to come to the plays, and another, Father X. says, to his certain knowledge advised his people from the altar if they did come, to bring eggs to throw. Mr. Hackett was sitting behind a woman who said in *Birthright* 'it's a pity it ain't Lady Gregory they are choking.' Mr. Quinn heard I held a salon at the theatre and it is wonderful how many people turn up or come to express sympathy. I got a good rehearsal to-day of *Mixed Marriage,* which I think might take very well here."

"26th. Plenty of booking for *Playboy* whether by friends or enemies. I went to lecture at Vassar yesterday. I had no idea the Hudson was so beautiful. The train was close to the brink all the way, and opposite are wooded cliffs and heights, and at night, coming back, the lighted towns on the other side gave a magic atmosphere. I find new scenery an extraordinary excitement and delight. I am going off just now to Oyster Bay for the night to visit the Roosevelts. I have been to church this morning and feel fresher."

"Algonquin, Monday, 27th. When John Quinn came yesterday afternoon, he brought Gregg with him. Both had heard from different sources that *The Playboy* is to be attacked to-night. The last *Gaelic American* says, 'The New York Irish will send the Anti-Players back to Dublin like whipped curs with their tails between their legs.' Quinn heard it from a man he knows well, who had called him up to say there is a party of rowdies coming to the theatre to-night to make their demonstration. They thought it possible this might be stopped by letting the enemy know we are prepared, but I thought it better to let them show themselves. They have been threatening us so long; we shall see who they are.

"This morning I saw Flynn and Gaston Mayer and told them the matter was out of my hands now, that we don't want interviews or argument, and that it is a question between Liebler and the mob. Flynn went off to the police, and I have not heard anything since. I have not told the players."

"Tuesday, November 28th. The papers give a fairly accurate account of what happened last night.[2] There was a large audience,

[2] See extract in appendix IV.

The Gaol Gate was put on first, which, of course, has never offended anyone in Ireland, but there was a good deal of coughing going on and there was unrest in the gallery. But one man was heard saying to another, 'This is all right. You needn't interrupt this. Irishmen do die for their neighbours.' Another said, 'This is a part of *The Playboy* that is going on now, but they are giving it under another name.' Very soon after the curtain went up on *The Playboy* the interruptions began. The managers had been taking much too confident a view, saying, 'These things don't happen in New York.' When this did happen there were plenty of police, but they wouldn't arrest anyone because no one gave the order, and the disturbance was let go on nearly all through the first act. I went round, when the disturbance began, and knelt in the opening of the hearth, calling to every actor who came within earshot that they must not stop for a moment but must spare their voices, as they could not be heard, and we should do the whole act over again. At the end Tyler came round and I was delighted when he shouted that it should be played again. O'Donovan announced this and there were great cheers from the audience. And the whole play was given then in perfect peace and quiet. The editor of the *Gaelic American* and his bodyguard were in the stalls, two rows of them. They were pointed out to me when I came in. The disturbers were very well arranged; little groups here and there. In the box office this morning they have a collection of spoils left by the enemy (chiefly stink-pots and rosaries). A good many potatoes were thrown on the stage and an old watch, and a tin box with a cigar in it and a cigarette box. Our victory was complete in the end.

"Ten men were arrested. Two of them were bar-tenders; one a liquor dealer; two clerks; one a harness-maker; one an instructor; one a mason; one a compositor; and one an electrician.

"Some of the police who protected us were Irish. One of them said to our manager, Mr. Robinson: 'There's a Kerryman says he has you pictured and says he'll have your life.' Mr. Robinson had had some words with this Kerryman and had said: 'We'll give you a supper when you come to Dublin,' and the Kerryman had answered, 'We'll give you a wake.'

"The disturbers were fined sums from three to ten dollars each."

"28th. I was talking to Roosevelt about the opposition on Sunday and he said he could not get in to the plays: Mrs. Roosevelt not being well, he did not like to leave home. But when I said it would be a help to us, he said, 'Then I will certainly come,' and settled that to-night he will dine with me and come on."

"Wednesday, 29th. I was in such a rush last night I sent off my letters very untidily. I hadn't time even to change my dress for dinner. It went off very well. John Quinn, Col. Emmet, grand-nephew of the Patriot, Mr. Flynn. I had asked Peter Dunne (Mr. Dooley) but he was engaged to dinner at eight at the Guinnesses. He came, however, at seven and sat through ours. He was very amusing, and he and Roosevelt chaffed each other. . . . When we got to the theatre and into the box, people saw Roosevelt and began to clap and at last he had to get up, and he took my hand and dragged me on my feet too, and there was renewed clapping. . . . Towards the end of *Gaol Gate* there was a great outbreak of coughing and sneezing, and then there was a scuffle in the gallery and a man throwing pepper was put out. There was a scuffle now and then during *The Playboy* but nothing violent and always great clapping when the offender was thrown out. We played with the lights up. After the first act I took my party on to the stage and introduced the players, and Roosevelt spoke separately to them and then made a little speech, saying how much he admired them and that he felt they were doing a great deal to increase the dignity of Ireland (he has adopted my phrase) and that he 'envied them and Lady Gregory for America.' They were quite delighted and Kerrigan had tears in his eyes. Roosevelt's daughter, who was with another party, then appeared and he introduced her to them, remembering all the names, 'This is Mr. Morgan, this is Miss Magee. . . .' I brought him a cup of tea and it was hard to tear him away when the curtain went up.

"I stayed in my room writing letters through the second act, and when I came back, a swarm of reporters was surrounding Roosevelt and he was declaring from the box, 'I would as soon discuss the question as discuss a pipe dream with an out-patient of Bedlam.' This was about an accusation they had just shown him in some paper, saying he had had a secret understanding with some trusts. He was shaking his fist and saying, 'I am giving you that straight; mind you, take it down as I say it.' When the play was over, he stayed in the box a few minutes discussing it: he said he would contribute a note on an article he wants John Quinn to write about us. When we left the box, we found the whole route to the door packed, just a narrow lane we could walk through, and everyone taking off hats and looking at him with real reverence and affection, so unlike those royal crowds in London. It was an extraordinary kindness that he did us."

The Mayor had received a protest against the play and on that second night he sent as his representative the Chief Magistrate, Mr. McAdoo, who had formerly been a member of Congress, had served as Assistant Secretary of the Navy and as Police Commissioner of New York, and is a leading citizen of the city.

The *New York Sun*, in the issue of November 30th, summarised his report:

"Chief Magistrate McAdoo, who was sent by Mayor Gaynor on Tuesday night to see *The Playboy of the Western World*, wrote to the Mayor yesterday that he had sat through the play and had seen nothing in it to warrant the fuss which some Irishmen were making. Magistrate McAdoo told the Mayor that it was not nearly as objectionable as scores of American plays he had seen in this city and that there was no reason why the Mayor should either order the withdrawal of the play or suspend the licence of Maxine Elliott's Theatre. The Mayor said that the letter had satisfied him that there was no need of any action by the city and that so far as he was concerned the matter was closed."

"Of the few arrested on the second night one was an Englishman, who objected to British soldiers being spoken of as 'khaki cut-throats,' and one was a Jew, who did not give his reasons. For the accusations were getting more and more mixed. A man was heard asking outside the Maxine Elliott Theatre during the riot, 'What is on to-night?' and the answer was, 'There's a Jew-man inside has a French play and he's letting on it's Irish, and some of the lads are inside talking to them.'

"I have had a nice letter from Rothenstein. He is here painting some portraits. He says, 'I would have been to pay you my respects but unhappily I have for the second time been laid up. I hope I may still get the chance, and that the charming and brilliant people I saw with such delight in London are getting their due. I want to bring some friends to see them this week, and am looking forward to the pleasure of seeing them again.' This was written on the morning of the 28th, and he adds a postscript: 'Since writing I see at breakfast an account of a big fuss you had last night. I think it is a fine thing that a work of art should have so vital an effect on people that they feel towards it as they do towards life, and wish to exalt or to destroy it. In these days when there is so little understanding of the content and so much said about the technique of these things, I do feel refreshed that such a thing can happen. I hope the physical experience was not too trying. I admire the courage and determination which both sides showed. If a country can produce so great a man as Synge and a public so spirited that it will protest against what seems a wrong presentment of life to them, then we may still have hope that art will find a place by the fireside. I take my hat off to you all.' "

"December 1st. All well last night. Galleries filled, and apparently with Irish, all applauding, not one hiss.

"I was asked at a tea-party 'what was my moral purpose in writing *The Playboy!*' "

Mr. Yeats wrote from Dublin when he heard of the riot: "December 3rd. What a courageous man Roosevelt is! I mean courageous to go so much beyond official routine. I think it is the best thing that has ever happened to us so far as opinion here is concerned. The papers here have been exceedingly venomous. I am having a baize-covered board with a glass frame to fit in it put up in the vestibule, and promised the audience yesterday, speaking from the stage, that I would put up the American notices as they reached us, good and bad alike. At present I have put up an old picture frame with the rather lengthy London notices of the row. I think it wise that our own people should know that they see there on the board some proof of the reception we are getting. . . . Shaw has just sent me a copy of an interview he is sending to the *New York Sun*. He says you are 'the greatest living Irishwoman,' and adds you will beat the Clan na Gael as you beat the Castle. He makes a most amusing and ferocious attack on the Clan na Gael, and says they are not Irish. . . . But I forgot, you will have read it before this reaches you. I hope he will not have left you all in the plight the little boy was in after Don Quixote had beaten his master. He will, at any rate, have amused New York, which does not care for the Clan, and all fuel helps when one wants a fire. I am pleased that he has seen the issue—that we are the true Ireland fighting the false."

I wrote home on December 1. "The Company have signed on till end of February, so I shall most likely stay till then. The only thing I am at all afraid of is want of sleep. I don't get much. Everyone says the climate here is exciting, but I may get used to it, and we have had exciting times.

"I have made my little room off the stage into a greenroom, and brought some books there and made regular arrangements for tea. There are no greenrooms in these theatres and the Company look rather miserable straying about. Mrs. G. is lending me her motor this afternoon and I am taking some of the players for a drive and to Quinn's for tea. He is such a help to me, so capable and kind. My December horoscope, I remember, said, 'Benefit through friends' and I think it comes about a month wrong and that things happen in the previous month, for in November I had help from him and Bernard Shaw and Roosevelt!

"A priest came in yesterday to express his sympathy, and attended the plays, and I took him round to see the players. So far 'the Church' has not pronounced against us, only individual priests. . . . The servant maids are told we are 'come to mock Ireland.' We are answering nothing now, just going on. Bernard Shaw's article is splendid, going to the root of the matter, as you say. I am just now going over to the theatre to see the start of the voice-production classes. . . . I determined there should be a beginning."

"Dec. 12th. The luncheon with the *Outlook* was great fun. There were present the editors, an Admiral, and some other military heroes, and after lunch some one called for silence 'that Lady Gregory might be questioned.' So they asked questions from here and there, and I gave answers. For instance, they asked if the riot had affected our audience, and I said, yes, I was afraid more people had come to see us pelted than playing. And that I had met a few nights before in Buffalo a General Green, who told me that when driving through crowds cheering for Roosevelt, he had said to Roosevelt, 'Theodore, don't you feel elated by this? And Mr. Roosevelt had said, 'Frank, I always keep in mind what the Duke of Wellington said on a similar occasion, "How many more would come to see me hanged" ' (great applause). . . . Someone asked me why I had worked so hard at the Theatre, and I quoted Blake:

I will not cease from mental strife
Or let the sword fall from my hand
Till we have built Jerusalem
In—Ireland's—fair and lovely land.

"For, I said, it was a part of the building of Jerusalem. This went very well, and in my lecture at Brooklyn in the evening I tried it again but it was received with roars of delighted laughter. It was explained to me afterwards that a part of Brooklyn is full of Jews, who are trying to turn it into a Jerusalem of their own!

"Oh, I am tired to-night!"

"Dec. 15th. Mrs. ——, the Catholic friend who is working for us, is sending to-day to the *Tablet* a very good notice of us written by a priest. She says educated priests and Catholics generally are so much ashamed of the riot that they give out it was got up by the management! She wanted me to have this contradicted, but of course it would be useless. I have just had the *Outlook* and will send it on to you. Roosevelt 'commanded' Quinn to write an article on us. He said he couldn't, but I think it is charming."

"Sunday, 27th. I don't think the Church will really turn on us. It would bring it into a fight with all the theatres and that would make it unpopular. Here Catholics take care to say, 'It is not the Church that is against you, only certain priests.' Father Y. telephoned me this afternoon, saying he was praying for us every day and for the success of our work, and that he thinks *Workhouse Ward* as fine as Shakespeare! Another priest, Father Z., Chaplain in the Navy, has asked me to tea, and says he will come to see the plays only not *The Playboy*."

"A nice matinée yesterday. My friend the wild Irishman who comes to the theatre, tells me the Irish are 'waiting for us' in Chicago, but I don't see what they can do.

"The *Gaelic American* is firing a very distant and random gun now though it has headed an article '*Playboy* as dead as a nail in a door.' I have just been reading Masefield's *Everlasting Mercy*. How fine it is, as fine as *Nan*, but leading to Heaven and the wholesomeness of earth instead of poison pies!

"Mrs. —— gave a tea for me yesterday, and people seemed enthusiastic and there is evidently a great deal of talk about us; but it is just like London, we are building downwards from the intellectuals. *Image* went so well last night I was glad I had put it on. Quinn was delighted with the scene grouping. He thought each scene like an Augustus John drawing. . . . I believe the critics are bewildered because of so much new work. Priests keep dropping in and seem to enjoy the plays, and O'S. told me last night all the young men are either coming to see us or if they have no money, are reading our plays at the library and getting up debates concerning them.

"A lady at Philadelphia said to another, 'What did you really think of *Lady Gregory's* play, *The "Cowboy" of the Western World!*'

"Many happy New Years to you!"

"December 29th. I am too tired to write a letter. This is just to say all is going well, big houses on these last nights. *Kathleen* and *The Playboy* both go extremely well. We have got the audience, and I believe, and everyone says we could now run for weeks, but the theatre is let to someone else. It is just as well leaving at the top of the wave. Next week six towns, then Philadelphia.

"January 2d. I had a talk with Tyler. He was nice, and they

want us to confirm the contract for next year. Talking of the opposition he said, 'The Irish seem to be always afraid of things.' . . . Last week was a real triumph."

"Philadelphia, January 9, 1912. I am staying here with Mr. and Mrs. Jayne, in a beautiful house, with great kindness from my host and hostess. We opened very well last night. We had a very appreciative audience. Mr. and Mrs. —— afterwards gave a supper for me and presented me with an immense basket of roses.

"We dined on Sunday night with Dr. Furness, the old Shakespearean scholar. We went by rail and had to walk a little way to his house. It was four degrees above zero but so still it didn't seem cold. There has been a good deal of snow, and the streets are very slippery. It is impossible to walk at all without goloshes.

"Mr. Jayne went after dinner to a meeting of a philosophical society founded by Franklin. He brought back philosophers and learned men of all sorts. We talked on astronomy. I told them I had once walked down the tube of Lord Rosse's big telescope. Mr. Jayne told of Herschel having his telescope brought to him when he was old that he might look at Orion and remember it as his last view of the heavens.

"The Jaynes and some of the philosophers went on to a ball at the Assembly Rooms, and I was invited. It gave me a sense of Philadelphia being a community of its own—very entertaining.

"A Rev. John —— called on me yesterday, sending in a message that I used to teach him his catechism at Killinane Church. I had forgotten, but remembered him as a little Protestant boy. Something made me ask what church he belonged to. 'Catholic.' I said: 'My catechism didn't do much good then?' 'Yes,' he said, 'I was an Anglican clergyman for a great many years.' 'Why did you change?' 'Because of authority. I wanted authority, and I cannot give up the belief in the divinity of our dear Lord.' 'But we believe that.' 'No, it's being given up little by little, and the bishops seemed uncertain. I wanted authority.'

"When we parted we talked about Roxborough thirty-eight years ago. I said, 'We must say a little prayer now and again for each other.' He said, 'Will you please say a great many for me.'

"By orders from New York two secret service men were sent to see me safely home from the theatre, quite unnecessary for Mr. Jayne, who is a leading lawyer, was sufficient escort."

"January 16th. We had a little trouble last night, the first of *The Playboy*. The first act hadn't gone far when a man got up and protested loudly and wouldn't stop. Others shouted to him to go out or keep quiet, and called out 'New York Irish,' but it was a good while before the police could be stirred up to remove him. By that time another man in the stalls was calling out 'This is an insult.' The men near were calling to him to clear out, but they didn't help to evict him. It was Robinson who came at last and led him out like a lamb, but I believe he made some disturbance in the hall. By this time others had started a demonstration in the balcony and there was a good deal of noise, so that for about ten minutes the play couldn't be heard. I went round, but didn't make the actors repeat it, for I thought the audience ought to be made to suffer for not being more helpful. About twenty-five men were ejected or walked out, but all were given back their money at the box office, and I am sure will think it a sacred duty to spend it in the same way again. Two were arrested for assault. Nothing was thrown but a slice of currant cake, which hit Sinclair, and two or three eggs, which missed him—he says they were fresh ones. I lectured at the University this afternoon; some of the students had come and invited me. A very fine attendance, many of the audience standing. I spoke only half an hour, but made quite a new little lecture and it held them. I gave eight tickets to be given to athletes among the Pennsylvania students as A. D. C.'s for me to-night. They would have been very useful putting out offenders and taking messages to the stage. I rehearsed this morning, and then lectured and went to a 'College Club' tea—and I am tired and won't write more."

"January 17th. The riot last night was not so serious as I had expected. The agitators had been so gently dealt with the first night and had had their money returned, one felt sure they would try again, and when I got to the theatre, one of the officials told me he had been watching the box office during the day, and had seen 'murderers' taking four or five seats together. The auditorium was very full, and at the back, where I sat, there were a great many suspicious-looking characters. One of them began to cough loudly during *Kathleen ni Houlihan* when Miss Allgood was singing the first little song, and to mutter, so that people near told him he was not the only person in the theatre. Others joined in coughing, but I sent a message round to have the lights put up, and the moment they were turned on, the coughs stopped. I pointed out this man, and was amused to see him sit through the play looking sullen but silent except for an occasional mutter or cough, which was stopped at once, for a policeman in plain clothes had been put on each side of him. Near the end, where all on the stage rush out after Christy when he is going to 'kill his father the second time,' he could not resist laughing, and then he walked out discomfited.

"There was a man behind me who coughed loudly at intervals all through and sounded as if making ready to spit, so that it took all my courage not to move. In the third act, when Christy boasts of having 'cleft his father to the breeches belt,' he called out 'Shame, shame!' several times and walked out. However, whether he repented or looked through the glass screen at back of the stalls and saw the father come to life again, I don't know, but he returned and stayed to the end.

"The first man who made a noise was the most difficult to deal with. He crooked his legs round the legs of his chair, and it took four men to take him out. One, with a large roll of paper in his hand, stood up and called out that he represented the County Down. There were fifteen evicted altogether, all from the stalls, and some others walked out shouting protests.

"The police were more energetic last night and did their work very well and with joy, as Irish policemen would. The inspector too was there and seemed very determined. Also, I had my eight young athletes from the University at hand, ready and willing to give aid. The play was not interrupted for more than a minute or two at a time. I told the players to stop speaking whenever there was a row, and to resume when it was over, so nothing was really lost. A good half of the protesters last night stayed till the end of the play. I think they were waiting for the bad bits to begin, so they saw it at all events. The papers say snuff was thrown, but I think not. I think it was premeditated coughing, but the throats didn't hold out very long. On the other hand, there were a lot of rough-looking Irishmen near me, three together on my bench, who did not take any part in the disturbance, and seemed to enjoy the play. I am sure, therefore, that there will be two parties. . . . I am having my University boys again to-night. Flynn had to leave in the middle of the evening and Robinson took Mrs. Flynn to the opera, so we were a little short-handed, but got on all right. John Quinn is coming from New York and will stay the night, so I shall be quite easy."

"January 17th. At two o'clock I was just finishing lunch alone, Mrs. Jayne lunching out and Mr. Jayne being in bed with a cold, when I was rung up by Mr. Bradford, our manager at the Adelphi, to say that he had warning from Lieblers that we might have to change the bill to-night and take off *The Playboy*. I said that could not be done, but he said it might be necessary. There is some legal point, and Mr. Bradford thought that we might all be arrested if we went on. I said I would rather be arrested than withdraw the play and could answer for the players feeling the same. He said there was also danger that Shubert, to whom the theatre belongs, might close it. I said that would be bad but not so bad as withdrawing *The Playboy*, for it would be Shubert's doing not ours, though that might not be much help in the public view. I was anxious, and I told Bradford not to consent to anything without consulting me. Then I called up John Quinn at New York, got him at his office, and asked him to see the Lieblers, and said that I need not tell him I would sooner go to my death than give in. He said he would see them at once, and that he would be here this evening, as he had intended. At 4 o'clock I heard again from Bradford. He said it had been decided to go on, and that a bail bond had been prepared. He asked if there was anyone to represent me in case of my arrest. I said I would wait to consult Quinn. It is such a mercy he is coming. My only fear is lest they should get out an injunction to stop the matinée to-morrow; even that would be claimed as a victory. They had told me at the theatre this morning there would probably be trouble to-night. The men arrested were let out, had their money returned, and were escorted through the streets by an admiring crowd. However, I should like to avoid arrest, because of the publicity; one would feel like a suffragette."

"Thursday, 18th. When Quinn arrived, we went straight to the theatre—it was then 7:15—and found the whole cast had already been technically arrested! The tactics of the enemy had been to arrest them in the theatre at 8 o'clock and so make a performance impossible. But the theatre lawyer had managed to circumvent them, and the Chief of Police, now our warm friend, had said he would not only refuse to let his men arrest the actors, but he would have anyone arrested who came on the stage to do so. In the end the warrants of arrest were issued and the manager of the theatre signed bail bonds for the appearance of the Company on Friday morning. The warrants are founded on a bill passed last year in the municipality before S. Bernhardt's visit, forbidding 'immoral or indecent plays.' Our accuser is a liquor dealer. I should have been completely bewildered by the whole thing, but Quinn seemed to unravel it. We had a consultation with the theatre lawyer, and Mr. Jayne's partners, Mr. Biddle and Mr. Yocum, to whom he had sent me. The question seems to be whether it is best to have the hearing put off and brought before a judge, or whether to have it settled straight off to-morrow. The danger is that our case may come up for trial after some weeks, bringing us back here, making it possible for the enemy to boast that we were under bail. Quinn is this morning seeing all the lawyers again, and some decision as to our course will be come to.

"The Commissioner of Public Safety attended the play last night, and said the attack on it must be a joke. . . . I have been interrupted in this by the correspondent of the *Telegraph* coming to ask if it is true, as stated by the Irish Societies, that I am an envoy of the English Government. I referred him to Mr. Bryce, who, I suppose, would be my paymaster!"

"Saturday, 20th. I have been too anxious and hard worked to write since Thursday. That was the last performance of *The Playboy,* and there was an immense audience. I could not get a seat. Even the little boxes at the top—it is a very high theatre with eight boxes at each side—were all taken. I had made appointments with reporters and others, and had to get a high stool from the office put in the passage and sit there or at the back of the stage. It was the record matinée of the Adelphi. There was tremendous enthusiasm and not a sign of any disturbance. Of course, we had a good many policemen in the house, to the great regret of the management, who had to turn so much good money away. So that was quite a cheerful day. Someone in the audience was heard declaring that the players are not Irish, but all Jews. I had an anonymous letter from some one, who accuses me of the usual crimes and winds up: 'The writer has never saw the play, but has read all about you and it'! That is the way with most of the letter writers, I think.

"Yesterday, Friday morning, we attended the Magistrate's Court at nine o'clock. We had to wait nearly an hour in a tiny, stuffy room. When the hearing began, I was given a chair behind the Magistrate, but the others had either to sit at the back of the inner room, where they could not see or hear, or stand as they did, for over an hour. The liquor-seller, our prosecutor, was the first witness. He had stayed only till Shawneen's 'coat of a Christian man' was left in Michael James's hands. He made a disturbance then and was turned out, but was able to find as much indecency even in that conversation as would demoralise a monastery. His brother, a priest, had stayed all through, and found we had committed every sin mentioned in the Act. Another witness swore that sentences were used in the play and that he had heard them, though they are not either in book nor play. Several witnesses were examined or asked to speak, all giving the same story, 'or if it was not the same story, anyway it was no less than the first story.'

"Our actors were furious. Kerrigan tried hard to keep from breaking out and risking all when the priest was attacking his (that is Shawn Keogh's) character and intentions. At last he called out, 'My God!' and the Magistrate said, 'If that man interrupts the Court again, turn him out,' forgetting that he was speaking of a prisoner at the bar! Indeed, as the prosecutors grew excited, the trial of the Irish Players seemed to be forgotten, and it became the trial of Christy Mahon for the attempted murder of his father. Mr. Gray demanded that the actors should be 'held for Court,' but Quinn, knowing what would happen, had arranged for this, and our lawyers 'sued out a writ of *habeas corpus*' (I hope this is the right expression) and had arranged with Judge Carr to try the case in the afternoon. Mr. Gray wanted then to have it tried at once. He said he had to leave town in the afternoon, but in the end the Judge said he could not arrange for the trial before three o'clock. This gave me time to telephone to John Quinn, who had thought the trial was not to be till next morning, and was attending cases of his own in New York. He answered that he would come if he possibly could. Then there was a message that he had missed the train by one minute, but had caught another, ten minutes later. At three o'clock we went to the Court, a large one this time. The Judge didn't know anything about the play, and had to be told the whole story as it went on, just like old Wall in Dublin at our first riot, so before the case had gone far audience and officials were in a broad grin. The liquor-dealer got a different hearing this time, was asked some pertinent questions instead of being simply encouraged, as he was by the Magistrate.

"The dramatic event was the arrival of Quinn while a witness was being examined. We had got leave from the Judge for him to cross-examine, and the witness had to confess that the people of Ireland do use the name of God at other times than in blessing or thanking those who have been kind to them, and in gratitude or prayer, as he had at first asserted upon oath. Also when he based his attack on indecency by quoting the 'poacher's love,' spoken of by Christy, he was made to admit that, a few sentences earlier, marriage had been spoken of, 'in a fortnight's time when the banns will be called.' Whether this made it more or less moral, he was not asked to say. He called the play 'libidinous.'

"J. Q. asked one witness if anything immoral had happened on the stage, and he answered 'Not while the curtain was up!' I think it was the same witness who said, 'A theatre is no place for a sense of humour.' The players beamed and the audience enjoyed themselves, and then when the Director of Public Safety was called and said he and his wife had enjoyed the play very much and had seen nothing to shock anybody, the enemy had received, as Quinn said, 'a knock-out blow.' He made a very fine speech then. There is just a little bit of it in the *North American*, but Mr. Gray made objections to its being reported, but, anyhow, it turned the tables completely on the enemy. It was a little disappointment that the Judge did not give his verdict there and then, that we might have cabled home.

"A lot of people have been expressing sympathy. A young man from the University, who had been bringing a bodyguard for me on the riot nights, has just been to say good-bye, and told me the students are going to hold an indignation meeting. The Drama League, six hundred strong, has so far done or said nothing, though it is supposed to have sent out a bulletin endorsing the favourable opinion of Boston upon our plays, a week after we came here, not having had time to form an opinion of its own. Can you imagine their allowing such a thing to happen here as the arrest of a company of artists engaged in producing a masterpiece, and at such hands! The Administration has been reformed of late and is certainly on the mend, but there is plenty more to be done, although the city has an innocent look, as if it had gone astray in the fields, and its streets are named after trees. The Company are in a state of fury, but they adore John Quinn, and his name will pass into folk-lore like those stories of O'Connell suddenly appearing at trials. He spoke splendidly, with fire and full knowledge. You will see what he said about the witnesses in the *North American* and even Robinson says he 'came like an angel.' "

"Sunday, 21st. Yesterday was a little depressing, for the Judge had not yet given out his decision; so we are still under bail and the imputations of indecency, etc. The Philadelphians say it is because the Act is such a new one, it requires a great deal of consideration.

"A reporter came yesterday to ask whether I considered *The Playboy* immoral. I said my taking it about was answer enough, but that if he wished to give interesting news, he would go to the twenty-six witnesses produced against us (we were not allowed to produce one on our side) and try to get at their opinions, and on what they were founded. He answered that he had already been to ten of them that morning, that they all answered in the same words, not two words of difference—that their opinion was founded on the boy and the girl being left alone in the house for the night. They can hardly have heard Quinn making the clerical witness withdraw his statement that immorality was implied by their being left together. I advised him also to look at the signed articles on the play in so many English and American magazines, and to remember that even here the plays have been taught in the dramatic classes of the University of Pennsylvania, that the President of Bryn Mawr had invited the players to the College for the day, and had sent a large party of students to the last matinée of *The Playboy,* leave being asked to introduce them to me. I told him he might print all this opposite the witnesses' opinions.

"Yesterday's matinée, *Rising of the Moon, Well of the Saints,* and *Workhouse Ward,* was again so crowded that I could not get a place and went and sat in the side-wings, where a cinematograph man came to ask if I would allow *The Playboy* to be used for a moving-picture exhibition, as it would be 'such a good advertisement for us!' Last night also there was a very good audience. We took just one dollar short of eight thousand dollars in the week. Such a pity the dollars were returned to the disturbers or we should have gone above it."

"I was advised to go to a certain newspaper office to get evidence that was considered necessary as to the standing of the magistrate who had issued the writ and before whom we had been brought (we had been advised to take an action for malicious arrest). John Quinn introduced me to the Editor. I have had some telephone talk with him during the day and he sent a young man with a message I had better come to the office after nine in the evening and I could get facts. So I went there from the Theatre, up to the eighteenth floor. He introduced me to a young man who had known Carey all his life and gave an astonishing account of the use made by him when in the police of Thugs, Pluguglies and other means of intimidating witnesses. Also said he had taken a regular tax from houses of ill-fame which he encouraged in his division, the Fifth Ward. He was forced to retire from the police and was made a magistrate after a while as a political job, and immediately became rich. He had begun life 'standing about saloons and anyone that would give him a drink he would make him welcome.' However this was not evidence, and I told the Editor so, and he telephoned down, 'Send up Jimmy Carey's Obituary'! (So like *Coats*!) He got an envelope full of cuttings, but I only wanted one, the most concise, and chose one dated Oct. 19, 1905, saying Carey had resigned from the police on the previous day rather than face his trial which was to take place before the Police Board that morning upon four charges: 1. Conduct prejudicial to good discipline in the police department; 2. neglect of duty; 3. disobedience of orders; 4. inefficiency. The Editor was loath to take this paragraph from those he is preparing the obituary, but he was generous and gave it at the last, and sent a sub to hunt up the other information. He meanwhile lamented his troubles of the evening before when he had gone for supper to the Bellevue where I had met him.[3] He had taken to the restaurant a young niece, who wanted something for supper, whereas the editor himself wanted two soft-boiled eggs with rice and cream. These simple dishes, however, could not be had at the fashionable Bellevue and he was able but to pick at a little of the delicate food. After he had taken the niece home, he made off to his own homely restaurant, where he secured his rice and eggs. This, and an interview I had seen with Yeats, who supposes that our arrest was due to the fact that Philadelphia is a Puritan town, brought back the rural atmosphere."[4]

Our friends at home were naturally amazed, especially in London where the posters of the newspapers had in large print,

[3] Lady Gregory had prepared for a further edition of this book by inserting some pages of typescript containing new material for this chapter which has been inserted here. This paragraph originally read as follows:

"I was advised to go to a certain newspaper office to get evidence that was considered necessary as to the standing of the magistrate who had issued the writ and before whom we had been brought (we had been advised to take an action for malicious arrest). The editor was generous enough to let me have the files, classified in the newspaper office as 'Obituary Notices', ready for use at the proper time an envelope containing the reports of some curious incidents in the record of the magistrates in question. The editor lamented his troubles of the evening before when we had gone for supper to the Bellevue where I had met him."

Clipped to these pages was a note "(It was with regret I left this out of my account of our time at Philadelphia . . .)".

[4] The typescript continued with the following text which Lady Gregory had later crossed out with blue crayon.

"(The young man brought the Grey divorce case typewritten, but I wouldn't take it. I asked for the paper with the Judge's summing up, and that has to be hunted up. It was Grey who divorced his wife, but they say it was a 'contest' which should divorce the other first, and that he was the worst, and that the Judge cleared the Court and would not let the evidence be published.) I only want a sentence for my cable. I was to have started with the Company this morning for another six towns, on the road to Chicago, but the delay in the Judge's decision keeps me here till tomorrow partly to be able to cable and partly another point. Quinn advised that as soon as we get the decision we ought to take an action in the name of the Players against McGarrity for malicious arrest. It would be a splendid dramatic coup. (He said we need not go on with it longer than we liked; it could easily be dropped after a while.) Mr. Jayne was well enough to see me yesterday, he is a very good lawyer and gives very clear advice, and he said he thought it an excellent idea, and that we should sue for 50,000 dollars, the cost of starting proceedings would be very [? small.]" The typescript ends with the word "very."

"ARREST OF THE IRISH PLAYERS." Mr. Yeats wrote from Dublin, January 21: "I need not tell you how startled I was when a reporter came to me on Thursday evening and asked me whether I had anything to say regarding the arrest of the Abbey Players. While I was talking to him and telling him I didn't really know anything about it (he was as ignorant of your crime as I was), a second reporter came in, equally urgent and ignorant. Then a wire came from the London correspondent of the *New York Sun*, asking for an opinion on the arrest of Abbey Players. We were speculating as to what it could mean, and I was surmising it was *Blanco*, when a telegram came from the *Manchester Guardian*, saying it was *The Playboy* and asking me to see their reporter. Then a young man arrived with a telegram, and I thought he was the reporter and became very eloquent. He was sympathetic and interested, and when I had finished, explained that he was only the post-office messenger. Then another reporter turned up and after that the *Manchester Guardian* man. You will have had the papers before this. I think for the moment it has made us rather popular here in Dublin, for no matter how much evil people wish for the Directors, they feel amiable towards the players. If only Miss Allgood could get a fortnight, I think the pit would love even *The Playboy*. However, I imagine that after a few days of the correspondence columns, we shall discover our enemies again.

"We have done very well this week with the school. I am rather anxious that the school, or No. 2 Company, as it will be, should have in its repertory some of our most popular pieces. . . . The great thing achieved is that if Philadelphia had permanently imprisoned the whole Company, our new Company would in twelve months have taken their place here in Dublin. We have now a fine general effect, though we have no big personalities."

"Philadelphia, Monday. I forget what I have written, and I don't know if I have explained that we were allowed no witnesses, either at the Magistrate's or the Judge's Court, and with our hastily instructed lawyers we should not have been able to make even any defence through them but for the miraculous appearance of John Quinn. And this is the fifth day we have been under bail on charges of indecency, and its like."

"January 22d, Hotel Algonquin, New York. Contrary to my directions Liebler's man had put on *The Playboy* for Pittsburg. It was asked for by some ladies who are taking the whole house for a charity performance. Now they have written to ask for another bill instead, *Hyacinth*, *Riders*, *Workhouse*; and the papers say that *The Playboy* has been taken off on religious grounds."[5]

"Richmond, Indiana, January 24th. The journey to Pittsburg is a quite lovely journey, like Switzerland but less monotonous; the sunshine and snow exhilarating. The plays had begun when I arrived. There was a very good audience and *Hyacinth* and *Workhouse Ward* made them laugh a great deal. Carnegie Hall is all gilding and marbles, and a gilded organ towers above the butcher's shop in *Hyacinth*. I had to make a little speech and was able to tell of the telegram from Philadelphia, saying the Judge had dismissed the case. We came on here through the night.

"An interviewer who came this morning has sent me an interesting book on Indiana book plates, and an old lady brought me an Irish Bible, and the jeweller who packed my watch would take nothing, and Miss Allgood has sent me a box of roses. So the stars must be in a good mood. I think we ought to start with *The Playboy* in Chicago and get that over. It would show we are not damped by Philadelphia."

We went on that night to Indianapolis. *The Playboy* had been specially asked for in Indianapolis. Protests against its production were made to the manager of the theatre by the Ancient Order of Hibernians and others, but the manager said he was powerless. They also called upon Superintendent of Police Hyland, who said: "I will have plenty of men at the theatre to quell a disturbance. I don't believe, however, that there will be any trouble. If there are persons who do not like the show, they can stay away. But there is one thing certain; if they do not stay away and come to the show to make trouble, they will find plenty of it on hand."

The Mayor was also appealed to, but he did not see his way to stop the play. The Irish Societies then decided to stay away, and though the theatre was packed, the play went through in perfect peace.

"Chicago, Hotel La Salle, January 26th. Tyler wired me to come on here, so I left the Company at Indianapolis this morning and came on. We don't begin playing here till the 5th. No theatre is ready. Gaston Mayer was very urgent we should stay another week on account of getting here so late. I told the Com-

5 Together with the typescript is a telegram. It reads:
PITTSBURG PENNA JANUARY 23RD 1912. JOHN QUINN, 31 NASSAU ST. NEWYORK. TRAVEL TO INDIANAPOLIS TONIGHT TWO DAYS THERE. LAFAYETTE CANCELLED. SPOKE FROM STAGE APOLOGISED FOR WITHDRAWING PLAYBOY DEFERENCE TO JUDGE CASE NOW DISMISSED LEAVE WITHOUT STAIN ON CHARACTER LIKE HYACINTH HALVEY. SAID WORKHOUSE WARD PARABLE OF IRELAND OUR ABUSE OFTEN PERVERTED AFFECTION, WE DONT MEAN ALL HARD THINGS WE SAY. MIGHT BE USEFUL IN PAPERS. FINE AUDIENCE TRY ARRANGE VISIT CHICAGO OPENING NIGHT FIFTH PROBABLY PLAYBOY TIRED OUT HAPPY AND CONTENT A GREGORY 150AM.

2. G. W. Russell (A.E.) by J. B. Yeats the elder. Courtesy of Senator M. B. and Miss Anne Yeats (to whom acknowledgement is made for their kind permission to include all the paintings by J. B. Yeats in this section) and to the National Gallery of Ireland.

3. Miss A. E. Horniman by J. B. Yeats the elder. Courtesy of the Abbey Theatre.

4. Edward Martyn by Sarah Purser. Courtesy of the Dublin Municipal Gallery of Modern Art.

5. William Fay by J. B. Yeats the elder. Courtesy of the Abbey Theatre.

6. Frank J. Fay by J. B. Yeats the elder. Courtesy of the Abbey Theatre.

7. Sara Allgood by Sarah Purser. Courtesy the Abbey Theatre.

8. Maire O'Neill by J. B. Yeats the elder. Courtesy the Abbey Theatre.

9. Lady Gregory in the title role in W. B. Yeat's play "Kathleen ni Houlihan". Courtesy of Gabriel Fallon.

10. John Quinn and W. B. Yeats.

11. J. M. Synge by J. B. Yeats the elder. Courtesy the National Gallery of Ireland.

12. Dr. Douglas Hyde (An Craoibhín Aoibhinn), by J. B. Yeats the elder. Courtesy of Miss Norah Niland and the Sligo County Library and Museum.

13. George Moore by J. B. Yeats the elder. Courtesy of the National Gallery of Ireland.

14. George Bernard Shaw.

15. Lady Gregory. The frontispiece to the first edition of *Our Irish Theatre*.

16. A photo of G. B. Shaw, W. B. Yeats and Lady Gregory with her grandson Richard, *c.* 1910. Courtesy Major R. Gregory.

17. Lennox Robinson by James Sleator. Courtesy of the Abbey Theatre.

18. Sara Allgood as Kathleen ni Houlihan. Courtesy of Gabriel Fallon.

19. Maire Nic Shiubhlaigh by J. B. Yeats the elder. Courtesy of the Abbey Theatre.

20. Dr. J. F. Larchet by Sean O'Sullivan. Courtesy of the Abbey Theatre.

21. Arthur Sinclair as James I in Lady Gregory's "The White Cockade" by Robert Gregory. Courtesy of the Abbey Theatre.

22. The cast of the first Abbey Theatre performance by W. B. Yeats's "The Golden Helmet", on 10th February 1910.

IRISH PLAYERS AND IRISH PLAYS FOR AMERICA
THE "ABBEY THEATRE PEOPLE" AT QUEENSTOWN

23. The Abbey Players before setting off for their second American tour. Photo: the *Cork Examiner*.

24. Lady Gregory seated at her desk in the drawing room of Coole Park, with the statue of Andromeda behind her: Photo: G. B. Shaw.

25. Duras House, home of Count de Basterot, where Lady Gregory, W.B. Yeats and Edward Martyn first discussed the idea of an Irish Theatre. Photo: Gabriel Fallon.

pany of this and they decided to stay. We shall therefore finish here March 2nd and sail on the 6th. We had no trouble at Indianapolis last night. The police authorities were very firm and the threats collapsed. I wish Philadelphia had been as firm. They are all afraid of the politicians. . . .

"I was sorry to leave the Company. I feel like Wilhelm Meister going through ever-fresh adventures with the little troop. As to the rows, I don't think there is anything you (Yeats) could have done, except that you would have done things yourself while others have done them for me. The Company insist on giving John Quinn a silver cup, in gratitude for his help. I haven't seen Flynn for a fortnight. He is astray among the one-night towns and talked to us at Indianapolis through the telephone, with a bad cold."

"25th or 26th. I see by the papers that at the La Salle Hotel, where I am staying, a meeting of Irishmen has been held at which an 'Anti-Irish Players' League' was formed, beginning with a membership of three hundred. Such a pity I couldn't have slipped in to the meeting! A petition had also been written and was being sent out for signature, demanding the suppression of *The Playboy*. This petition was said to have been signed by eight thousand persons, and twenty thousand signatures were expected. Meanwhile the Anti-Cruelty Society of Chicago, at the head of which are various benevolent ladies, had asked leave to buy up the whole house for the first performance of *The Playboy of the Western World*. They meant to resell these seats at an increased price for their charity and believed it was likely to draw the largest audience. So they have taken the theatre for Tuesday, February 6, and the public performance of *The Playboy* will take place the next day."

"January 29th. My typewriter is mended at last, and I am getting settled. Last night one of the boy interviewers—they are all boys here—came in from one of the papers. He showed me two statements written by Liebler's manager here, one colourless, the other offering a reward of five thousand dollars to anyone who could prove the management had bribed rioters for the first night, as has been stated in the papers. I advised that this be put in, as people really seem to believe it is true. This young man had been to see many of the objectors. They said Synge was a 'degenerate,' who had lived abroad to collect a bad atmosphere, which he put round Irish characters afterwards. A nice young interviewer; he wants to write a play round his mother's life, to show what a mother's devotion can be. Another of them is twenty-five and is going to be married next summer. He showed me his fiancée's portrait, and another went and hunted for a Don Quixote I wanted, to distract my mind from present-day things.

"This morning one came who is in with the Irish Clubs and had all the objections, but now seems quite friendly. He says one of the chief officers of the 'Anti-Irish Players' League' is a man called H., a son of old Mrs. H.! He has hinted that my sympathies are with the landlord side, and that he could tell tales of hard treatment. The interviewer wanted to know if a rehearsal could be held for the Mayor so that he might judge the play, but I said the first night under the patronage of the Anti-Cruelty Society would give him his opportunity. A lady interviewer then came, but I made her take her pencil and write down what I did say, which is more than the boys do. I tell them I put in my pig and it comes out sausage."

"Tuesday, January 30th. I am so tired! Last night I dined with the Hamills, friends of John Quinn. It was a very pleasant dinner and we all went afterwards to see *The Woman*, a good play in its realistic way. I came home quite cheery but found in the passage one of my young interviewers, who told me the Town Council had unanimously voted against *The Playboy* being put on. He had been sent to ask me for a statement, but advised me not to make one, and there was nothing to say. I was going to bed near midnight when another interviewer arrived, and said the Mayor had acted on the recommendation of the Council and suppressed the play. He showed me an article which was to appear in the morning issue of his paper telling this. I was very sad for it seemed as if there was an end of the fight. The hot water-apparatus in my room, which is always out of order, began grunting and groaning between one and two when I was asleep and wakened me; so I got no more sleep till late morning, and then was awaked by interviewers at the telephone. They even knocked at my door while I was dressing.

"When I went down, however, I found that the Mayor had not ordered the play off, and the article in the paper had had to be reprinted. Also Flynn arrived and was a help with the army who came in, entertaining them while I typed out a statement about the adventures of *The Playboy* so far, and this statement I gave them. Then I 'phoned to Mr. Hamill, who is a lawyer and who had said last night he would help me in any legal difficulty. He came at once and was splendid. He went into the law of the case, and believes that if the Mayor does forbid it, we can take him into the Federal Court, and go on all right. He says another lawyer, who was at the dinner last night, has also volunteered to serve. He went to try and see the Mayor but missed him. He is, however, to see him at noon to-morrow. He came back at five for another talk, and says he doesn't think the Mayor has power to stop it. He has seen the Corporation lawyer.

"I was engaged to lunch with a nice Mrs. —— at one, but got there after the hour and had to be back here before two, and it was an absurd thing: I had had my room changed. I had suffered so much from the unmanageable hot water that I threatened the manager that I would tell the interviewers about it, and he at once gave me another suite. My things were being brought up, and I couldn't find hat or coat, therefore had to go just as I was. However the lunch was very pleasant and good, what I had of it. . . .

"I came back to find a Mr. Field, editor of one of the papers, who had brought 'an enemy,' who announced he had come but for five minutes to hear my views, and spent at least ten in giving me his own. Then Liebler's local manager came in. He also thinks we shall be able to circumvent the Mayor. He believes, however, the Mayor will give the order for political reasons, though he has some culture and would not like to be classed with the Aldermen. A couple of ladies called. One comfort of being attacked is that one finds friends to help. . . .

"I have nice rooms now on the ninth floor—there are twenty-two floors altogether—the place riddled with telephones, radiators, etc. I was glad to hear the voice of a fat housemaid from Mayo a while ago.

"It is a strange fate that sends me into battle after my peaceful life for so many years, and especially over *Playboy*, that I have never really loved, but one has to carry through one's job. One of the accusations has been that there are no Irish persons connected with the company, and my answer is given accurately in one of the papers 'The Players are all Irish by birth. They had never left Ireland until they came to England on the tours made by us. With two exceptions all are Roman Catholics.

" 'I believe the play is quite honestly considered by some of my countrymen out here to be injurious to Ireland and her claim for self-government, but I know that such an assumption is wrong and that the dignity of Ireland has been very much increased by the work of the Theatre, of which the genius of Mr. Synge is a component part.' "

"February 1st. Yesterday morning I took a holiday, went to see a little amateur play in a private house. It was on suffrage, called *Everywoman*, very short and rather amusing. It was given at 11 o'clock and afterwards there was an 'informal lunch,' rather a good idea,—little tables, not set out, here and there. There were first cups of delicious soup, then vegetable sandwiches with little cases of hot mince, and peas, just a plate and fork, then ices and black coffee, and bonbons. It was much pleasanter than sitting down to a table; one could move about. The luncheon was all over by 1:30, and then a Mrs. R—— took me for a drive in her motor. We drove about thirty miles about the park and town and along the lake side, but never really away from the town, which is immense. The lake is lovely, a soft turquoise blue, not the blue of the sea, and there was floating ice near the shore. It was luckily a bright day, the first we have had. To-day there is snow again and darkness.

"When I came home, I set to work to correct a copy of *The Playboy* according to the prompt copy I had sent on by the Company, in case the Mayor wanted it. A journalist came in who wanted to know about the cuts, and I got him to help me. Then Mr. Hamill came; he doesn't think there will be trouble. Then I took up a lot of telephone addresses that had been left for me to call up, and found one was from 'W. Dillon.' It was a Mr. Dillon representing the enemy, who had been brought to see me on Tuesday. My interview with him had appeared in a very mangled form next day and I found only then that he was a brother of John Dillon, M.P., and the Corporation lawyer. I called him up, and he answered from the City Hall, and said he was writing a report on the legal aspect of the case for the Mayor, and wanted to know if I was sure certain words had been left out of the acting version, as I told him had always been done. I said yes, and I could now bring him the prompt copy. He assented and I went round to the City Hall. Mr. Dillon was sitting in his office, dictating to a shorthand writer. He said, 'You may listen to what I am dictating, but you must treat it as confidential.' I said, 'I will go away if you wish,' but he said, 'No, I will trust to your honour as a lady.' He was just finishing his statement, as printed in the papers this morning, denouncing the play but saying that, though in his opinion it might lead to a riot, he did not think the Mayor had power to stop it. I showed him the prompt copy. He asked if we could not strike out still more. I said the passages we had changed or left out had been changed in Mr. Synge's lifetime and with his consent, and we did not feel justified in meddling any more. I think he expected me to make some concession, for he said then, 'I think you would do much better to take the play off altogether.' I said we were bound by contract to Liebler to put on whatever plays they asked for. He said, 'Then it is not in your power to remove it?' I answered, 'No,' and that ended the matter. I felt sorry for the moment, for it would have been gracious to make some small concession, but afterwards I thought of Parnell. . . . We may bring that play some other time, and there are many who think his betrayal a greater slur upon Ireland than would be even the real killing of a father.

"The *Examiner* announces that the Mayor won't stop the play. He has said. 'I do not see how the performance can be stopped. I have read part of it and its chief characteristic seems to be stupidity rather than immorality. I should think it would take more than a regiment of soldiers to compel an audience to fill the Grand Opera House to see such a poor production. I certainly shall not see it.'

"I hope I may get some breathing time. The idea of a day spent playing with little Richard seems an impossible heaven! And I feel a little lonely at times. It is a mercy this will be the last fight. I don't think it is over yet. . . . I like to hear of the success of the school. It will be a great enjoyment sitting down to listen to a verse play again if I survive to do it!"

"Feb. 3rd. I dined with the McC——s, and went on to the Opera, *Tristan and Isolde*, which I had never seen. It was a great delight, a change from worries. I like the people here. They are more merry than those of the other cities somehow, at least those I have fallen amongst. They are vital. They don't want to die till they see what Chicago is going to do.

"There is snow on the ground and yesterday when I went for a walk, the cold frightened me at first,—such pain in the face, but I went on and got used to it. The thermometer has been six below zero."

"Feb. 8th. I seem to have been busy ever since. The first night of *The Playboy* was anxious. I was not really anxious the Anti-Cruelty night, and it went off quite peaceably, but I was last night, the open one, for, as I quoted from *Image*, 'There are always contrary people in a crowd.' But the play was acted in entire peace. I nearly fell asleep! It seems complete victory. The Corporation had to rescind their resolution against it, and I suppose the objectors found public opinion was too strong to permit any protest to be made. It is a great mercy. I did not know how great the strain was till it was over.

"On Monday we opened to a fairly large house with comedies and they were well received. The Hull House Players came and gave me a lovely bunch of roses. They have been acting some of my plays. When I got back to the hotel, I found a threatening letter written in vile language, and with picture of coffin and pistol, saying I would 'never see the hills of Connemara again,' and was about to meet with my death. It seemed a miracle to have got through such a Wood of Dangers with flags flying."

"Feb. 12th. Everything goes on so peaceably we are astonished. *The Playboy* finished its five days' run on Saturday with never a boo or a hiss. I believe the enemy are making some excuse for themselves, saying they won't riot because it was said they were paid to do so, but it is an extraordinary defeat for them. Quinn was much excited over it when he was here, and he did not know the extent of our victory. He thinks it the pricking of the bubble of all the societies that have been terrorising people. Fibs go on, of course, and a Mrs. F—— told me that her Irish maid said she had been forbidden to go to *The Playboy* 'because it runs down the courage of the Irish.' She was sad, and said 'The Irish always had courage.'

"It makes one think *The Playboy* more harmless even than one had thought, their having to make up these inventions. One is glad to put it on for them to see. I feel like Pegeen showing off Christy to the Widow Quinn, 'See now is he roaring, romping?' The author of 'An Open Letter to Lady Gregory' came to me at some Club to ask if I had seen it. I said yes, and that the paper had telephoned to know if I would answer it but I had said no, and that I wished all my critics would write me open letters instead of personal ones, as I could leave them unanswered without discourtesy.

"We have a good following among the intellectuals, and a good many Irish begin to come in. We know that by the reception of *Rising of the Moon*.

"Coming back from my lecture at Detroit, I was to have arrived at Chicago at eight o'clock. I awoke to find we were in a blizzard. The train got stuck in a suburb of Chicago, and after hours of waiting we had to wade across the track, ankle deep in snow, I in my thin shoes! After fighting the blizzard, we had to sit in a shed for another hour or two. Then they said we must wade back to the train. They thought it could be run to the station. I thought I might as well wait for my end where I was, as I could not carry my baggage and there was no one to help me, so stayed on my bench. After a bit some omnibuses came to our relief, and I being near the door was put in first, and got to the hotel at three o'clock. I had not had breakfast, expecting we should be in, and when I asked for it later, the car had been taken off, so all the food I had was a dry roll I had taken from the hotel on Sunday. However, I was none the worse, and glad to have seen a blizzard. It was the worst they had had for many years, deaths were caused by it, and much damage was done.

"I have been walking to the theatre every night as usual in spite of the threatening letter. I don't feel anxious, for I don't think from the drawing that the sender has much practical knowledge of firearms.

"I can hardly believe we shall sail next week! It will be a great rest surely. . . . Well, we have had a great victory!"

EDITORS' NOTE

Lady Gregory's own copy of *Our Irish Theatre*, has inserted in it a much revised version of *The Binding*, which is given below. Variations are noted and marked as in Chapter V.

THE BINDING

"I HOPE you do not think that we Americans helped in these attacks on you" was often said to me in New York and other cities. And I would say "No, our countrymen made that clear by throwing the national potato; if you had attacked us you would have thrown pumpkins; we should have felt like Æsop's philosopher under the oak tree."[1]

I think the account I have given shows that the opposition was planned and ordered even before we landed,[2] and by a very small group working through a political organisation. As to the reason and meaning of that attack, it is for those who made it to set that out. I think sometimes of Alexander Hamilton's words in Washington's time[3]: "After this war is over will come the real war, the great battle of ideas;" and that the long political war in Ireland may be, and seems to be nearing its end. And I remember Laeg[4] looking out from the wounded Cuchulain's tent and making his report at Ilgaireth "I see a little herd of cattle breaking out from the West of Ailell's camp and there are lads following after them and trying to bring them back, and I see more lads coming out from the army of Ulster to attack them," and how Cuchulain said "That little herd on the plain is the beginning of a great battle." The battle of ideas has been fought elsewhere and against other writers; was[5] not Ibsen banished from his country and Molière refused Christian burial?

[1] "I had just written these pages and put together these letters when in last Christmas week we set out again for America. We spent there the first four months of this year, but this time there were no riots and we were of the happy people who have no history, unless it may be of the continued kindness of America, and of the growing kindness and better understanding on the part of our own countrymen.

"Last year, it was often said to me in New York and elsewhere, 'You must not think that we Americans helped in these attacks.' And I would answer, 'No; our countrymen took care to make that clear by throwing our national potato. If you had attacked us you would have thrown pumpkins, and we should have fared worse than Æsop's philosopher under the oak.' "

[2] "I think the facts I have given show that the opposition was in every case planned and ordered before the plays had been seen—before we landed."

[3] "I cannot but remember Alexander Hamilton's words when the building of America began:"

[4] "I think too of Laeg"

[5] "other dramatists. Was"

Sometimes it seems to be the old story, the[6] two sides of the shield. Some who are lovers of Ireland say[7] we have lessened the dignity of Ireland by showing upon the stage countrymen who drink and swear and admire deeds of violence and are misers or covetous or thirsting after land.[8] We who are lovers of Ireland believe that our Theatre with its whole mass of plays has very greatly increased its dignity; and we are content to leave that judgment to the great Arbitrator, Time. And amongst the Irish in America it was easy to rouse feeling against us. Is not the new baby always the disturber in the household, and our school of drama is the newest product[9] in Ireland, that Ireland which had become almost consecrated by distance and by romance. An Irishwoman who loved[10] her country very much said while I was in America: "I don't want to go back and see it[11] again; it is a finished picture in my mind." But Ireland cannot always be kept as a sampler on[12] the wall. It has refused to be cut off from the creative work of the intellect, and the other countries who are creating literature have claimed her as of their kin.

[We were never stopped for a single night; our curtain was never lowered till the end of the act.] I wish my countrymen before coming into the fight had known it to be so unequal. They had banished from the stage one or two plays they had found offensive, and no one greatly cared.[13] But works of imagination such as those of Synge could not be suppressed even if burned on[14] the market place. They had not realised the tremendous support we had, that we were not fighting alone but with the intellect of America as well as of Europe at our back.

There was another thing they had not reckoned with. It had been put down in words by Professor William James. [He said:] "Democracy is still upon its trial. The civic genius of our people is its only bulwark and neither laws nor monuments, neither battleships nor public libraries, nor churches nor universities can save us from degeneration if the inner mystery be lost. That mystery, at once the secret and the glory of our English speaking race, consists in nothing but two common habits, two inveterate habits, carried into public life. One of them[15] is the habit of trained

6 "It is after all the old story of the"
7 "believe"
8 ", or who are misers and covetous or hungering after land."
9 "newest birth"
10 "And old Irishwoman who loves"
11 "Ireland"
12 "upon"
13 "no one had greatly cared."
14 "in"
15 "these"

and disciplined good temper towards the opposite party when it fairly wins its innings. The other is that of fierce and merciless resentment towards every man or set of men who break the public peace." ¶ The civic genius of America had decided that not we but our opponents had broken the public peace.

Now, little Richard, that is the story[16] *of my journey, and I wonder if by the time you read this*[17] *you will have forgotten my coming home with a big basket of grapes and bananas and grape fruit and oranges for you and a little flag with the Stars and Stripes.*

[*And all you heard of the fighting was the little song you learned some words of, hearing me say it so often, and that someone else was singing just then in America:*

Every time I come to town
The boys keep-a-kickin my dawg aroun'
Makes no difference if he is a houn'
They got a-quit kickin my dawg aroun'

Every time I go to school
The teacher lams me with a rule
Makes no difference if I am a fool
She's got a-quit lammin' me with a rule . . .

But] *I was very glad to be at home with you again while the daffodils were blooming out, and to have no more fighting, perhaps for ever. And if it is hard to fight for a thing you love, it is harder to fight for one you have no great love for. And you will read some day in one of those books in the library the story*[18] *of a man who was said to be mad but has outlived many who were not, and who went about fighting for the sake of someone who had maybe "her match in every parish and public" from El Toboso to Valladolid; though he still called out after every battle*[19] *"Dulcinea is the most beautiful woman in the world." So think a long time before you choose your road, little Richard, but when you have chosen it follow it on to the end.*

COOLE, July 24, 1913.

16 *"the whole story"*
17 *"by the time you can read it"*
18 *"in the library that are too high now for you to reach, the story"*
19 *"some one who was maybe 'the fright of seven townlands with her biting tongue' though he still called out after every battle"*

THE IRISH THEATRE AND THE PEOPLE[1]

I WAS asked the other day to tell when the Irish Theatre had come into being. I said I could tell the very day, almost the moment, and that was true in a sense—I was as it were present at its birth. But it was not all true, for nothing comes into the world of itself. We take sudden notice of grey buds on the willow, but the stirring of sap had begun long before, when Brigit brings the birthday of the year. Is not life itself but a preparation for the time we shall cross the mering that divides the worlds?

The nineteenth century was a chilly and scanty one where Irish literature is concerned. I myself delight in Miss Edgeworth's novels, and could keen after Lady Clonbrony's yellow satin chair-covers, pushed out for the sake of "painted velvet." But as regards the life of Ireland and the people of Ireland, they are patronising, artificial, taking a bird's-eye view of a simple peasantry, grateful for small mercies, and an impulsive, prodigal landlord, who, repentant, leaves the husks of London, and wins Heaven in eating his own mutton at home. Mr. and Mrs. S. C. Hall wrote in the same patronising strain. Carleton, born of the people, parades their qualities as a showman his wares. Lever started the Dublin carman on his road of manufactured jokes; novelists to the end of that century took the same detached, distant view. As to songs, Moore's melodies were the only ones belonging to Ireland I ever heard in my childhood. Those who sang them and those who listened would have been very much surprised if they had been told that songs of far higher literary value were being sung by every hearth-fire on the estate.

I myself went a little farther towards knowledge; for either from the wild beauty of my home, or the traditions of an old nurse who remembered the landing of the French at Killala, or the natural tendency of the younger member of a family to kick against the opinions of its elders. I grew up with something of a romantic love of Ireland which led me to read histories never taught by my English governesses, and to buy the little green-

[1] First published in *The Yale Review*, January 1912. In a typescript of this article belonging to Captain T. M. MacGlinchey, the title is "The Irish Theatre and the Return of the People."

covered books that contained the ballads of the '48 time. Some of these, some of Davis's especially, were stirring and beautiful; some were doggerel, little more than a list of names of the "felons of our land." I still care for them; they are in the tradition, they are roughly hammered links on the one chain. But any potato digger could have given me songs with more of the true expression of grief and love and the pain of partings, with more disclosure of the individual soul.

It was in 1880, just at the time of my marriage, that the Land War began. For the ten or twelve years that followed, the imagination and passion of Ireland was thrown into that fight. The farmer fought to keep his holding, the landlord fought to save his heritage, there were some who fought for a vision that had appeared to them, who would not set bounds to the march of a nation. Through those years I used to look week after week through the Nationalist newspapers, thinking to find some verse, some poem that would, as in the '48 time, put hopes into stirring words. But I found none such through those years. The first lines I tore off from a paper and kept—I have them still—were those written by Katherine Tynan on Parnell's death.

Parnell's death. That was the unloosing of forces, the disbanding of an army. In the quarrels that followed and the breaking of hopes, the imagination of Ireland had been set free, and it looked for a homing-place.

When the Prophet Elijah called out that he was the only servant of God left in Israel, he was shown a cave where forty other prophets were hidden for a while. And so it had happened in Ireland. Through all those years we had thought so barren, a group of scholars had gone on with their work, the translation of the old Irish manuscripts. O'Curry in his "Manners and Customs of Ancient Ireland" had given fine pages of history or romance; O'Donovan and O'Daly did the same. Standish Hayes O'Grady in his "Silva Gaedelica" gave the great deeds of the Fenians and their leader. This mass of material had begun to find its way into poetry, that of Sir Samuel Ferguson, of Aubrey de Vere. Mr. Yeats founded his first long narrative poem on it, the "Wanderings of Usheen." But even those poets and some at least of those translators would have wondered had they been told that the old culture they were bringing to light had never died, but was fresh and living in the country still.

It was soon after Parnell's death that the miracle happened. The Gaelic League was set on foot by Mr. Douglas Hyde. It was a movement for keeping the Irish language a spoken one, with, as a chief end, the preserving of our own nationality.

Meetings were established through all the Irish-speaking districts, where men and women, boys and girls, recited poems and stories and songs in the Irish tongue, and were given praises and rewards. That does not sound like the beginning of a revolution, yet it was one. It was the discovery, the disclosure, of the folk learning, the folk poetry, the folk tradition. That culture, that tradition of learning had never been forgotten. Poems were still being made that were part of a lyric literature that had existed in Ireland before Chaucer was born, and was there in gentle Spenser's time, as he well knew when he advised that the poets should be harried out of Ireland. It was not England that had brought in learning, it was England that had made it hide its head. We are able to claim for Ireland the oldest European literature written in the language still spoken, except that of the Greeks.

The excitement of the discovery was enormous. I can but speak for myself. I set to work to learn Irish. I had wished to do so long before, but was discouraged, first by the advice of a Chief Commissioner of Irish Education who had told me it would be a waste of time to learn a language which had "no literature," and again by the shyness of the people about teaching a language they had felt was looked down on. Now the table of values was changed. It was the Irish speaker who was envied. No more little green song-books, not much more of books of any sort. What do I want from them with all the learning of the ages walking our roads?

Our Theatre, when it set out, had in its repertory Mr. Yeats's beautiful verse-plays, and some prose ones in the Ibsen tradition, written by Mr. E. Martyn. But it was caught into the current, and it is that current, as I believe, that has brought it on its triumphant way. It is chiefly known now as a folk theatre; it has not only the great mass of primitive material, of primitive culture to draw on, but it has been made a living thing by the excitement of that discovery. Mr. Yeats himself was swept into the current. Compare his "Land of Heart's Desire," written a little from the outside, with his "Kathleen ni Houlihan." You may like one better than the other, but you see what the influence has been. Mr. Synge was caught in, and with him it was all for good. In his return to Ireland just at that time of imaginative awakening, he found fable, emotion, style. He tells what he owes to that collaboration with the people; and in spite of all attacks, he has given back to them what they will one day thank him for. He has put into perfect and lasting form in his "Riders to the Sea" the sorrow, the struggle against a force too strong for them, of those islanders among whom he made his dwelling for a while. Their Gaelic songs are full of the pity of the unequal fight; he has shaped it so that there are now many who cannot hear Aran spoken of without a pulling at the heartstrings. The return to the people, the reunion after separation, the taking and giving again, is it not the perfect circle, the way of nature, the eternal wedding ring?

THE COMING OF THE IRISH PLAYERS[1]

At the beginning of 1898 [1897] I was in London, and I find a note written in a diary I have kept from time to time: "Yeats and Sir Alfred Lyall to tea. Yeats stayed on. He is very full of play-writing. . . . He with the aid of Miss Florence Farr, an actress who thinks more of a romantic than of a paying play, is very keen about taking or building a little theatre somewhere in the suburbs to produce romantic drama, his own plays, Edward Martyn's, one of Bridges's, and he is trying to stir up Standish O'Grady and Fiona Macleod to write some. He believes there will be a reaction after the realism of Ibsen and romance will have its turn. He has put 'a great deal of himself' into his own new play, *The Shadowy Waters*, and rather startled me by saying about half his characters have eagle's faces."

A Successful Start

A little time after that I had come home to Coole, and Mr. Yeats came over there and we wrote a programme or circular. It began:

"We propose to have performed in Dublin in the spring of every year certain Celtic and Irish plays, which, whatever be their degree of excellence, will be written with a high ambition and so to build up a Celtic and Irish school of dramatic literature. We hope to find in Ireland an uncorrupted and imaginative audience trained to listen by its passion for oratory, and believe that our desire to bring upon the stage the deeper thoughts and emotions of Ireland will insure for us a tolerant welcome, and that freedom to experiment which is not found in theatres of England, and without which no new movement in art or literature can succeed. We will show that Ireland is not the home of buffoonery and of easy sentiment, as it has been represented, but the home of an ancient idealism. We are confident of the support of all Irish people, who are weary of misrepresentation, in carrying out a work that is outside all the political questions that divide us."

[1] First published in *Collier's National Weekly,* October 21, 1911.

We asked for a guarantee fund of £300 to make the experiment, which we hoped to continue during three years.

We gave our first performance in May 1899, at the Ancient Concert Rooms. Mr. Yeats's "Countess Cathleen" and Mr. Martyn's "Heather Field" were the plays given. There was real excitement over the experiment, and after the first night London papers sent over representatives to make a report. There was enthusiasm for both plays, and this we had expected, but what we had not expected was that at the last moment a political enemy of Mr. Yeats's had sent out a pamphlet in which he attacked the "Countess Cathleen" on the ground of religious unorthodoxy. The pamphlet was sent about; sentences spoken by the demons in the play were detached and given as Mr. Yeats's own opinions, and a Cardinal, having read the pamphlet but not the play, condemned it on the strength of these quotations. Young men from the Catholic University were roused to come and make a protest against this "insult to their faith," and in the end the play was given under police protection, an attack on the actors—English actors who had been brought over for the performances—being feared. They found it hard to understand the excitement, but went through their parts very well.

The next year we again collected English actors and again played in the spring, taking the Gaiety Theatre this time. "The Bending of the Bough," written by Mr. George Moore and Mr. Yeats on Mr. Martyn's play, "The Tale of a Town," afterward published, was given, and also "Maeve," Mr. Martyn's symbolic play concerning the idealism of Ireland, and a one-act play by Miss Alice Milligan, "The Last Feast of the Fianna." In our third year, 1901, Mr. F. R. Benson took the burden of our enterprise on his shoulders and produced "Diarmuid and Grania," a heroic play by Mr. George Moore and Mr. Yeats. This time also we produced "The Twisting of the Rope," by the founder of the Gaelic League, Dr. Douglas Hyde, the first time a play written in Irish had been seen in a Dublin theatre. He had written it in two or three days, while staying with us at Coole, on one of the Hanrahan stories written by Mr. Yeats. He acted in it himself with other Irish speakers, and it was a delight even to those who knew no Irish—it was played with so much gaiety, ease, and charm.

Our three years' experience had ended, and we hesitated what to do next. But a breaking and re-building is often for the best, and so it was now. We had up to this time, as I have said, played only once a year, and had engaged actors from London, some of them Irish, certainly, but all London-trained. The time had come to play oftener and to train actors of our own. Mr. Yeats had never ceased attacking the methods of the ordinary theatre, both in gesture and staging, and wanted to try for more simple ones. It happened there were two brothers in Dublin, William and Frank Fay, who had been in the habit of playing little farces in coffee palaces and such like in their spare time. William had a genius for comedy; Frank's ambitions were for the production of verse. They or one of them had thought of emigrating, but had seen our performances, and thought something might be done in the way of creating a school of acting in Ireland. They came to us at this time and talked matters over. They had work to do in the daytime and could only rehearse at night. The result was that Mr. Yeats gave his "Kathleen ni Houlihan" to be produced by Mr. Fay at the same time as plays by Mr. George Russell and Mr. Ryan, first at St. Theresa's Hall and then at the Ancient Concert Rooms.

Encouraging Contributions

That was the foundation of an Irish dramatic company. I have given these beginnings of our theatre in some detail, as they are apt to be forgotten. It has grown steadily since then. We worked on with Mr. W. Fay as producer, and when all his time was needed for our enterprise we paid him, a part coming from the earnings of the company, a part from me, and a part from Mr. Yeats. Toward other expenses we were given £50 by an American friend, Mr. John Quinn. Mr. Fay and his brother left us in a moment of discouragement and of trouble with the company, but not until we had been several times to London and had found good audiences and been given good notices. These London visits led to generous help from Miss Horniman, who bought and reconstructed the Abbey Theatre in Dublin and gave us free use of it, together with a subsidy, which was promised until the end of 1910, when our patent came to an end.

Our Own Theatre

We have now with our savings, however, been able to buy the Abbey Theatre and to bear the cost of obtaining a new patent. We have asked for an endowment of £5,000 to enable us to continue our work, and independence through the next half dozen years, and of this sum a considerable part has been given.

As to our players, they have won their own admirers, and I, for one, owe them very many thanks for the way they have made the characters of my comedies laugh and live.

The name that justifies the creation of our theatre most of all is perhaps that of the late J. M. Synge.

At the time of his first visit to Coole he had written some poems, not very good, not so good as those which have been published, and a play which was not good at all. I read it again lately when helping Mr. Yeats in sorting out the work to be published in Synge's collected edition, and again it seemed without merit. He was collecting folklore and studying dialect. Later when my "Cuchulain of Muirthemne" came out, he said to Mr. Yeats that he had been amazed to find in it the dialect he had been trying to master. I say this with a little pride, for I was the first to use the Irish idiom, as it is spoken, to any large extent and with belief in it. Dr. Hyde has used it with fine effect in his "Love Songs of Connacht," but gave it up afterward on being remonstrated with by a Dublin editor. The next thing Synge wrote was, I think, his book on Aran, but he could not find a publisher. I myself took it to London and had it retyped, and both Mr. Yeats and I offered it to publishers, but it was rejected, and it had to rest until his name had gone up. Then one day he brought us two plays, "The Riders to the Sea" and "The Shadow of the Glen," both masterpieces, both perfect in their way. It was the working in dialect that had set free his style, and the dramatic method he had mastered had made the fitting mould.

Organised Opposition

We put these plays on as soon as possible in Dublin. We took some trouble about the staging; I had Aran costumes copied, and bought some in Galway pawnshops, and I found in the country a spinning-wheel that had been in the same family for over a hundred years.

The other play, "The Shadow of the Glen," was attacked by a few as a libel on the Irish peasant, but that cry soon died away. "The Well of the Saints" passed without much comment, but with a very small audience, for those were early days at the Abbey. It was different when "The Playboy of the Western World" was put on. On the first night, a Saturday, there was a very large audience. Mr. Yeats was away, Mr. Synge was there, but not very well, and nervous, as he always was at a new production. It began well, the first act and the second got their applause, though one felt the audience were a little puzzled, a little shocked at the wild language. As the third act went on there was some hissing, and the end of the play was rather disturbed. On Monday night, "Riders," which preceded it, went very well indeed. But in the interval after it I noticed at one side of the pit a phalanx of men sitting together, not a woman among them. I told Synge I thought it looked like some organised disturbance, and he telephoned to have the police at hand in case of an attack upon the stage. The first part of the first act went undisturbed. Then suddenly an uproar began. The group of men, about forty altogether, booed, hooted, blew tin trumpets; it was impossible to hear a word of the play. The curtain came down for a minute, but I went round the actors to tell them to go on playing to the end even if a word could not be heard. There were very few people in the stalls, but among them was Lord Walter Fitzgerald, grand-nephew of the patriot, the beloved Lord Edward. He stood up and asked that he and others of the audience might hear the play, but that was refused. The police, hearing the uproar, came in, but we sent them out again; we wanted to see how far the obstruction would go. It lasted to the end of the evening; not one word had been heard after the first ten minutes. Next day Mr. Yeats arrived and took the management of affairs. There was a battle of a week. Every night protesters with tin trumpets came and interrupted; every night the police carried some of them off to the police courts. We determined to hold on for the week we had announced the play for. It was a definite fight for freedom from a mob censorship.

A part of the new national movement had been and rightly, a protest against the stage Irishman, the vulgar and unnatural butt given on the English stage to represent our countrymen. We had the destroying of that scarecrow in mind among other things in setting up our theatre, and there is no doubt he has all but disappeared in these last years. But the Nationalist Societies were impatient; they began to dictate here and there what should or should not be played. At Liverpool a priest had got up an entertainment, and they did not like one of the plays and hooted, and the priest appeared and apologised and said he would remove the piece they objected to. In Dublin Mr. Martin Harvey, an old favourite, had been forced to take off a little play because it dealt with Irish belief in witchcraft. The widow of a writer of Irish plays that had been fairly popular was picketed through Ireland with her company, was nearly ruined—no one being allowed to enter the doors—and finally at, I think, Athlone was only allowed to produce a play after it had been cut and re-arranged by a committee improvised from the shopkeepers of the town.

If we had been obliged to give in to the dictation of any organised group we should of necessity have closed the theatre. I respected the objections of those among that group who were sincere. They, not used to works of imagination and wild fantasy, thought the play a libel on the Irish peasant, who has not put parricide upon his list of virtues; they thought the language too violent or it might be profane. There was no room for argument: they had their principles, we had ours, both to be respected. The methods were another thing; when the tin trumpets were blown and brandished we had to use the same loud methods and call in the police. We lost some of our audience by the fight; the pit was weak for a while, but one after another said: "There is no other theatre to go to," and came back. The stalls, curiously, who appeared to approve of our stand, were shy of us for a long time; they got an idea we were fond of noise and quarrels. That was our second battle, and at the end of the week we had won it.

We were accused for a while of burying the work of young authors, of giving it no chance to be seen. No one knew all the time how Mr. Yeats and I, and for a while Mr. Synge, read and reread play after play, hoping to find something possible to produce. We had already some known writers, Mr. Boyle and Mr. Colum, but in these last few years young men who had not written at all until they saw our company play began to send us good drama—Mr. Robinson, our present manager; Mr. Murray, a national school-master; Mr. Fitzmaurice, Mr. Ray, Mr. Irvine, son of a Belfast workingman. They have all written with power in a rather harsh and realistic way, and are still at the beginning of their work, as we think. If it were only to develop this genius for drama in the young generation, I think our theatre has justified its existence.

As to myself, as time went on, I began to choose and criticise and advise on plays, and to stage-manage and produce and organise, because there was no one else to do it at the moment. And at last, for the same reason, to write.

The plays I cared most for wanted comedy after them to relieve the tension of listening to closely packed verse. I began by writing scenarios for one friend and dialogue for another, and then I wrote my own "Seven Short Plays," and some longer ones, historical for the most part, according to the folk history I take as authority. As the young authors write more and more of the tragic side of life, my little comedies are put on more and more to balance them, and then people say, or are said to say: "Too much Lady Gregory." But it cannot be helped yet a while till some of our youngsters grow old enough to allow themselves to laugh.

Our latest battle was with Dublin Castle and the official world. Mr. Bernard Shaw's play, "Blanco Posnet," was refused by the censor. We thought this hypocrisy, for we remembered many offensive plays that had been passed and guaranteed, and we saw this to be a profoundly moral and religious one. Mr. Yeats and I put the play into rehearsal and announced it for the week of the Horse Show. Then the offices of the Crown began to rumble and mutter, and then they threatened to use "all the power of the law" against us if we put on the play. At the last we were threatened not only with the loss of the patent but with the infliction of a fine so heavy that it would sweep away the little sum of money we had saved, and with which we might have made provision for our players till they had found other work.

That evening, for the first time, we hesitated. We were at rehearsal, and we felt we had taken our people from their other work and ought not to endanger their future. But later we decided that we had given our word, that at all risks we must keep it or we should never be trusted again—that we must in no case go back. We put on the play at the date announced. There was an immense audience. At the end, there was a tremendous burst of cheering, and the cause was won. There was a large crowd outside the theatre. Some stranger asked what was going on inside. "They are defying the Lord Lieutenant," was the answer. When the applause inside was heard, the crowd took up the cheering and it went through the street. That was our most amusing battle, and I hope though I would not dare prophesy, it may be our last.

EDITORS' NOTE

The Archives of the Abbey Theatre contain the press cutting books of its early years, including those of the tours in the U.S.A. All have been stuck in by Lady Gregory.

The American cuttings include many interviews with Lady Gregory and reports of lectures that she gave. One such lecture was called "How to Found a National Theatre," and in the publicity brochure for the Coole Edition it was announced that this would appear in *Our Irish Theatre*. As there will be a further volume in the Edition containing Lady Gregory's lectures, in place of the Robert Gregory volume (XV), this lecture will appear there.

A selection of the interviews are given here, the lectures will appear in a separate volume.

The Evening Post (New York) 6.12.1911

SURE THE IRISH PLAYERS WILL SUCCEED

Lady Gregory Doesn't in the Least Mind the Fighting Evenings

The scrambled egg evenings at the Maxine Elliott Theatre do not bother Lady Gregory in the least. As she says "I am of a fighting race," and later adds that she is "quite Irish," never having left her native soil until she was nearly ten and when married going to live seven miles from her girlhood home.

Lady Gregory admits grey hair and the fact that she is a grandmother, the latter fact softened by the fact that she is a very new one, this milestone in her career having been passed only a week before her departure to the New World.

It is her first trip across the ocean, but she expects to make many more, as the reception accorded her and her company of Irish players, she thinks, seems to warrant this prediction. So little did the stormy voyage harass her that she wrote a play coming over and corrected proof-sheets of a new book, besides outlining scenarios etc.

Lady Gregory's hair is parted and waved, fastened in the nape of her neck in a Grecian knot. Over this she wears a black lace scarf which falls low in the back over a simple black gown. This is the costume in which she has already become familiar to theatregoers, whether she is standing in the wings looking on at a specially vital scene, in the chintz hung salon of the theatre, as hostess in a box entertaining celebrities, going and coming from the stage door in the energetic fashion that never destroys her serenity.

She has been interviewed since her arrival and reinterviewed. She adapts herself with grace and ease to the process. "There is only one misconception," she says smilingly, "which I had to correct. As a general thing the interviewers have been kind and veracious. But my little company of players do object to being called peasants, perhaps for the reason that they are not peasants, and the morning after our first appearance when the newspapers spoke of them as such I explained to them at rehearsal that I had been equally misrepresented; that they had referred to my blue eyes and to my grand daughter as 'he'."

In regard to the fighting scenes that lent additional colour to the first evenings of Synge's "The Playboy of the Western World" Lady Gregory admits that so often has rioting disturbed the stormy tenor of the Irish Players' way that it has now become part of the mosaic of their dramatic life. "I can't say anything more illuminating on this subject than W. B. Yeats just after an appeal for an endowment for the Irish Theatre:

"In England the artist has to fight with apathy, but in Ireland his enemies are mistaken enthusiasms, old ideals that have outlived their use and the violent prejudices that must exist in every country where the mass of the people have no half interests. Everything becomes vital when it comes to Ireland. It takes to itself wings or claws. Passionate opposition is inspiring, but it makes financial independence essential."

"Those are my ideas exactly!"

Lady Gregory makes a verbal departure for a moment, saying that she believes the time is not far distant when people will have on their note paper and business cards "Telephone hours so and so," and it will be understood that the dominating wire can rule only during these intervals. Her need of this has been particularly acute recently, owing to the many calls from friends, acquaintances and even strangers requesting to know if she is "all right," if she has been unduly frightened and what she thinks of the "Playboy" disturbances.

"My only disquietude was not at the riot itself but at what it signified; that my people had not freed themselves entirely from the yoke of those traditions which seem so incompatible with your broad free life here. But I may be doing a great injustice to think even that 'my people' have been in any way at fault in this matter. One firecracker under a tin pan can create a terrible din, and one drunken or disorderly person in a crowded gallery is equally disturbing to the general peace.

"The first real riot which we passed through quite unscathed, not even our feelings lacerated, occurred at the Ancient Concert Rooms in Dublin in 1899, where the Irish Players made their first real essay. This opposition was made to Mr. Yeats's play 'Countess Cathleen.' One of his admirers, Horatio Krans, wrote of it that 'no drama had ever before been presented in Ireland so inspired with the spirit of the race and so subtly and beautifully steeped in national dyes.' The scene of 'Countess Cathleen' is laid in old Ireland. She is the great lady of the district, fighting with the conditions of plague, poverty and of demoniac powers which finally, to thwart her good intentions, strip her of her wealth. She at length sells her soul to these demons for gold to relieve her beloved people, but a vision at the end of the play tells that she is forgiven, because God judges the intention, not the deed.

"Some rough and ready theologians saw fit to object to the suggestion that God had forgiven a woman who so far forgot her duty, intimating it as a reflection upon those of Catholic orthodoxy. Their banding together to break up the performances, interfered with by the police who acted in the interests of law and order, really made thinking people wonder what time of day it was with certain people in Ireland.

"Several other battles have marked our steady ongoing, the most severe that which raged about the production of Bernard Shaw's 'Blanco Posnet,' which had been refused by the censor. We believed this act to be purely hypocritical and stood firmly by our intention. It required courage to do that, because we were threatened by the officers of the Crown with the loss of our patent and a fine so heavy that it would eat up all profits. We put the play on at the Abbey, billing it for the week of the Horse Show. We had committee meetings up to the last rehearsal debating whether we should fly in the face of this powerful opposition, but the Irish blood was up and we stood by our guns manfully. Heaven is on the side of the strongest battalions, said Napoleon; our battalions were strong in conviction if not in numbers, and we won out triumphantly. The theatre was crowded every night and 'Blanco Posnet' was one of our biggest successes.

"You can understand how tremendous the feeling in Ireland has been over these plays by this incident. There is a certain public house in a certain back street in Dublin where a few months after the trouble over 'The Playboy' the owner's wife for some reason or other, possibly a sudden fit of housewifely industry, ordered one of her potboys to take our bills of that drama out of the window. He said 'If they go, I go.' A second potboy was called and to the request he made the same answer. Finally the owner came downstairs and shouted 'Leave the damn things where they are.' They stayed."

It is with great difficulty that Lady Gregory can be induced to leave the interesting topic of the achievements of those who have been associated with the success of the National Theatre, Yeats, Synge, Douglas Hyde and others, and tell something about her own personal work.

"There are many moments when I feel as if I shall have to leave all this theatrical work, the writing of scenarios, for others, the time killing processes of organisation, stage managing, rehearsing, to devote myself entirely to the study, collecting, translating and the purely literary functions of the Gaelic work. There are such stores of material yet untouched, such wonderful volumes written only in the memories of the old who are fast passing on, leaving nothing tangible behind them, such marvellous possibilities, and the day is so short, its demands so insistent. One cannot do everything!

"I made three attempts to learn Gaelic. The laughter of a large family, the cruel blast that has destroyed so many tender flowers, prevented the first from fruition. After my early marriage I made a second trial, choosing for school teacher an old labourer, but my innocent ambition was misconstrued. Ireland was at that time a hot bed of suspicion. What did such an unprecedented act imply? For the sake of peace I dropped my primer efforts and it was not until Ireland was torn apart after the Parnell imbroglio, when all tables of value were changed, that the old idea was resurrected, and this time I studied and learned unmolested.

"It is not an easy language to learn; it is unbelievably difficult. Rules of grammar and construction have had to be made to suit a language which went merrily on during its formative time without regard to set forms. Consonants have been dropped at will so as to make the rhythm more perfect, and in consequence the written and the spoken words are so strangely different that you doubt their relationship all the time. The taking away of the consonants left nothing to hang your hat on.

"I was the first to write in the Irish dialect—that is, the English of Gaelic thinking people. I wrote in it before Synge did. He said he was amazed to find in my 'Cuchulain of Muirthemne' his desired dialect.

"Seven of my plays, published in book form, are in the repertory of the National Theatre. 'Twenty Five,' my first, has had a chequered career, suppressed because it was too sensational. I am rewriting 'The Workhouse Ward.' I believe in rewriting and bringing out again plays that have had changes made in them to suit the dramatic demand which a literary production does not always meet. Intention and desire come, you press your idea, then comes the iron hand of technique forcing that expression into the mould of convention. The play I wrote on the steamer is to be published in the *Outlook,* and I have with me a short unpublished play which is to come out before long.

"The original incorporators of the Irish National Theatre Society have never been paid for their services, as such. By our new contract we cannot, if we would. We have only the small royalties that come when any of our plays are produced, but the criticism that has been made that we are not seeking new material is unfounded. We read and search anxiously in the mass of manuscript that comes in, much of it available for other theatres than ours which have not a distinct purpose to fulfil.

"Those that have answered successfully these requirements, besides some already mentioned are T. C. Murray, who wrote 'The Village Schoolmaster;' Mr. Irvine, son of a Belfast workingman; Mr. Robinson, a Cork man; Miss Alice Milligan, who wrote 'The Last Feast of the Fianna;' 'The Bending of the Bough,' by George Moore, was very popular, as was 'Maeve' by Mr. Martyn. The first Gaelic play written as such was given at a Dublin theatre when we produced 'The Twisting of the Rope,' by Douglas Hyde. This was an adaptation made in three or four days by him at my home at Coole from one of the Hanrahan stories of Mr. Yeats. 'Diarmuid and Grania' was a heroic play that Yeats and Moore wrote in collaboration. This was produced under the temporary chaperonage of Mr. F. R. Benson, the Shakespearean manager who relieved us of our onerous duties for a time.

"Briefly, many of the requirements of these plays may be summed up in the statement that they must present Ireland past and present to the sympathy of the world and throw a light on all the phases of Irish character, not entirely cutting off those with which we are so familiar on the stage, but adding to them, interpreting them anew.

"I have been asked why we do not present these plays as curtain raisers. To do that would defeat the whole object of our plan. Charles Frohman saw that when a few years ago he brought over the clever Fays, connected in the beginning of our work with us at the Abbey Theatre. He gave these plays by themselves, thus preserving the atmosphere, and while they did not make a great success they no doubt helped to pave the way for this, the second appearance of the Irish Players.

"The failure then to make a big success may have been due to the fact that they were given a large theatre. In the beginning of our productions Mr. Yeats objected strongly, as did I, to the stagy methods of the London actors, and it was not until we had advanced far enough along to have our own people interpret them that we were satisfied. Our people do not seem to play to the audience, but the audience seems to be looking on at the unfolding of the scenes. A small theatre helps this illusion.

"When I saw the Sicilian players I was immensely impressed with one salient point, the perfection of gesture. Gesture to the Latin race is as natural as breathing. Our people do not gesture and to try and make them would be foolish.

"The material we have is the voice. The Irish people have beautiful rhythmic voices, and we have made these our component of value. Since we have been here I have had many letters commenting on this fact.

"All through the country I have found a new interest in the Gaelic movement. Prof. Baker of Harvard has done much to further our work. I lectured at Smith, Wellesley, Yale and other educational centres. In every place I was surprised and pleased at the attention and information I found. In Boston many of the tenants on our estate in Ireland, emigrants to the New World, came to the theatre and then to visit me. With several of them I took tea. I find them often homesick, but I have noticed that when they come back it is usually for a visit. The old homes, transfigured by their vivid imaginations, seem woefully small and uninviting. Once a strange woman came to our place at Coole and asked to see my husband. When she had an interview she put some money in his hand, about $20 as I remember, and then went away. We never knew who she was, apparently some one executing a dying request, which may have meant the return of a 'conscience' fund. She said that she had come from America to do this and was going right back again. She looked out of the window and commented on the disappointment it had been to her to see the places she had left as a child. That was the only clue we had to her mysterious coming and we never found out anything else but there is an Irish play in that incident.

"Your country was the first to help the Irish Theatre. Our first £50 was the gift of John Quinn, a well known lawyer of New York city, who has always been interested in the Gaelic movement, is a friend of Douglas Hyde and of Mr. Yeats, and sent in answer to our first request for funds to carry on the work of protest against the current belief that Ireland is the home of buffoonery. We have since then bought the Abbey Theatre and have a large part of the £5,000 contributed, which seems necessary to carry on the enlarged work which commenced in concert hall rooms and which has now its season every year in London at the Court Theatre, Sloane Square, and will apparently have an American season as well. That is not doing so badly in thirteen years, is it? It was through the influence displayed by Miss Horniman, who became interested in our London work, that we went into the Abbey Theatre of Dublin, reconstructed and given rent free, with the addition of a subsidy which expired in 1910."

Lady Gregory places no time limit on the duration of the

American tour. "I came over at a week's notice," she says, "and just as long as the interest of the people holds out we shall remain. At present the Abbey Theatre is tenanted by a class of sixty under Norman Muncke and from these pupils we shall draw for a second company, so that when we come again our own playhouse will not have to be closed, as happened this time."

Boston Transcript 29.9.1911

WRITES PLAY ON STEAMER

Lady Gregory, Irish Dramatist, Arrives.
Son of Charles Dickens Also on Cymric
Each Visits America for First Time
Liner Was Delayed by Gales and Head Seas.

Lady Augusta Gregory, the Irish dramatist, and Alfred Tennyson Dickens, oldest son of Charles Dickens, the famous author, reached Boston to-day on the White Star liner Cymric, which arrived from Liverpool and Queenstown. Neither of the distinguished passengers had ever before been in the United States. Lady Gregory comes in connection with the tour of the Irish players. Her desire to direct the rehearsals of "The Playboy of the Western World," which is to be produced in about two weeks, is her chief reason for making the trip. E. F. Flynn, manager of the Irish Players company, and William Butler Yeats, the Irish poet, went down the harbor on the revenue tug Winnisimmet to meet her.

Lady Gregory felt that had the voyage required three more days she would have been able to finish a play which she started on board ship last Sunday. The title is to be "McDonough's Wife," and it is possible that the piece may be staged here. The play is founded on a true story. When his wife died McDonough was unable to get anybody to carry her body to the grave, and it was necessary for him to go through the countryside playing his pipe to attract body bearers. McDonough was the son of a piper who was supposed to have received his gift of piping from the fairies. McDonough himself played his pipe at Lady Gregory's home when she was a child and at her wedding. He died about ten years ago, she said.

Lady Gregory's departure from Queenstown on the Cymric was preceded by a wild automobile ride across the Emerald Isle. The strike on the Irish railways tied transportation up and to reach Queenstown from her home, Coole Park, in Gort, County Galway, Lady Gregory borrowed the automobile of Lord Gough, a neighbor. The route lay through the counties, Galway, Clare, Limerick and Cork. Tires were punctured frequently, and owing to his ignorance of the country the chauffeur drove ten miles beyond Queenstown before realizing the mistakc. When within about a mile of their destination on the return the petrol gave out it was necessary to walk.

A short time before he left London preparatory to taking the steamer, Mr. Dickens was afraid that he would have to cancel or postpone his American lecture tour, because of the effects of a slight sunstroke which he suffered. He consulted a specialist and was advised to take a good rest, which he did so far as he was able. His father's life and works constitute the subject of his lecture, which includes the reading of a letter from his father, one of the last that the author wrote before his death.

Mr. Dickens's home is in Melbourne, Australia, Alfred Tennyson was his god-father and Mr. Dickens, who is sixty-six years old, is named after him. Through a spirit of adventure he went to Australia when he was twenty years old and has made that country his home ever since. Mr. Dickens will give his first lecture at the Middlesex Women's Club at Lowell on Oct. 9. After that he will visit the principal cities in this country and Canada and will return in May.

The Cymric docked about eight o'clock, after having remained at anchor off Boston Light all night. She was about twelve hours late in reaching the Light, owing to head seas and moderate gales and fog during considerable of the passage, which required eight days and ten hours. She brought 152 saloon and 576 steerage passengers. More than a hundred who had expected to sail from Queenstown were delayed by the railway strike and missed the boat.

Boston (Mass.) Evening Globe 30.9.1911

COMES TO DIRECT IRISH PLAYERS

LADY GREGORY WROTE NEW PLAY WHILE ON STEAMER—CHARM OF HER PERSONALITY LIKE THAT OF HER WRITINGS.

Everyone who has been delighted by reading or seeing the comedies of Lady Augusta Gregory will thoroughly appreciate what is meant when it is said that the personality of this highly accomplished woman possesses the very same charm that makes her dramatic writings so enjoyable.

Her ladyship lacks nothing of the dignity becoming her rank, but thoughts of the peerage flee when one is privileged to engage in conversation with her. Lady Gregory is first a grand-mother—a fact which she announces with smiles and tenderness—and everyone knows how sympathetic and interesting all grandmothers are.

But a very active grandmother is Lady Gregory. As is well understood, she is here to direct productions of the Irish players, at present appearing at the Plymouth theatre, which involves no end of work. Furthermore, she is finishing another play, written largely during her trip over on the Cymric, on which steamer she arrived here early yesterday morning.

Directly after leaving the ship Lady Gregory proceeded to the Plymouth theatre, there to plunge into the labors incident to preparing coming performances and rehearsing actors for various and to some of them new roles.

Made Dublin Theatre a Reality

Lady Gregory is of stately figure, with the grace and beauty of a true gentlewoman. She dresses entirely in black, which emphasizes the rosiness of her complexion, for Lady Gregory is as fair as the bloom of a flower.

Her head is crowned with a wealth of luxuriant hair that was once a deep velvety black, but which is now fast turning to a silvery gray. Two very kind, very merry and indeed very young brown eyes look out at you and smile a cordiality which heightens your pleasure.

In company with William Butler Yeats her associate in the managerial affairs of the Irish players, Lady Gregory was strolling about the lobby of the hotel Touraine when found by an interviewer. It was entirely too rainy to go outdoors before dinner, so her ladyship was finding recreation in a necessarily short walk through the hotel office and corridor.

Lady Gregory is the widow of Sir William Gregory, who was governor of the island of Ceylon. Her creative work in literature has been entirely since the death of her husband. As Mr. Yeats says, she made the Irish players and their theatre in Dublin a reality by her practical ideas her energy and her influence.

Surprising indeed it will be to many to learn that Lady Gregory began writing comedies only when it was found that the repertory of the newly organized company was in need of light plays. In fact, not until then did Lady Gregory—she a grandmother—find her remarkable power as a dramatist.

Her First Work writing Charades

Yesterday's interviews with the press representatives who boarded the Cymric was Lady Gregory's first experience with reporters. She had never been interviewed by newspaper writers before. "What bright young men and women they were," she said enthusiastically, "and so interested in one. It was a positive pleasure to meet them."

Glancing over the afternoon papers that lay in her lap, Lady Gregory said, "I am going to send these home, my friends will be so interested, too. See there's a picture of me and my umbrella. I'm glad to have that picture of my umbrella, for I have since lost it and I don't expect to get it again."

Urged to tell of her life, Lady Gregory laughed, and replied: "O, my life has been such a very long one that were I to begin at the beginning I'm afraid I should not get through for a very long time. Think of it, I had a very old nurse who used to tell me that she remembered the landing of the French on the west coast of Ireland in 1798. This old nurse was very young at the time, but never forgot how the people at a theatre cheered when the news of the landing of the French was brought to them. You know it meant so much to those opposed to England's rule.

"As a young girl I took part in charades. I can well recall that I was not good at acting, but I was thought very apt at inventing plots and stories for the charades. That was the first display of my dramatic instinct, but it was so very small, so very trifling —indeed, only fun and play—that it isn't worth mentioning.

Husband Friend of O'Connell

"I married and my family took all my attention until after my husband's death. My first literary work was editing his autobiography. My husband was a friend of Daniel O'Connell, yet he opposed as a candidate on one occasion the candidate whom O'Connell indorsed.

"O'Connell thought much of my husband and often called him over, saying: 'Now, see how much better you look on this side.' Strangely enough, my husband finally stayed on O'Connell's side, eventually becoming a liberal."

"Was it from conviction or friendship that Sir William changed his politics?" was asked.

"Friendship, largely, I think," answered her ladyship, "for he was very fond of Daniel O'Connell.

"After completing the editing of my husband's autobiography I worked on many of the papers that he had left. You see, his grandfather was under secretary of Ireland from 1813 to 1839 and these documents and many others were of great historic value, and to all of them I gave my best in the interest of Irish history. After that I did considerable work on translations. It was then that I became aware of the movement to organize the players which you have seen in Boston."

At this point Mr. Yeats begged to interrupt that he might praise Lady Gregory's efforts on behalf of the Irish theatre.

"You see," he said, "I had the plan in my mind; I knew what I wanted to do but not until Lady Gregory joined us did we do anything practical. I had no sooner enlisted her aid than we had formed a company and began accomplishing things."

"It was within a week," added Lady Gregory, "that we had obtained a charter."

Gives Story of Her New Piece

"Yes," agreed Mr. Yeats, "and Lady Gregory was our greatest help. You know that she not only did the practical things that were necessary, but when we found that we needed comedies in our repertory she was the one to whom we turned, for she was able and willing to write them for us."

"That's all within a very short time, a decade or so?" the interviewer queried.

"Yes," both answered, while Mr. Yeats hastened to supply the additional information that Lady Gregory "wrote a comedy on shipboard."

"No, no, it isn't a comedy," insisted her ladyship. Thereupon she discussed the new piece, which is called "McDonough's

Wife." It has for its foundation a true story of one McDonough, who, when his wife died, was unable to secure body bearers and so went about the countryside playing his pipe to draw together the body bearers. McDonough's father was a piper and was supposed to have received his gift of piping from the fairies. Curiously enough, McDonough played his pipe at the home of Lady Gregory when she was a child and at her wedding. His death occurred about 10 years ago.

"Will the play be produced here?" asked the interviewer.

"I'm not sure," replied Lady Gregory. "There are so many plays it is difficult to find opportunity to try a new one."

Speaking of J. M. Synge, author of a number of the plays in the Irish players' repertory and until his death an associate of Lady Gregory and Mr. Yeats in the new theatre enterprise, Lady Gregory, after paying a tribute to his high character and his merit as a writer, referred to his visit to the island of Aran.

Will Not Write About America

"I had gone to Aran, which is on the west coast of Ireland," said Lady Gregory, "to hear the purest speech that it is possible to hear. I did not then know Mr. Synge and I was indignant when I learned that he was there for the same purpose. And he, too, was indignant when informed of my errand.

"Often, when later we were introduced and with Mr. Yeats worked for the new theatre, we laughed over the incident."

"This is your first visit to this country?" asked the reporter.

"Quite the first," answered Lady Gregory.

"How long shall you remain here?"

"I think three or four months."

"Are you going to write a play about America and Americans, Lady Gregory?" was the next question.

"Ah, that makes me think of the English tourists who come to Ireland and then go back and write what they think about us, and tell us how we ought to live. No, I shall not write about America or Americans. I quite think you are able to govern yourselves and your country, without advice from me," and her ladyship laughed as though the very idea were a joke.

Boston Evening Transcript, 7.10.1911

THE ABBEY THEATRE

Lady Gregory on its ways and methods

How It Began and Grew—The Advent of Synge—Her Own Part as Helpful Critic—Her First Comedy, and How Mr. Yeats Condemned It—How the Young Irish Playwright Develops—How the Abbey Theatre Mounts Its Plays Cheaply—The New Home Industry It Has Brought Ireland.

Under the shadow of her wide hat, her still-rounded cheeks bright with the earnestness of her subject, Lady Gregory talked to me of the new Irish drama and its playwrights. And although Lady Gregory is no longer a young woman, it was of Romney that I thought as I looked at her, and of how he would have painted her—the eagerness, the bloom, and the tantalizing shadow of the hat. Then she lifted her head and I saw her kind-shrewd eyes. "Franz Hals!" I exclaimed to myself, and that time I was sure. Even then perhaps I was forgetting her scholarship, of which, as every one who has read "Gods and Fighting Men" knows, she has a great deal. I was thinking only that Lady Gregory represents the common sense as she does the sense of humour of the Irish movement.

For it is not as a scholar, nor a grand-mother, nor the widow of a statesman, nor the administrator of a household and an estate—though she is all of these—that Lady Gregory comes to America, but simply as a playwright and a producer. It may be that she wishes we would respect that fact a little more strictly. "A young woman of the press called on me today," she said, with her quaint, surprised accent, "to ask me what I thought of love in schools. She showed me a clipping from the paper, and she said, 'What are the qualities of friendship?' But really, as I told her, I could not see how that was connected with our Irish drama."

It was of playwrights and playwrighting chiefly that Lady Gregory spoke to me. "Someone was telling Mr. Yeats the other day," she said, "of the Arabic Theatre—a kind of theatre of the people which always has been; and Mr. Yeats was feeling sorrowful that we had had no such institution with which to begin. For when we started, England, France and Germany each had its national theatre, but, Ireland, like America today, had none. But I told Mr. Yeats that there would have been no creation in getting our drama into an established national theatre. It was having to form the theatre that made it interesting.

"At first, when we started we had no new playwrights. For two or three years we had only Mr. Yeats's 'Countess Kathleen' and some plays by Mr. Martyn. Then Mr. George Moore came into the movement and Dr. Douglas Hyde with his Gaelic plays. For in the beginning we dreamed of a national drama arising in Gaelic. But the use of Gaelic is dying out in Ireland. Few of the people now speak it, and though prizes for drama have been offered each year, aside from Mr. Hyde's plays there has been nothing of mark in Gaelic.

"Then came Mr. Synge, quite unknown. He had written a book of folklore of the Aran Islands, which I myself took around to all the London publishers, only to have it rejected; and he had written some poems and plays of no value. It was while he was staying with me at Coole that Mr. Yeats and I suggested that he should make drama of the peasant life he knew so well. His plays were the first fruit of the new movement. He never would have expressed himself in any other medium.

"I started myself, by helping others. I think, by altering and mending other plays, by writing sceneries for Gaelic plays and dialogue for others. My first play, 'Twenty-five,' was a sentimental comedy. A poor man and woman are obliged to sell their place. A young man who has cared for the wife comes back from America and wants to give her the money, which she refuses. Keeping his identity from the husband, he plays with him at cards and loses. Mr. Yeats laid a heavy hand upon his effort. He criticised it severely as too sentimental. But I think now I have sufficiently laid its ghost by writing a comedy without sentiment, 'The Jackdaw,' which is to be given here next week."

Although Lady Gregory protested her indebtedness to Mr. Yeats, she said nothing at all of the help she has given him through her knowledge of the folk life and speech—a knowledge as broad and accurate probably as that of Synge. She knows not only the peasant mind but "that mass of imaginations and traditions made by princes, saints and sages hundreds of years ago." Alone and with Mr. Yeats she has gone from cottage to cottage in Ireland, amassing a great volume of folklore. Mr. Yeats told the other day of how they stopped once at a little inn in north-west Galway where lived a girl famous for her beautiful voice. She sang to them not alone the old ballads, but songs made quite lately in the village, one of them mocking a young man who had gone to another village for a sweetheart. "It had," said Mr. Yeats, "the simplicity of great literature. One felt that in that village a miracle might at any time happen and some beautiful thing be born." It is folk like these that Lady Gregory knows; and it is in the idiom of their speech that her plays are written, and that her Molière is translated. It is perhaps not fair to refer to "The Kiltartan Molière"—little known in this country—as a translation. Lady Gregory wrote it for the Abbey Theatre at a time when there were few new plays, translating not so much the words of "Les Rogueries de Scapin" and the other plays it contains, as their spirit into the speech of the Irish villages.

But the Abbey Theatre has not fallen upon many days of dearth of plays. Almost from the beginning it has been overwhelmed with manuscripts. The labour has been in the choosing. "If a play is merely imitative, if it shows no quality of style, no sign of temperament, we send it back with a printed form," said Lady Gregory. "When we see that the writer has personality, a vision of life, we send him another slip, which we call 'Advice to Young Playwrights.' If, best of all, a play shows that the author has the essential qualities of a dramatist, we write to him personally, criticising, commending what we can, and asking him to try again. Usually we suggest that he send the scenario of a new play before he writes the dialogue, because it is so much easier to take out an act, to arrange a different ending, to make any one of the possibly necessary changes, in that form. We never attempt to influence an author by asking him to make his play realistic, romantic or fantastic. Our criticisms are only from the technical side, to see whether the author's intention—if he has an intention—is sufficiently carried out."

According to Lady Gregory, that unofficial school of playwriting, which is the Abbey Theatre, has one great advantage over all other similar institutions—(Harvard course please note and copy)—in that it gives its best pupils a chance to see their work upon the stage. "It is one value of our theatre," said Lady Gregory, "that we are able to put on a new play without great expense. Here in America, I understand, production is so expensive that a manager thinks a long time before he puts a play on the stage. At our theatre it is quite different. To us the play itself is the essential; the scenery we keep very simple. For Mr. Yeats's 'Deirdre' and 'Shadowy Waters' and for some of my plays, my son, who is an artist, has given his services in making the designs. Mr. Yeats and I have always been quite unpaid; and in these ways we have been able to keep down the expense so that we are constantly changing and putting on new plays.

"There is no kind of teaching that will do so much for the playwright. The most experienced dramatist cannot prophesy how a play will go until he has seen it on the stage. An audience cannot tell a lie. Critics may lie from the best of motives, but if an audience is bored, it will cough, if it is amused, it will laugh. Immediately it rewards you, or convicts you of sin. You may have been told not to use repetitions, but there is no argument like that of seeing your repetition on the stage. Then if you have repeated, your transgression seems to jump out and strike you in the face. If you have said anything illogical or superfluous, you cannot escape it there. There is one phrase in 'Hyacinth Halvey' that, as often as I see the play, hits me, and I haven't had the moral courage, or the determination, or whatever is necessary to take it out yet.

"Almost always we change a play very much after it has been performed. Mr. Yeats has rewritten all of his. He is just now at work on the final version of his 'Countess Kathleen,' written twelve years ago. My plays and those of Mr. Yeats are often changed in rehearsal, but our young dramatists, most of them, live too far away in the country to have that advantage. We ask them, though, to come to the first performance. After Mr. Murray had seen 'Birthright' he knocked out an unnecessary character, making the play three times as powerful. Another dramatist cut off an entirely superfluous first act. 'You will lose something by taking it out,' we wrote him—we pay more for three acts than for two—'but we should not be able to take the play on tour, had you left it in.'

"We never accept a play that we do not believe worthy of a place in our permanent repertory. We have made mistakes, but we have never taken a play without believing in it. Our object in our own writings and in those of others is to make them as perfect as possible. And I believe that if Mr. Yeats and I should be obliged to leave the work to-day, the theatre has already accumulated such a mass of fine work that it would go on of itself. Many of our audience already know whole plays by heart, and it has often happened when a new player has missed a line that he has been prompted from the gallery."

On the younger and more realistic writers whose work is being seen here, Lady Gregory commented briefly. Mr William Boyle, the author of "The Eloquent Dempsey," "The Building Fund" and "The Mineral Works," was, until he saw the Irish players in London, a short story writer. He has contributed an immense mass of plays, most of them comedies. Mr. Lennox, Robinson who is both manager and playwright, saw the plays of the Abbey Theatre first at Cork when he was twenty years old. Almost immediately he submitted a play which, while it had too many characters and a too elaborate action, nevertheless showed vitality. Lady Gregory and Mr Yeats wrote him their criticisms. He revised his play and it was put upon the stage. His "Harvest" and "The Crossroads" will be seen here next week. Perhaps most interesting of all is the case of Mr. T. C. Murray, one of the best of the new dramatists and the author of "Birth-right," who is a village schoolmaster. Mr. St. John Ervine, the author of the grim and realistic play, "Mixed Marriage," is the son of working people.

"There is another point," said Lady Gregory, "that may not seem important to you but which means a great deal to us—for Ireland is poor—and that is the fact that our theatre has created a new home industry, bringing into the country thousands a year. Before when the English companies came, they brought with them their scenery, their costumes, their playbills. But we employ local players, printers, carpenters and charwomen. The money that is paid in Dublin is spent in Dublin; and money from England, and we hope from America, comes back to our Irish drama too. For it is our desire to enlarge our company, so that we can put on more plays side by side. It is always a temptation when we make our English tour to the four literary centres—London, Manchester, Oxford and Cambridge—to give only our greatest successes. But to do so would be to spoil the idea of our repertory theatre, and we have never yielded.

"We have been abused also for not sticking to Ireland altogether, but we could not make enough money in Dublin to stay there all the time. Besides we need the impersonal criticism which we cannot get in Dublin. We expect a great deal from that in this American tour; and I want to say that it is our greatest encouragement that the greatest intellectual work we have given here—Mr. Synge's 'Well of the Saints,' has met with the most enthusiastic popular reception."

Eunice Fuller

The Washington Times, 14.11.1911

LADY GREGORY, HEAD OF IRISH PLAYERS, REGRETS HOSTILITY

Writer and Manager Denies Statements in Circular Given Out

STAGE PICTURES NOT OFFENSIVE, SHE SAYS

Just Appealing Scenes From Life of Peasants, Familiar to Irish Born.

By Julia Murdock

"I honestly do not know, and I am at a loss to account for the objection of some of the Irish societies to the plays we are to put on this week by our company of Irish Players."

So spoke Lady Augusta Gregory, director of the National Theater Society this morning as she sat in her room superintending the opening of her large volume of mail, and transacting the business connected with the opening appearance of the Irish players in the Belasco Theater tonight.

"You may say that if we were hissed out of Dublin nobody connected with the Irish Players knows of the fact, and certainly the players themselves would have heard the hisses, would they not?

"You may also say that if we were denounced by the theatrical critics of Boston we have not heard of it.

"You may say likewise that now, since we have been accused of producing 'immoral,' 'vulgar,' 'vile,' 'hell-inspired' plays, we shall certainly be obliged to go on and produce them here in Washington, in order to convince the public that they are decent and true to life as it is lived in Ireland.

"I have never heard of the general attack that has been made on our plays," continued Lady Gregory, "except as I have heard of it through these silly handbills that were distributed on Sunday." She unfolded one of the circulars that had been passed out to the public calling upon the Washington public to refuse to support the plays.

All Officials Cordial

"I am going to send this to the manager of our theater in

Dublin, and ask him to have it framed and hung up in the lobby of the house so that Ireland may see how our plays are received by a certain class of people in America," said Lady Gregory.

"In all of the educational centers, like Boston and New Haven we have been well received, in fact our reception has been most cordial, not only by the intellectual people, but also by the municipal authorities and the police commissioners whose attention has been called to our plays. These gentlemen have visited our performances, and have declared that they have found nothing in them that is at all offensive.

"There has been, in the past, objection to some of the passages that occur in 'The Playboy of the Western World,' but these passages appear only in the book. They have been cut from the dialogue of the plays, and never have been spoken on the stage by members of the company. We are ready at any time to show our prompt books to the public as verification of this statement. Had any of the people who have taken upon themselves the task of objecting to our plays, taken the trouble to come to the theatre and see for themselves, they would know better than to object to anything in them.

"This is the reason there was hostility against our plays in Boston at first," Lady Gregory went on. "Some of the members of the Irish societies of that city objected to our 'Playboy,' but that passed away after it had been produced and it became as popular in that city as it was in Dublin.

Soul of the Race

"People of Irish blood have come to understand that to produce a great play the artist does his country more good than to represent it upon the stage with all its conventional virtues. They understand too, that we are not trying to give them a guide book of Ireland, but are trying to show the soul of a race.

"Our Dublin theater has opened the door of opportunity to the young men and women of Ireland who have genius or talent for writing. Now we are getting manuscripts of good plays from all parts of Ireland. It is as though Ireland had discovered a forgotten gift.

"We have brought a large repertoire of Irish plays to America, and while it is easier, of course, for a Dublin audience to understand our work, I am sure Americans will understand us, too. We thought it well to bring over here only our plays of peasant life in Ireland, though in Dublin we give other plays, historical dramas, like Mr. Yeats' plays of the Irish heroic age."

Lady Gregory is a typical Irish woman a native of County

Galway. She has been a devout student of what may be called the prehistoric period of the Irish imagination, fiction, and religion. In the four volumes of plays she has recently published she has retold in interesting fashion the old stories that have been familiar by peat fires in Ireland for many generations. She also has been a successful and industrious playwright, and though she is nearly seventy years old, she is present daily at rehearsals of the Irish Players Company.

Popular in Dublin

Among the words produced by the Royal Theater Company of Dublin none are more popular than those from her pen. In her "Book of Seven Plays," which illustrates the sentiments, religious feeling, and consciousness of the presence of mystery which characterizes the Irish plays and sets them in broad contrast to the humorous or purely tragic plays, perhaps none is more characteristic than, "The Travelling Man," a modern miracle drama which is a striking example of a play temperamentally Irish in its simplicity of staging, its mysticism, and its poetry.

Lady Gregory contributes her time and labor to the joint management, with Mr. William Butler Yeats, of the Abbey Theater in Dublin because, as she says, "We love our theater and the effect it is having on the life of Ireland." She smilingly refuses to discuss her own work.

Aside from her professional duties, Lady Gregory has accepted several social invitations, and also will appear before the Gaelic Society of Washington Wednesday at its meeting in the Cabinet room of Willard's Hotel, when she will make a short address to the members.

The Evening Post, New York 6.12.1911

LADY GREGORY

Patron and Directress of the Irish Players Draws a Distinction Between National Drama and a National Theatre—Germany.

Lady Gregory, playwright, and organizer and patron of the Irish Players, sat in a little dressing room just off the wings in the theatre. Through the stage entrances and exits came the voices of the actors and actresses, speaking the lines of Synge's "The Playboy of the Western World," amidst the frequent laughter of the audience. Many times the audience laughs at the wrong place—but no matter; at first the people misunderstood the whole purpose of this attempt to give expression of the Irish spirit through the medium of the drama, and in the end, perhaps, they will understand it all in complete sympathy.

For this day Lady Gregory is prepared to wait in wise patience, fortified by a ready humor; and, after seeing the Celtic players, one reflects that this last quality, coupled with a quaint fancy, is, in large measure, the sum of the Irish contribution to dramatic literature. These little plays are not dramas; the form of them virtually admits their limited appeal from the stage. But Ireland speaking is Ireland as it is. So much for a first impression.

Lady Gregory begged only that the interviewer would not ask her to review the history of the Irish theatre. To a request that she say something of the German national movement in the theatre, as compared with the Irish, and of the possibilities of development of a national school of drama in this country, she responded readily.

"In this country you have great opportunities for founding a drama, a theatre which shall give you expression," she said. "Only yesterday I was talking to one of your playwrights about it. One of your characteristics delights me especially. You cherish history and make little places to be known and loved. You mark with tablets and monuments the spots where great men were born, or where events have taken place. And that is evidence of a something in your national spirit which might express itself in drama. You have had three great wars, a picturesque, dramatic past, a great and interesting present, and a future. Why cannot the story of that be told upon the stage?

"To draw out this material you should have little theatres in many places, with companies of actors drawn from sources near at hand and trained to the work. Now, if you knew that you could write a short play about American life, and could have it played in a small theatre, your younger writers would try to write for the stage. The important thing is that the ventures should be small. It is no matter if the plays fail, for the expense has been small and no one is ruined.

"We have produced many little plays that have failed, and have given them up, and the loss has been of no consequence. Don't try to write big things, expensive to stage. Just a few days ago some one here sent me a play and asked me to read it and let him know what I thought of it. A short piece, and yet the directions called for a sheepfold with live sheep in it in the first scene, and in the last a more elaborate scene of the fold, with lambs gambolling about. It would have cost a great deal to put it on the stage—too much, and so I told him.

"In Germany there are many little theatres in the national movement. But the aim of the German national movement is quite different from ours in the Abbey Theatre. There, you know, the theatres are local, municipal enterprises, and are not limited in their subjects as we are, to dramas of the life of the country, but present plays by German writers of life in other countries. Theirs is a theatre of national playwrights, not of national life. The Irish players observe as a rule the stricter limitations of producing only plays by Irish writers of Irish scenes and subjects. It is better that we should limit ourselves so. Of foreign countries we know only by book or hearsay, or at best, by observation, which may not grasp the inner life of the people. It would be just as a book about a book, a copy of a copy, for instance like that portrait of myself which I would so glady suppress. It travels on from reproduction to reproduction, and each time more unlike me."

Actually, Lady Gregory is quite unlike her published portraits. You would guess her to be a grandmother, even if she were not quick to tell you so herself. A kindly, gracious presence puts you at your ease immediately and her ready humor, always evident in her eyes, invites you further. She speaks simply and directly.

"The limitation of the subjects of our plays," she went on, "was forced on us at first by a lucky accident, the jealousy of other theatres in Dublin. A too successful venture in their fields might have harmed their business, and they are quite influential in preventing the granting of a Government patent, which is necessary before one can produce plays in a public theatre. I believe in the wisdom of such limitations of subjects of plays, in a national theatre. Mr. Synge believed in them passionately. When it was suggested that the Irish Players might imitate the German example he wrote me a long letter about it, and that meant a great deal because he did not like to write letters. He said that it would be a terrible misfortune to go abroad for plays.

"One of your dramatists was showing me yesterday a paragraph in a paper he had written about the importance of historical drama in the national theatre. It was our first hope in Dublin to present historical plays. I have written several myself, and they have been acted in Dublin. But for the present the historical drama, which in the main implies something of the romantic, has been pushed aside by the realism of the younger writers, who are eager to write of life as it is about them. At the same time we have a number of historical plays and shall present them. I hope for an enlargement of the company after this visit to the United States. Perhaps we shall have one company to send over here, for we must come again and frequently—and, of course, we cannot leave Dublin without a company of the Irish players."

The Indianapolis Star, 26.1.1912

NO RIOT HALTS IRISH PLAYERS

Presaged Trouble Over "Playboy" Production in Local Theater Does Not Develop.

DIRECTOR DISCUSSES DRAMA

Lady Gregory Says National Society Has Developed New Literature in Isles

The presaged riot at the initial appearance of the Irish players from the Abbey Theater, Dublin, at English's Theater last night failed to develop, as throughout the evening's entertainment there scarcely was an uncomplimentary sound from the big audience.

Indianapolis folk of Irish descent were scattered in several parts of the theater, and at one time, during the second act, an outburst of giggling and laughing in a part of the gallery drew the attention of the audience in the pit for a few moments. The two plays produced are "The Playboy of the Western World" and "Riders to the Sea." Objections had been made to the former.

Policemen in plain clothes, four sergeants and sixteen patrolmen were stationed in various parts of the theater, and none of them was called on during the performance. Lady Gregory, director of the Irish National Theater Society, and well-known author, occupied a seat at the performance and interestedly watched for signs of an outbreak.

Brings Forth Plays

Lady Gregory believes that the branching out of the Irish dramatic project has had a favourable effect on the hitherto scanty literature of the Emerald Isle. She declared that, because the Irish players have been held down to productions either written by Irish authors, or written with Irish subjects as the basis, there has been an inrush of literature from the pens of hitherto unknown writers of the isle.

Since the days of Goldsmith, Sheridan and Oscar Wilde there have been few writers in Ireland whose efforts were worth dramatizing, Lady Gregory says. Since the Irish National Theater

Society started the movement for Irish plays, written in the simple and sincere style of Irish life, by Irish authors, the island has begun to produce another real crop of dramatists, she said last night.

Lady Gregory met J. M. Synge, author of "The Playboy of the Western World," in the Aran Isles, off the coast of Galway, where the islanders speak little but the old Gaelic tongue. The two discovered that the Isle of Aran was a gold mine of unadulterated Gaelic folk lore and some of the plays written by Mr. Synge will live in Irish literature, Lady Gregory believes.

People Know Lines

"We are tremendously pleased with the results of our efforts in America," she said. "We are pleased to see the audiences prepared for us. The people already have read and studied the plays and they know them by heart before we appear in them. The esthetic atmosphere of the American college cities, wherever we have gone, has been alive with appreciation of our efforts and it has been deeply gratifying to us.

"At Harvard and Yale and in New York our audiences were deeply appreciative of the simplicity and sincerity which we have been fighting for as a real exemplification of the new era in Irish drama. I really shouldn't call it a new era, for there has been no Irish drama heretofore.

"Since we were forced to use only Irish dramas, or plays written by Irishmen, it has been astounding to watch the opening up of the literature of Ireland. Not long since the son of an Irish laboring man produced a play, which was not only accepted, but was one which will exist. Many instances of a renaissance in Irish literature are constantly being brought to view."

Lady Gregory discussed briefly the various disturbances which have been aroused where the Irish Players performed and said she believed the educational campaign that is being carried on against adverse criticism of the dramas presented is bearing fruit.

New York Clipper, 27.1.1912

Conductor of Irish Players Asserts Critics Are Confused as to Intent of Author; Surprised at Opposition.

By Roswell Field

"If I thought there was anything immoral in the play; if I believed that in any way it could harm man, woman or child, I certainly should not ask that it be played."

Lady Augusta Gregory sat in the Rookwood Room of the Hotel La Salle, drinking tea and otherwise recuperating from the effects of the ride from Indianapolis. She did not have the appearance of a woman who had passed through a variety of ordeals, both of a hospitable and threatening nature. She was as serene as the best article of sky in her native Ireland and ready to talk of her travels and her mission—even of that formidable topic "The Playboy of the Western World."

"I tell you," she repeated, "as I tell everybody who asks me —and I am asked very often—that if anything in 'The Playboy' could harm man, woman or child, I should be the first to protest against its appearance.

"Then you ask me again if it would be judicious as a matter of expediency to drop the play from our list while in the States. To that I reply we have both artistic and sentimental reasons for not doing so. We had our great fight over 'The Playboy' while Synge was alive, and we won the fight and made the world receive it on its artistic basis.

"And now that Synge is dead it is not for us to weaken or to intimate by our action that we do not firmly believe and indorse our opinions formerly upheld and fought for."

Among Great Plays

"But suppose we had omitted the play over which so much hubbub has been raised. It is among the greatest of modern plays.

"What would your scholars and people of culture have thought of us? You certainly do not think that we should be taking you at your proper valuation if we offered a variety of plays and omitted a masterpiece.

"All through the East the people have received us as intelligently, as cordially, and such opposition as has been manifested is really only the expression of an insignificant minority—never to be compared to the real sentiment of the communities we have visited when judged by the character of our audiences and the verdict of the intelligent authorities."

The question of opposition having come up, Lady Gregory was asked if she did not recognize some reason for the impatience of her Irish critics.

"It is all based on complete misunderstanding of the text and a confusion as to the intent of the author," she replied. "The play represents a phase of life which happens to be placed in Ireland.

Question of Morality

"The question of the morality of the play may be left safely to the authorities that pass upon it and to the people who see it, and that has been done triumphantly so far as we are concerned. It is not our fault, it is not Mr. Synge's fault, if certain persons unintelligently persist in twisting about scenes and situations, notably that scene where the young girl is advised to remain in the hut with the young man; no carnal purpose is intended or suggested.

Lady Gregory has the eye with the proverbial Irish twinkle. She described the first night in New York, which, after an attempted outbreak, the police arrested seven malefactors, which included three literary bartenders, a harnessmaker and a printer. On the second night two Englishmen and a Jew were taken up for creating a disturbance. The Englishman explained, that they objected to the characterization of British soldiers as "khaki cut-throats."

Antagonism Puzzled

"We were puzzled, however," said Lady Gregory, "to account for the antagonism of the Jew, who came, it seems from St. Joseph, Mo. But the clouds rolled away when he explained to the judge that 'Callahan gave me a seat.' "

"Will you do me a favor?" said Lady Gregory as she started to make ready for the guests of the evening. "Will you please say that the 'y' in Synge is short and 'g' hard? I am asked that question every day, and I should like to settle it once and for all. Synge himself answered the question himself in his poem where he says:

" 'Lord, your judgment quickly bring,
And I'm your servant, J. M. Synge.' "

The Sunday Record-Herald, Chicago, 4.2.1912

WOMANS SECTION

By Mary O'Connor Newell

Certain prominent personages belonging to a Chicago society for improving things—this time by way of the Drama League—were much in evidence the afternoon when I called to see Lady Gregory by previous appointment.

While the clerk was getting Lady Gregory's room on the telephone for me they pushed their cards over to him and in voices not loud but peremptory demanded that Lady Gregory should be apprised immediately and without further delay of their arrival, and when the clerk tried to plead the previous motion they announced themselves again as personages whose business with Lady Gregory brooked no delay. They scurried into the elevator ahead of me and down and around the corridor leading to Lady Gregory's suite like two rabbits of "Alice in Wonderland" preoccupations, and when we were severally assembled "in the presence," so to speak, they forthwith announced to the distinguished visitor that neither they nor she could go on with the work of improving things right here in Chicago "as long as there was a reporter present."

What could Lady Gregory do?

You know if you have ever stood in the way of the majestic barge of reform when manned by determined femininity.

She asked me if I could wait a few minutes.

Behold me, therefore, still breathless from the impact with the wedge of the society for improving society, seated a few minutes later on a divan down and around the long corridor by the elevator, to which Lady Gregory had quietly continued to accompany me in spite of assurance on my part that I knew the way perfectly and would not for worlds take her away from the League for Improving Things. Behold me with five or ten minutes on my hands with which to brood over the inscrutable mystery surrounding many women in public life.

Why do they so often think—ask any innocent bystander—that membership in an uplift society is a patent exempting them from courtesy's common code, when to be courteous would be inconvenient?

Almost her first words on returning to me were on the beauty of punctuality in keeping engagement. It appeared by this that the members of the society for improving society were late by several quarters of an hour for their original engagement with Lady Gregory.

"Busy people are always prompt in keeping engagements," she said. "Sir John Millais told me that Gladstone—then prime minister and the busiest man in England—was punctual to the second at sittings for his portrait. 'If you wish to know who waste my time, look to the idlers in society,' he said."

There seem to be two types of Irish face, that which is so often caricatured on the stage and the straight-featured, high-cheeked type. Lady Gregory's face is of the American Indian type of Irish face, to use an Irishism. Her eyes are clear hazel and need no aid from glasses in reading, I observed. A woman on the sunny side of 55, she has the manner of one born into a world in which there is time enough for everything. She is not in the least languid. She speaks vividly, decisively, yet quietly and with a distinct Irish inflection.

She wore a plain black gown that day, bearing no Parisian cachet. The unusual thing about her dress, and at that it was not conspicuous, was the fine black lace veil which hung well back from the part in her gray hair to below her shoulders. The line of the veil imparted a curious distinction to Lady Gregory's not overly tall figure, adding dignity and softening her profile.

We talked incidentally of many things—of makes of type-writers, overheated rooms and current newspaper comment on "The Playboy." Once she lifted the heavy typewriter from one table to another to show the repairer who came in just what seemed to be wrong with it. He laid his big topcoat and his hat on the chair on which she had been sitting. When she came back to it she picked them up, carried them across the room to another chair and laid them down. A newspaper was wafted from the table at which the man was working to the floor. She stooped before he could and picked it up.

Simple natural acts, you say; why mention them? Why shouldn't Augusta, Lady Gregory of Coole Park, Gort, County Galway, Ireland, daughter of a former deputy lieutenant of that county, widow of Rt. Hon. Sir William Gregory—former member of parliament for County Galway and for Dublin and one-time Governor of Ceylon—essayist, dramatist, writer of fairy tales, patroness and director of the Abbey Theater movement and stage manager of the Abbey Theater Players on their present American tour, act as a well-bred woman?

No reason in the world. But somehow the frequent interviewer of much advertised women was surprised to find one who did not summon a servant to attend to every hitch in the business of living in a hotel and had self-helpfulness written large upon her. And it was consoling to find one famed for many missions of social improvement—helping a nation's stage, its literature and its industries—coming with the improved personality vital to ultimate success.

* * *

At first Lady Gregory was not inclined to enter into a discussion of "The Playboy of the Western World."

"If I thought it indecent and unfit for presentation, is it necessary to ask if we would produce it?" she said, answering rather the public's attitude than any question of mine.

"Give me an opinion of 'The Playboy' in your own words, an affirmation about it," I requested.

"It is a masterpiece of literature," she answered, "extraordinarily human, full of poetry and imagery, written in language finely attuned to character. The question is not whether you like it or not. I do not ask people to like it. As a matter of fact, there are other plays in our repertory I much prefer, but it has been made necessary for us now to give 'The Playboy' in order to show that it is not what it has been called, indecent, unfit for presentation. Everywhere it has been seen it has been pronounced by the official censors—the chiefs of police, etc., who were called in to decide upon it—entirely harmless.

"Although they are attacking our organization," continued Lady Gregory, "we believe that the objectors are quite as sincere in thinking that our theater is injuring Ireland as I am that it is helping Ireland.

"Their contention is that in showing this fantastic picture of Irish life in which the characters cannot be said to be examples of the highest principles, we are 'showing up' Ireland, showing the country to be unfit for self-government.

"Now I have seen the play acted in all the intellectual and social centers of England and in several large cities of America and I have never found that that impression has been made on any single person in the cultivated audience.

* * *

"I not only believe, but know, that our theater taken as a whole and Mr. Synge's genius is a component part of our theater —has enormously raised the dignity of Ireland. Both in England and on the continent the Abbey Theater is constantly being written upon as an example of how other national theaters should be founded.

Lady Gregory derives great comfort from a review of the Abbey Theater's activities by ex-President Roosevelt in a December review. She read excerpts from it aloud to me, stressing the paragraphs to the effect that "the Abbey Theater is one of the healthiest signs of the revival of the ancient Irish spirit that has been so marked a feature of the world's progress during the present generation," and, "it is especially noteworthy and proof of the general Irish awakening that this vigorous expression of Irish life, so honorable to the Irish people, should represent the combined work of so many different persons and not that of only one person."

"The last sentence," said Lady Gregory, "puts very clearly an argument I am often using. It is not right to pick out one play or one writer to be condemned. Our mass of work must be taken as a whole. We cannot expect to please everybody. There is an old proverb in Ireland that hits off the situation exactly:

If you wish to grow old
You must eat hot and cold.

"We have been almost as violently attacked by unionists for the nationalist character of some of our plays as we are now being attacked by nationalists. An English man walked out of the Abbey Theater in Dublin denouncing my 'Rising of the Moon' as anti-English, and saying that until he saw it he intended to send a contribution to some Irish literary fund."

* * *

To a clipping from a Chicago newspaper, which declared that "a play which depends upon Irish scenes, Irish characters and Irish players must fail unless it is patronized by the Irish," Lady Gregory answered:

"Our appeal is to intellectual America. Naturally we prefer to interest the Irish. We should like to show the Irish a new school of drama that is Irish; still, if they will not come, we hope to interest others.

* * *

"Our players have never been on any other stage. They have always played together, and therefore play like the five fingers—in harmony, unlike the ordinary company which is made up of many people who have different methods. All are Irish born, all under 30, and none has ever left Ireland save to play with this company."

Wednesday March 6, 1912, Boston Evening Transcript

A whole page interview with Lady Gregory, who sailed with the Abbey Theatre players from New York for Ireland yesterday, appears in the "North American."

"You want to hear about our Irish girls, what we have in store for them?" she asked, recently. "Well, let me tell you, I never fully appreciated what this great land was doing for our colleens, and I didn't relish the American influence either, until I came here. But now it is different. Inwardly I had rebelled against our young and pretty girls, the future womanhood of Ireland, coming to this country in such large numbers. It seemed like a crime.

"Why, from the time a girl is the height of the table, her own ambition, her future hope, is America. And it used to fairly make my heart ache to hear so much talk of this great country. Not that I was opposed to it, remember; but I couldn't bear the thought that it was taking our most ambitious and energetic girls, the very pick of the land.

"And while my tenants and everyone I came in contact with were talking of America, I never had any thought of crossing the ocean until I found that I was obliged to do so, even against my wishes. But it has indeed been a great joy to me to see the country that I had heard so much about, and my feelings naturally turn to gratitude.

"There is no nation that is so bound to our country as America," Lady Gregory went on. "Why, there are more Irishmen and Irishwomen in this country than there are in Ireland. And the sending of our girls to this country to be educated, and the introduction of American teaching methods would be royally welcomed.

"On my return to Ireland I intend to give historical plays, those dealing with this native history, and produce them in all the large cities. The Irish are good listeners, and have a passion for oratory, and this will satisfy their cravings. The realistic plays are in vogue there now."

The Cork Examiner, 20.12.1912

ABBEY THEATRE CO.
DEPARTURE FOR AMERICA.
INTERVIEW WITH LADY GREGORY.

Queenstown, Thursday

In response to what has proved a genuinely enthusiastic invitation the famous Abbey Theatre players, accompanied by Lady A. Gregory, whose enthusiasm in the up-building of the National Theatre is boundless, left Queenstown today by the White Star steamer Majestic for New York. The company which left here consist of the following: – Miss Sara Allgood, Miss Mona Bierne, Mr. M. J. Dolan, Miss Kathleen Drago, Mr. H. E. Hutchinson, Mr. J. M. Kerrigan, Miss Eithne Magee, Mr. Nugent Monck, Mr. Sydney Morgan, Miss Eileen O'Doherty, Mr. Frederick O'Donovan, Mrs. Frederick O'Donovan, Mr. J. A. O'Rourke, Mr. Arthur Sinclair, Mr. Adolphus Wright.

On their arrival at Queenstown last night, the company proceeded to the Queen's Hotel, where they remained overnight. The arrangements connected with their embarkation were made by Messrs. James Scott and Co., agents of the White Star Line, who at Queenstown and on board the Majestic, devoted attention to the comfort of Lady Gregory and the company, for which suitable acknowledgment was made.

Before leaving, your correspondent met Lady Gregory at the Queen's Hotel, and there listened to the gifted authoress detail her impressions of the work to which she has rendered such priceless service, while she also referred to the tour, in which Lady Gregory takes as deep interest as the youngest member of the distinguished company of players whom she accompanies, and of whom she is naturally proud, as the players are, of the connection with Lady Gregory, whose desire is to achieve even still greater things for the brilliant Irish company so closely associated with her name.

In the course of the interview, Lady Gregory said she is looking forward to a great success in America, where they did very well last year. They had many friends in America, all of whom were anxious to welcome them back. They were taking with them on this tour a great deal of new work. The "Playboy" would always be in their repertoire. Some of the new work is by Cork authors, including "Patriots," by Lennox Robinson, which was a very great success, and deals with the present political conditions, and represents a dying away of the old physical force movement in favour of more practical work. It is a simple, candid production, and shows how things have worked out in Ireland. They are also taking with them T. C. Murray's powerful play, "Maurice Harte," which was a big success in London and Dublin. It was during its production in London that Mrs. Asquith asked to be introduced to the author, which Lady Gregory had pleasure in complying with.

Lady Gregory likes America very much, and has many personal friends there whom she will be glad to see again. In her wanderings there before she met many of her tenants' children who went out from Ireland, and was glad to find them, all doing well.

Amongst other plays they are taking with them are "Family Failing," by Boyle, which is a Northern play, and deals with the Protestants of Belfast; the two act comedy, "Damer's Gold," by Lady Gregory herself, will be amongst the number. The Abbey Theatre will be carried on by the No. 2 company in their absence.

Their American contract lasts to the 1st of May, and they will be back for the Oxford Eights week, which they were specially booked for, and where they have had big successes in the past.

Their second company visited several Irish cities and towns in the present year, including Belfast, Galway, Longford, Doneraile, etc., and did very well in all.

Considering the high quality of the players, they are glad to have them appear before large audiences, though, of course, the Irish productions in Dublin and the country interested them most. They got more money, too, by going to America, for until the Abbey Theatre is enlarged their receipts would continue small. Before enlarging the Abbey they hoped to devote their efforts and resources to having continuous plays. At present they play only half the week. Later, they will have more players, and with sufficient rehearsals they would do much more work. Their venture had opened up a new profession in Ireland, both for dramatists and players and its success was beyond question.

With the advent of Home Rule, Lady Gregory says she believes the imaginative stir that will be caused by a National Parliament in College Green will greatly help every intellectual or imaginative movement. Everyone will be interested in the building of the Nation, and she believes this National Theatre a very important stone in that building.

Mr. Roosevelt wrote an article, added Lady Gregory, some time ago, in the "Outlook," saying how much the Irish National Theatre and Dramatic movement had added to the dignity of Ireland. They heard of the same in foreign countries—France, Germany, and Italy—and the question asked by those interested in Drama is not, what is the English Theatre doing, but how is the Irish Theatre doing, as they find it the most interesting expression of National Dramatic Art to be found in any country.

At Kingsbridge yesterday, they got a most enthusiastic and encouraging farewell, and were assured of an equally enthusiastic reception home. To the American people Lady Gregory wished to say, before leaving Queenstown, that the company looked forward with great delight and pleasure to the appreciative audiences and the kindliness and friendship of the American people, and not even the raging gale blowing now at Queenstown on their departure by the Majestic can quite depress their spirits. They open at Chicago on the 30th inst., with "Kathleen Ni Houlihan," "Maurice Harte" and "Spreading the News," and in the second half of the week in Chicago their plays would include "Mixed Marriage," by a Belfast author, which was very successful in Chicago before, so that all Ireland will be well represented in the productions.

Lady Gregory will remain with the company throughout the tour.

Miss Allgood, like her associates, looks forward to a thoroughly successful tour in the States. Speaking of the parts, she thought the part of the Mother in "Maurice Hart," and next to that, the "Patriots" and "Mixed Marriage," suited her best.

On arrival on board the Majestic, Lady Gregory and the company were specially introduced to Captain Haddock and the officers, and their comfort on board carefully provided for.

Australia has sent an invitation to the Abbey Company for an extended tour in that country.

Bettaine No. 2, February 1900

LAST YEAR

The Irish Literary Theatre, at its first performances in May, 1899, produced two plays, *The Heather Field*, by Mr. Edward Martyn, and *The Countess Cathleen*, by Mr. W. B. Yeats.

An Irish audience does not need to be reminded of their reception and of their success.

It is not for any of us, who have been concerned in the project from its beginning, to speak of the merits of these plays. *The Countess Cathleen*, now in its third edition, has so often been reviewed as a poem that it does not need any new criticism. *The Heather Field* was given, after its success in Dublin, at a matinée at the Strand Theatre in London, by Mr. Thomas Kingston. It has now been translated into German, and is to be produced, with Mr. Martyn's permission, at Berlin, at Vienna, at Breslau, and at Dresden. In America it is to be produced by Mr. Metzler at New York, Boston, Washington, and Philadelphia.

Readers of Irish newspapers will remember the many columns in every paper in which the plays were discussed, always with warm interest and almost always with warm appreciation.

I may, however, give extracts from a few of the many English papers in which articles on the Irish Literary Theatre appeared.

The *Speaker* said: "Intellectual and artistic Dublin is this week following with keen interest and an excitement almost national in its depth and intensity the somewhat daring experiment of the promoters of the Irish Literary Theatre. Readers of the *Speaker* are not unaware of the extent and nature of our neo-Celtic Renaissance—of the significance not merely of the mystical and spiritual note in such literary work as that of Mr. Yeats and A. E., but also of the growth here on native soil of a spirit of associative production in the fine arts as represented in our *Feis Ceoil, Oireachtas*, and local assemblies making for a culture racy of our traditions. The dramatic blossoming is the latest fruit of this new generation; and its importance lies just in this—that while many, and those well-wishers of the movement, thought that the appeal of such plays as *The Countess Cathleen* of Mr. Yeats, and Mr. Martyn's *The Heather Field* was too esoteric a cult, the event of their actual production in this city has so belied these anticipations as to ensure the permanent success of the Irish Literary Theatre....

"There was certainly no meretricious element in the presentation of *The Countess Cathleen* or *The Heather Field* as seen on Monday and Tuesday nights respectively at the Antient Concert Rooms. The hall is designed as a concert-hall—and a small one at that—the platform is ill-adapted in size and shape to the purpose of a stage; the scenery and accessories, in fine, were bald to a degree. All this threw an immense ordeal not merely on the players themselves but even on the audience. Both, however, came through the test with a success verging on triumph. Fine acting there no doubt was. Mr. Thomas Kingston and Miss May Whitty in especial were really superb; but nevertheless the literary beauty of *The Countess Cathleen* and the marvellous dramatic power of *The Heather Field* fascinated an audience as I have seldom seen an audience affected.... All this wonderland of imaginative symbol and spiritual thought has come home to men's bosoms here in Dublin with an enchanting naturalness. The Celt breathes this air by birthright. The only doubt was whether the acquired appetites and vitiated taste of playgoers surfeited on 'musical farces' and other variety entertainments—Dublin's normal dramatic diet for some years past—would not be inhibited from the enjoyment of more ethereal fare. This misgiving has proved without foundation. 'The intellect and spirit' of Dublin's culture has responded most hopefully to the artistic stimulus of the Irish Literary Theatre, and it would be rash to set limits to the literary and ethical influence which the unequivocal success of the 'new drama' may exert on the evolution of the dramatic art far beyond the bounds of Ireland."

The *Outlook* said: "Some who greatly admired the really beautiful traits of Mr. Yeats's play, *The Countess Cathleen*, had misgivings as to its effectiveness in places as acting drama. It is pleasant to find that the actual representation at the Irish Literary Theatre this week in Dublin has shown these fears to be groundless. The beginning has been, upon the whole, most auspicious. For the rest, many Irish Catholics have been amazed and then amused, at the objection to the play made by a certain small section on religious grounds—a section whose conception of art is primitive. As a matter of fact, Mr. Yeats knows a great deal more than his critics about the real mind and imaginings of the Irish peasantry.... But he appreciates the difference between religion and fantasy.... Stiff and formal minds who would have things otherwise may next require that Ariel be taken to church, and Puck made orthodox."

"Max," who came to Dublin on behalf of the *Saturday Review*, wrote in it: "In writing *The Countess Cathleen*, and in starting the Irish Literary Theatre, Mr. Yeats's aim has been to see whether beauty be not after all possible on the stage. Every one who cares about the stage ought to be grateful to him, whatever the outcome of his experiment. If I were asked what were the two elements furthest to seek in the modern commercial drama, I should have my answer pat: 'truth and beauty.' I should, however, hasten to admit that there is some considerable attempt at the former element. . . . About beauty I have said nothing. To say anything about it could have served no practical purpose; for there is no faintest effort among ordinary modern dramatists to attain any kind of beauty. In the ordinary modern theatre, beauty begins and ends with the face of the leading lady. . . . For the rest Mr. Yeats has written a poem of exquisite and moving beauty. . . . He is pre-eminently a poet; and for him words and the ordering of words are always the chief care and delight. His verses, more than the verses of any other modern poet, seem made to be chanted; and it is I fancy this peculiar vocal quality of his work, rather than any keen sense of drama, that has drawn him into writing for the stage. It is this peculiar quality also which differentiates the *Countess Cathleen* from that intolerable thing, the ordinary 'poets play'. . . . Despite the little cramped stage, and the scenery which was as tawdry as it should have been dim, I was, from first to last, conscious that a beautiful play was being enacted. And I felt that I had not made a journey in vain.

"I regret that I have not left space in which to write of the other play presented by the Irish Literary Theatre—Mr. Martyn's *Heather Field*. Not long ago this play was published as a book, with a preface by Mr. George Moore, and was more or less vehemently disparaged by the critics. Knowing that it was to be produced later in Dublin, and knowing how hard it is to dogmatise about a play till one has seen it acted, I confined myself to a very mild disparagement of it. Now, that I have seen it acted, I am sorry that I disparaged it at all. It turns out to be a very powerful play indeed. For the benefit of my colleagues I may say that it has achieved a really popular success—a success which must be almost embarrassing to the founders of a Literary Theatre."

To-Day says, quoting a correspondent in Dublin: "Edward Martyn's play, *The Heather Field*, was an unqualified success, and a popular success. It was well acted, and caught the attention of the audience. I was astonished at the attention with which it was listened to. The first act I feared would bore, but people were attentive, and, after that, when the second act began, there was no further question. Martyn's popularity was unbounded; the crowd was never tired shouting for him. . . . The hall was very fairly filled each day, though it is the off season in Dublin, and the whole venture was a decided success, and the *Heather Field* is sure to see the light in London."

A second article in *The Outlook*, entitled "Billy Kelly and the Irish Literary Theatre", said: "Well, I needn't tell you much about the plays. The papers let you know how Dublin, for once in its forlorn life, had a peep into fairyland. Never in the loneliest night, lookin' over the starlit valleys from the woods of Ballyvogne, an' the world so quiet that you could hear the grass growin', till the fairy fiddles tuned up beyant over the ford of Graignenagall—never in these nights did I see anything like what I saw in the *Countess Cathleen*. . . . I had a talk with Misther Yeats, an' he said a lot I didn't quite grasp about simbles an' other outlandish things that he didn't learn in the South. 'Cathleen is a simble,' says he, 'an' you'll find her in your own heart, Billy Kelly,' says he. 'I wish to God I did, Misther Yeats,' says I, 'I'd keep her there,' says I, 'an' some Dublin Jackeens wouldn't see so much of her as they do.'

"An' the next night, whin Misther Martyn's play kem on—well, all I have to say is, I didn't think that any Irish landlord, that ever stood in two shoes, had the makins of sich things in him. I'd bear eviction by sich a man with a light heart."

AUGUSTA GREGORY

The Arrow, June 1, 1907

AN EXPLANATION

I wish to explain on behalf of myself and the players to some whose opinion we respect, why, having been attacked for the performance of the "Playboy" in Ireland, we have decided to bring it to England. We would rather have given Ireland another opportunity of judging it when the heat caused by the collision of organized interruption and organized force had cooled down. But some attacks published, the latest through an English paper, have been of such an unworthy nature that we felt it would be necessary either to take the play into the Courts as the subject of a libel action or to some calm audience, and this audience we hope to find in Oxford, and in London.

I may say that the play was never acted as it is printed. I know, though I was not present, that it was considerably cut in rehearsal; and after the first public performance, we, the players and I, went through it and struck out any expressions that had given offence, and which were not necessary to the idea. It was so played during its Dublin week, and so it will be played in England. We did nothing, however, to soften or to hide the central idea; we felt that would be an insincerity. This idea may be taken very seriously if taken as a yet to be fulfilled prophecy, and is it not said that every work of art is either a memory or a prophecy? It is a fore-shadowing of what will happen if emigration goes on carrying off, year by year, the strongest, the most healthy, the most energetic. Often looking at our fields and farms I think of war time in ancient Rome.

> "The harvests of Arretium
> "This year old men shall reap;
> "This year young boys in Tiber
> "Shall fling the struggling sheep."

The old are always left to us, and the very young, the weakly in body or in mind. Some day it may be not a prophecy but a commonplace that a man coming with a name for strength and daring even in crime may take the mastery of a feeble countryside. Can anyone say that such a tragedy is impossible? And if the idea be a mere fantasy, who is so thin-skinned as to take offence? There are some critics, town dwellers for the most part, who would be "more royallist than the king," and cry out if the Irish peasant is represented with the lack of any virtue, no, if he be even called a peasant. And what then about other classes? The first play produced by our Irish Literary Theatre was Mr. Edward Martyn's "Heather Field," the subject of which is the driving of a husband from idealism to madness, by the narrow and vulgar conventionality of a woman of my own class. The "Bending of the Bough," founded on his "Tale of a Town," had the same idea differently treated. Protestant friends of mine have been able to admire, as I do, the spiritual beauty of Father Dineen's "Faith and Famine," though, we believe, its picture of Protestant bigotry to be not only a caricature but an impossibility. A Unionist paper made an attack upon the "Rising of the Moon," on the ground of its belittling the Royal Irish Constabulary, and yet I have been told that there was "never such great laughing" as when the little comedy was read in a Belfast Police Barrack. The plays we have produced must be taken as a whole; there are types of nobility in them as well as of greed or folly. Seanchan's high pride stands against Dempsey's ignoble bendings.

I am sorry Mr. Synge laid the scene of his play in Mayo if Mayo people are offended. He might have mentioned some undiscoverable Irish district. Yet if Mayo has cause to complain it may remember that Mr. Yeats has made his young bridegroom, who gives up love, home and all to follow Cathleen ni Houlihan, a Mayo man. I am not sure there are not counties which would adopt the "Playboy" and his whimsical admirers into their baronies, if they might also claim Michael Gillane as of their kin. I do not think it will be very long before Mayo, while thanking Clare and Galway for well meant resolutions of denunciation and of patronage, will say that in such questions it will prefer taking its soul upon its own shoulders, and judging not by hearsay but for itself—A. GREGORY.

Private and Confidential

PARAGRAPHS FROM SAMHAIN, 1909[1]

At the close of 1910 Miss Horniman's generous subsidy of £800 in money and the free use of the Theatre, which costs her in rents and rates about £200 more, comes to an end, together with the Patent.

We opened at the Abbey Theatre at Christmas, 1904, and during the first years we had but small audiences, for it is well known that a theatre audience takes a long time to build up; and the whole of the £800 was spent on the payment of actors, the takings of the theatre doing no more than paying for advertisements, scene shifters, attendance, etc. But during our last financial year, which closed at the end of August, we have been able to put more than £800 to capital, and by the close of 1910, should our present audiences continue, for our season has begun much better than any previous one, we shall put to capital more than the £800, and the money value of the free use of the theatre. We are, in fact, at the present rate of expenditure, making a small profit.

There will be however, should we apply for a new Patent for another period of six years, certain exception expenses. There will be legal expenses for the application for the new Patent; a considerable sum must be paid to Miss Horniman for the Theatre (though she is prepared to give it to us at cost price of the leases, without charging anything for the alteration and enlargement of the building, which was once the shabby little hall of the Mechanics Institute), and the interior must be redecorated and cleaned. This is an exceptional outlay, but a permanent addition

[1] *Paragraphs from Samhain 1909* is printed on handmade paper and has a smaller block of Elinor Monsell's device on the front cover than that which appears on the cover of the later version of this booklet *Paragraphs written in November 1909* (Wade, 3rd edition, no. 244b). There are a number of differences in style: the type width is smaller on the former which has no printer's imprint. The play list in the latter is set in a smaller typeface, the date of the latest of which is 2nd March 1910, whereas in the first issue the last play is dated 11th November 1909. From these indications and changes in the text (given below) *Paragraphs from Samhain 1909* should be considered the earlier and numbered Wade 244b, whereas *Paragraphs written in November 1909* should be Wade 244c.

to our expenses will be payment of authors and the appointment of a general manager. We did not, until the beginning of the present season, pay authors anything, as we did not think it right to do so until the actors were properly paid. But from this on, authors, with the exception of ourselves and of Mr. Bernard Shaw, who will not at present take payment for our work, must receive a percentage of the gross takings. The managerial work, which grows heavier from year to year, can no longer be borne by us at present, for it would require the entire time of one or other, and we have our own work to think of. Our Auditors warn us that in view of all this, our savings, which amount at present to about £1,200, are insufficient, if we are to apply for a Patent for another period of six years, and that we require a sum of £5,000 as guarantee, endowment, or in some other form. A third Director, bringing capital, might, perhaps, take a share in our work. Our Secretary, in consultation with the Auditors, Messrs. Kean & Co., is working out an account in detail, which can be seen by anyone who feels inclined to help us.[2]

We may point out that our Theatre spends in Dublin over £2,000 every year, not only in salaries, rents, and rates, but on orchestra, typewriters, carpenters, tailors and dressmakers, stage hands, advertisements, printing, and the many small expenses connected with such a business. None of this money is taken out of the country, as is the case with the companies who visit the other Dublin theatres. This expenditure will, we hope, increase with the increase of our audience, which will make possible the enlargement of our Company, and more continuous playing.

The list of Plays published with this shows something of

[2] There are a number of differences between the two versions of the third paragraph of the booklet and the later version is given here.

There will be, however, should we apply for a new Patent for another period of six years, certain exceptional expenses. There will be legal expenses for the application for the new Patent; a sum of money must be paid to Miss Horniman (see supplement), and the interior of the theatre must be re-decorated and cleaned. This is an exceptional outlay, but a permanent addition to our expenses will be payment of authors and the appointment of a general manager. We did not, until the beginning of the present season, pay authors anything, as we did not think it right to do so until the actors were properly paid but from this on, authors must receive a percentage of the gross takings. The managerial work, which grows heavier from year to year, can no longer be borne by us as at present, for it would require the entire time of one or other, and we have our own work to think of. Our Auditors warn us that, in view of all this, our savings, which amount at present to about £1,200, are insufficient, if we are to apply for a Patent, and that we require a sum of say £5,000 as guarantee, endowment, or in some other form. A third Director, bringing capital, might, perhaps, take a share in our work.

what we have done since we began in a concert hall ten years ago our work of creating a dramatic movement in Ireland. Our principal achievement has been the foundation of a school of Irish writers and actors who have given a distinguished and powerful representation of Irish country life. The works of the late Mr. J. M. Synge are recognised everywhere now by students of dramatic literature as among the most important that have been given to the theatre in our time. The representation of these plays which, being true works of the theatre, can never give their full meaning to the reader alone, probably depends upon the continuance of our Company. The actors of the English stage can never have the minute knowledge of the folk life of Ireland which they make necessary, and the representations of them which have taken place upon the Continent have been, and probably always will be, re-statements in the idiom and manners of a folk life very different from ours.

But the folk drama, for which our Theatre has given the opportunity, has a number of writers, and especially of late there have arisen young men of great promise whose future is probably bound up in the future of our Theatre. The creation of a folk drama was, however, but a part of the original scheme, and now that it has been accomplished we can enlarge our activities, bringing within our range more and more of the life of Ireland, and finding adequate expression for the acknowledged masterpieces of the world. A theatre, as we conceive it, should contain in its repertory plays from the principal dramatic schools. We have begun with three plays by Molière, as their affinities with folk drama have made them easy to our players. During our next season we shall add to them one of Goldoni's comedies. Our players have, however, given a good deal of their time to the speaking of verse, and we are about to produce "Edipus Rex" of Sophocles. A French classical play, and one of Calderon's should come next;[3] and when we apply for a new Patent we shall hope to remove the limitation of our present one, which prevents us from performing any Elizabethan work. We wish, in fact, while keeping the bulk of our work as Irish as possible, to enlarge gradually the experience of our players until the day has come when it will be possible to find in our repertory examples of the great schools, chosen as impartially as if they were pictures in some national gallery.

[3] Two sentences have been changed here. ". . . and we are about to produce "Œdipus the King." A French classical play, and one by Calderon, should come next;"

All the laborious building-up, the slow amassing of a large repertory of Irish plays, the training of actors, the making of a reputation with the general public, has been accomplished, or all but accomplished, and there is little needed to make the Abbey Theatre a permanent part of Irish life, the centre of a distinguished school of players, playwrights and translators. We ourselves are ready to accept much or little influence and any arrangement that will keep the Theatre intellectual and courageous. We would sooner it came to an end than see the tradition we have created give place to one less worthy.

W. B. YEATS
A. GREGORY

ABBEY THEATRE,
DUBLIN *November, 1909*

THE IRISH NATIONAL THEATRE: ITS WORK AND ITS NEEDS

"Those who may think of starting Repertory Theatres could not have a better example of a modest enterprise than that afforded by the Irish National Theatre, which they owed to Mr. Yeats and his comrades."—Mr. WALKLEY AT THE ROYAL THEATRICAL FUND DINNER, JUNE 12TH, 1910.

"It would be indeed difficult to mention any other contemporary Theatrical Repertory which has enriched the British Stage with so much modern work of a high order as that of the Irish National Theatrical Society."—*Pall Mall Gazette*, JUNE 13TH, 1910.

"I don't think there has been anything like it in the world."—FORD MADOX HUEFFER IN THE *Daily News*, JUNE 20TH, 1910.

It was in 1899 that we began in a Dublin Hall our attempt to found an intellectual theatre in Ireland, and we have worked hard through eleven years to this end. The list of plays printed with this shows something of what has been done. Our principal achievement has been the foundation of a school of Irish writers and actors, who have given a distinguished and powerful representation of Irish country life. The works of the late Mr. J. M. Synge are recognised everywhere now by students of dramatic literature as among the most important that have been given to the theatre in our time. The representation of these plays which, being true works of the theatre, can never give their full meaning to the reader alone, probably depends upon the continuance of our Company. The actors of the English stage can never have the minute knowledge of the folk life of Ireland which they make necessary, and the representations of them which have taken place upon the Continent have been, and probably always will be, re-statements in the idiom and manners of a folk life very different from ours.

But the folk drama, for which our Theatre has given the opportunity, has a number of writers, and especially of late there have arisen young men of great promise whose future is probably bound up in the future of our Theatre. The creation of a folk drama was, however, but a part of the original scheme, and now that it has been accomplished we can enlarge our activities, bringing within our range more and more of the life of Ireland, and finding adequate expression for the acknowledged masterpieces of the world. A theatre, as we conceive it, should contain in its repertory plays from the principal dramatic schools. We already produce, and find an audience for, some of the plays of Molière, akin to the folk drama, and of Goldoni and other foreign writers.

Six years ago, we were enabled by a generous subsidy from Miss Horniman, to play upon a regular stage. We have had to fight against apathy and prejudice, and at one time or another against patriotic cliques or against government officials. But our Dublin audience is steadily increasing, and we find support and a welcome, not only in the chief towns of Ireland, but in the English intellectual centres, London, Manchester, Oxford and Cambridge. All the laborious building up, the slow amassing of a large repertory of Irish plays, the training of actors, the making of a reputation with the general public, has been accomplished or all but accomplished.

Our subsidy, including the free use of the Abbey Theatre, comes to an end, as well as our Patent, in this year. We have saved enough money (£1,900) to take over the Abbey Theatre and pay for a new Patent, a somewhat heavy expense; but a permanent addition will be the payment of authors and of a general manager. We did not, until the beginning of the present season, pay authors anything, as we did not think it right to do so until the actors were properly paid, but from this on, authors must receive a percentage of the gross takings. The managerial work, which grows heavier from year to year, can no longer be borne by us, for it would require the entire time of one or other, and we have our own work to think of. Our business advisers tell us that a sum of £5,000, which would hardly support a London Theatre for a season would enable us to keep our Theatre as we wish, vigorous, intellectual and courageous, for another half-a-dozen years. We believe that within a few years we shall be independent of outside aid, for our takings in our last financial year equal all the takings put together of the three previous years. We need not be ashamed to wait another few years, for the celebrated Moscow Art Theatre is, after ten years still carried on at a loss.

Towards the £5,000 we need as endowment, we have already been given £2,000, among the donors being Mr. J. M. Barrie, Mr. A. Birrell, Col. Hutcheson Poe, Lord Pirrie, Lord Iveagh, Mr. Wilfrid Blunt, Lady Bell, Lord Dunsany, Mr. F. Huth Jackson, the Duke of Leinster, the Duchess of Sutherland and Lady Tennant. Should we receive no more than this £2,000, we shall still go on for as long as we can, but we shall be crippled and not able to carry out plans for the strengthening and widening of our work, and we shall have, as in the years past, to give up to the actual business of the theatre so great a part of our own time as to interfere with our personal and creative work. We feel that we have almost pushed the stone up the hill. We shall be grateful to any friends of our enterprise who will help us to keep it from rolling down.

W. B. YEATS
A. GREGORY

ABBEY THEATRE,
June 21st, 1910

This article appeared as a booklet (8 pp. + cover) similar to *Paragraphs written in Nov., 1909* with a list of first performances at the Abbey Theatre and is not in the third edition of Wade's bibliography of W. B. Yeats' writings: its probable number would be 244d. It is dated June 21, 1910 and is a revised version of the letter, entitled "The Irish National Theatre" which appeared in *The Times* of June 16, and elsewhere in the London Press, and in *The Irish Independent* of the same date where it was headed "The Future of the Abbey Theatre."

At the end of the article there is a note to the effect that Lady Tennant of 34 Queen Anne's Gate, London S.W. was acting as Treasurer to the Fund. Some copies, presumably those distributed in Ireland, have a note stuck over this, which says that "Subscriptions may be sent to The Rt. Hon. W. F. Bailey, C.B., 3 Earlsfoot Terrace; Mr. Philip Hanson, 28 Clare Street; or Mr. Edmund Bourke, Royal St. George Yacht Club, Kingstown; who have consented to act as Treasurers and Trustees of the Abbey Theatre Endowment Fund."

APPENDICES

APPENDIX I

PLAYS PRODUCED BY THE ABBEY THEATRE CO. AND ITS PREDECESSORS, WITH DATES OF FIRST PERFORMANCES

IRISH LITERARY THEATRE AT ANTIENT CONCERT ROOMS

May 8th, 1899	"The Countess Cathleen"	W. B. Yeats
May 9th, 1899	"The Heather Field"	Edward Martyn

IRISH LITERARY THEATRE AT THE GAIETY THEATRE

Feb. 19th, 1900	"The Bending of the Bough"	George Moore
Feb. 19th, 1900	"The Last Feast of the Fianna"	Alice Milligan
Feb. 20th, 1900	"Maeve"	Edward Martyn
Oct. 21st, 1901	"Diarmuid and Grania"	W. B. Yeats and George Moore
Oct. 21st, 1901	"The Twisting of the Rope"	Douglas Hyde

(The first Gaelic Play Produced in any Theatre.)

MR. W. G. FAY'S IRISH NATIONAL DRAMATIC COMPANY AT ST. TERESA'S HALL, CLARENDON STREET

Apr. 2nd, 1902	"Deirdre"	"A.E."
Apr. 2nd, 1902	"Kathleen Ni Houlihan"	W. B. Yeats

IRISH NATIONAL DRAMATIC COMPANY AT ANTIENT CONCERT ROOMS

Oct. 29th, 1902	"The Sleep of the King"	Seumas O'Cuisin
Oct. 29th, 1902	"The Laying of the Foundations"	Fred Ryan
Oct. 30th, 1902	"A Pot of Broth"	W. B. Yeats
Oct. 31st, 1902	"The Racing Lug"	Seumas O'Cuisin

IRISH NATIONAL THEATRE SOCIETY, MOLESWORTH HALL

(The first prospectus of the Society, dated March, 1903, and signed by Mr. Fred Ryan began as follows: "The Irish National Theatre Society was formed to continue on a more permanent basis the work of the Irish Literary Theatre.")

Mar. 14th, 1903	"The Hour Glass"	W. B. Yeats
Mar. 14th, 1903	"Twenty-Five"	Lady Gregory
Oct. 8th, 1903	"The King's Threshold"	W. B. Yeats
Oct. 8th, 1903	"In the Shadow of the Glen"	J. M. Synge
Dec. 3rd, 1903	"Broken Soil"	Padraic Colum
Jan. 14th, 1904	"The Shadowy Waters"	W. B. Yeats
Jan. 14th, 1904	"The Townland of Tamney"	Seumas McManus
Feb. 25th, 1904	"Riders to the Sea"	J. M. Synge

IRISH NATIONAL THEATRE SOCIETY AT THE ABBEY THEATRE

Dec. 27th, 1904	"On Baile's Strand"	W. B. Yeats
Dec. 27th, 1904	"Spreading the News"	Lady Gregory
Feb. 4th, 1905	"The Well of the Saints"	J. M. Synge
Mar. 25th, 1905	"Kincora"	Lady Gregory
Apr. 25th, 1905	"The Building Fund"	William Boyle
June 9th, 1905	"The Land"	Padraic Colum

NATIONAL THEATRE SOCIETY, LTD. (ABBEY COMPANY)

Dec. 9th 1905	"The White Cockade"	Lady Gregory
Jan. 20th, 1906	"The Eloquent Dempsy"	William Boyle
Feb. 19th, 1906	"Hyacinth Halvey"	Lady Gregory
Oct. 20th, 1906	"The Gaol Gate"	Lady Gregory
Oct. 20th, 1906	"The Mineral Workers"	William Boyle
Nov. 24th, 1906	"Deirdre"	W. B. Yeats
Dec. 8th, 1906	"The Canavans"	Lady Gregory
Dec. 8th, 1906	New Version of "The Shadowy Waters"	W. B. Yeats
Jan. 26th, 1907	"The Playboy of the Western World"	J. M. Synge
Feb. 23rd, 1907	"The Jackdaw"	Lady Gregory
Mar. 9th, 1907	"The Rising of the Moon"	Lady Gregory
Apr. 1st, 1907	"The Eyes of the Blind"	Miss W. M. Letts
Apr. 3rd, 1907	"The Poorhouse"	Douglas Hyde and Lady Gregory
Apr. 27th, 1907	"Fand"	Wilfrid Scawen Blunt
Oct. 3rd, 1907	"The Country Dressmaker"	George Fitzmaurice
Oct. 31st, 1907	"Dervorgilla"	Lady Gregory

Nov. 21st, 1907	"The Unicorn from the Stars"	W. B. Yeats and Lady Gregory
Feb. 13th, 1908	"The Man who missed the Tide"	W. F. Casey
Feb. 13th, 1908	"The Piper"	Norreys Connell
Mar. 10th, 1908	"The Piedish"	George Fitzmaurice
Mar. 19th, 1908	"The Golden Helmet"	W. B. Yeats
Apr. 20th, 1908	"The Workhouse Ward"	Lady Gregory
Oct. 1st, 1908	"The Suburban Groove"	W. F. Casey
Oct. 8th, 1908	"The Clancy Name"	Lennox Robinson
Oct. 15th, 1908	"When the Dawn is come"	Thomas MacDonogh
Oct. 21st, 1908	New Version, "The Man who missed the Tide"	W. F. Casey
Feb. 11th, 1909	Revised Version of "Kincora"	Lady Gregory
Mar. 11th, 1909	"Stephen Grey"	D. L. Kelleher
Apr. 1st, 1909	"The Cross Roads"	Lennox Robinson
Apr. 1st, 1909	"Time"	Norreys Connell
Apr. 29th, 1909	"The Glittering Gate"	Lord Dunsany
May 27th, 1909	"An Imaginary Conversation"	Norreys Connell
Aug. 25th, 1909	"The Shewing-up of Blanco Posnet"	Bernard Shaw
Sept. 16th, 1909	"The White Feather"	R. J. Ray
Oct. 14th, 1909	"The Challenge"	Miss W. M. Letts
Nov. 11th, 1909	"The Image"	Lady Gregory
Jan. 13th, 1910	"Deirdre of the Sorrows"	J. M. Synge
Feb. 10th. 1910	"The Green Helmet"	W. B. Yeats
Mar. 2nd, 1910	"The Travelling Man"	Lady Gregory
May 12th, 1910	"Thomas Muskerry"	Padraic Colum
May 26th, 1910	"Harvest"	Lennox Robinson
Sept. 28th, 1910	"The Casting-out of Martin Whelan"	R. J. Ray
Oct. 27th, 1910	"Birthright"	T. C. Murray
Nov. 10th, 1910	"The Full Moon"	Lady Gregory
Nov. 24th, 1910	"The Shuiler's Child."[1]	Seumas O' Kelly
Dec. 1st, 1910	"Coats"	Lady Gregory
Jan. 12th, 1911	"The Deliverer"	Lady Gregory
Jan. 26th, 1911	"King Argimenes and the Unknown Warrior"	Lord Dunsany

[1] First produced by an amateur company at the Molesworth Hall in 1909.

Feb. 16th, 1911	"The Land of Heart's Desire"[2]	W. B. Yeats
Mar. 30th, 1911	"Mixed Marriage"	St. John G. Ervine
Nov. 23rd, 1911	"The Interlude of Youth"	Anon., first printed 1554
Nov. 23rd, 1911	"The Second Shepherd's Play"	Anon., *circa* 1400
Nov. 30th, 1911	"The Marriage"	Douglas Hyde
Dec. 7th, 1911	"Red Turf"	Rutherford Mayne
Dec. 14th, 1911	Revival of "The Countess Cathleen"	W. B. Yeats
Jan. 4th, 1912	"The Annunciation"	*circa* 1400
Jan. 4th, 1912	"The Flight into Egypt"	*circa* 1400
Jan. 11th, 1912	"MacDarragh's Wife"[3]	Lady Gregory
Feb. 1st, 1912	Revival of "The Country Dressmaker."	George Fitz-maurice
Feb. 15th, 1912	"The Tinker and the Fairy" (Played in Gaelic)	Douglas Hyde
Feb. 29th, 1912	"The Worlde and the Chylde"	15th century
Mar. 28th, 1912	"Family Failing"	William Boyle
Apr. 11th, 1912	"Patriots"	Lennox Robinson
Apr. 15th, 1912	"Judgment"	Joseph Campbell
June 20th, 1912	"Maurice Harte"	T. C. Murray
July 4th, 1912	"The Bogie Men"	Lady Gregory
Oct. 17th, 1912	"The Magnanimous Lover"	St. John G. Ervine
Nov. 21st, 1912	"Damer's Gold"	Lady Gregory

TRANSLATIONS OF THE FOLLOWING HAVE BEEN PRODUCED

Apr. 16th, 1906	"The Doctor in spite of Himself"	(Molière.) Translated by Lady Gregory
Mar. 16th, 1907	"Interior"	(Maeterlinck.)
Mar. 19th, 1908	"Teja"	(Sudermann.) Translated by Lady Gregory
Apr. 4th, 1908	"The Rogueries of Scapin"	(Molière.) Translated by Lady Gregory

[2] First produced at the Avenue Theatre, London, in 1894.

[3] Although the title was changed to "MacDonough's Wife" before it was performed, the first edition of this volume gives it as above. Lennox Robinson in his "Ireland's Abbey Theatre" (1951) also gives the title as "MacDaragh's Wife".

Jan. 21st, 1909	"The Miser"	(Molière.) Translated by Lady Gregory
Feb. 24th, 1910	"Mirandolina"	(Goldoni.) Translated by Lady Gregory
Jan 5th, 1911	"Nativity Play"	(Douglas Hyde.) Translated by Lady Gregory

NEW PRODUCTIONS

Nov. 21st, 1912	"The Hour Glass" Revised	
Nov. 21st, 1912	"Damer's Gold"	
Jan. 23rd, 1913	"The Dean of St. Patrick's"	G. Sidney Paternoster
Feb. 6th, 1913	Revival, "Casting-out of Martin Whelan"	R. J. Ray
Feb. 20th, 1913	"Hannele"	Gerhardt Hauptmann
Mar. 6th, 1913	"There are Crimes and Crimes"	August Strindberg
Mar. 13th, 1913	"The Cuckoo's Nest"	John Guinan
Apr. 10th, 1913	"The Homecoming"	Gertrude Robins
Apr. 17th, 1913	"The Stronger"	August Strindberg
Apr. 24th, 1913	"The Magic Glasses"	George Fitzmaurice
Apr. 24th, 1913	"Broken Faith"	S. R. Day and G. D. Cummins
May 17th, 1913	"The Post Office"	Rabindranath Tagore

APPENDIX II

THIS letter is reproduced by permission of the Board of Trinity College Library, Dublin, where it forms part of the J. M. Synge archives. The original letter to Robert is in the possession of his son Major Richard Gregory. Lady Gregory had put it into her copy of *Our Irish Theatre* and there it still is.

Nassau Hotel
Tuesday

Dear Mr. Synge,

The meeting last night was dreadful, and I congratulate you on not having been at it. The theatre was crammed, all the stalls had been taken at Cramers (we made £16). Before it began there was whistling &c. "Pat" made a good chairman, didn't lose his temper and made himself heard but no chairman could have done much. Yeats' first speech was fairly well listened to, though there were boos and cries of "What about the police?" &c. and we had taken the precaution of writing it out before and giving the reporters a copy. No one came to support us, Russell (A.E) was in the gallery we heard afterwards but did not come forward or speak. Colum "had a rehearsal" (and didn't speak or come). T. W. Russell didn't turn up. We had hardly anyone to speak on our side at all, but it didn't much matter for the disturbances were so great they wouldn't even let their own speakers be well heard. Lawrence was first to attack us, a very poor speech, his point that we should have taken the play off because the audience and papers didn't like it . . . then a long rigmarole about a strike of the public against a rise of prices at Covent Garden and a medal which was struck to commemorate their victory. But he bored the audience. You will see the drift of the other speakers, little Beasleys was the only one with a policy for he announced his intention of never entering the place again, and called upon others to do so, but the cheering grew very feeble at that point. A Dr. Ryan supported us fairly well. Though it was hard to get speakers to come forward, at the thick of the riot Mrs. Duncan sent up her name to the platform offering to give an address! but Pat sent back word he would not like to see her insulted! A young man forced his way up and argued with Dossy till a whisky bottle fell from his pocket and broke on the stage, at which Dossy flung him down the steps and there was a great cheering and laughing, and Dossy flushed with honest pride. Old Yeats made a very good speech and got at first a very good reception though when he went up there were cries of "Kill your Father" "Get the loy" &c. and at the end when he praised Synge he was booed. The last speakers could hardly be heard at all. There was a tipsy man in the pit crying "I'm from Belfast! Ulster aboo!" Many of our opponents called for order and fair play and I think must have been disgusted with their allies. The scene certainly justified us in having called in the police. The interruptions were very stupid and monotonous. Yeats when he rose for his last speech was booed but got a hearing at last and got out all he wanted to say. He spoke very well, but his voice rather cracked once or twice from screaming and from his sore throat. I was sorry while there that we had ever let such a set inside the theatre, but I am glad today, and I think it was spirited and showed we were not repenting or apologising. Pat came in here afterwards, very indignant with the rowdies. It is a mercy today to think the whole thing is over.

I had a wire from Fay yesterday, "Tabby completely upset Boyle. No use waiting here" and he came back this morning and has been here. He could do nothing with Boyle. Says it was temper roused by Miss Horniman's letter of cock-crows that roused him to write first, but now he won't withdraw unless Yeats will make a public declaration that we made a mistake in putting on the Playboy. Fay said of course that was impossible and Boyle won't give in. He seems to have no reason but Fay thinks had an uneasy feeling he didn't know where we might be leading him. He refused to read the scraps. Fay would like to kick him which is a healthy sign, and we have been arranging the programme for the rest of the season without his work which is rather a comfort. Boyle is being encouraged by a Mrs. —— who is collaborating with him in a play and who was the critic who cried him up so much in the Morning Post. He landed Fay in to see her, and she was very indignant at our having withstood the press.

I was writing the above account to Robert and took a duplicate for you. I am afraid you are very unwell and would have gone down to Kingstown to see you but thought I mightn't be let in. Please let us know how you are going on. I really count the loss of Boyle among our assets: Fay thinks he will give us back the plays when he finds he can do nothing with them, but he is hoping to place the "Mineral Workers" in America. We have settled "Pot of Broth", "Doctor" and "Kathleen" for next Saturday. "Cockade" and "Jackdaw" for Saturday or week after that. Yeats will go to Wexford tomorrow and see Mayne act.

Yours sincerely, A. Gregory

APPENDIX III

"THE NATION" ON "BLANCO POSNET"

We have often spoken in these columns of the condition of the British drama and the various ways of mending it. But there is one of its features, or, rather, one of its disabilities, as to which some present decision must clearly be taken. That is the power of the Censorship to warp it for evil, and to maim it for good. There can be no doubt at all that this is the double function of the Lord Chamberlain and his office. The drama that they pass on and therefore commend to the people is a drama that is always earthly, often sensual, and occasionally devilish; the drama which they refuse to the people is a drama that seeks to be truthful, and is therefore not concerned with average sensual views of life, and that might, if it were encouraged, powerfully touch the neglected spheres of morals and religion. As to the first count against the Censorship there is and can be no defence. *Habemus confitentem reum*. The man who would pass *Dear Old Charlie* would pass anything. He has bound himself to tolerate the drama of Wycherley and Congreve, of which it is a fairly exact and clever revival, suited to modern hypocrisy as to ways of expression, but equally audacious in its glorification of lying, adultery, mockery, and light-mindedness.

The case on the other count is, we think, sufficiently made out by the Censor's refusal to license Mr. Bernard Shaw's one-act play, *The Showing-up of Blanco Posnet*. It is fair to the Censor to explain the grounds of his refusal. Mr. Shaw has been good enough to let the editor of this paper see a copy both of his drama and of the official letter refusing a "license for representation" unless certain passages were expunged. There were two such passages. On the second Mr. Shaw assures us that no difficulty could have occurred. It raised a question of taste, on which he was willing to meet Mr. Redford's views. It seems to us outspoken rather than gross, but as it was not the subject of controversy we dismiss it, and recur to the critical point on which Mr. Shaw, considering—and, in our view, rightly considering—that the heart and meaning of his play were at issue, refused to give way. In order that we may explain the quarrel, it is necessary to give some slight sketch of the character and intention of *The*

Showing-up of Blanco Posnet. We suggest as the simplest clue to its tone and atmosphere that it reproduces in some measure the subject and the feeling of Bret Harte's *Luck of Roaring Camp*. It depicts a coarse and violent society, governed by emotions and crude wants rather than by principles and laws, a society of drunkards, lynchers, duellists at sight, and, above all, horse-stealers—in other words, a world of conventionally bad men, liable to good impulses. The "hero" is something of a throw-back to Dick Dudgeon, of the *Devil's Disciple;* that is to say, he is reckless and an outcast, who retains the primitive virtue of not lying to himself.

The scene of the play is a trial for horse-stealing. Blanco is a nominal—not a real—horse-stealer, that is to say, he has committed the sin which a society of horsemen does not pardon. He has run away with the Sheriff's horse, believing it to be his brother's and taking it on account of fraudulent settlement of the family estate. A man of his hands, he has yet allowed himself to be tamely captured and brought before a jury of lynchers. Why? Well, he has been upset, overtaken, his plan of life twisted, and involved out of all recognition. On his way with the horse, a woman met him with a child dying of croup. She stopped him, thrust the sick child on to the horse, and "commandeered" it for a ride to the nearest doctor's. The child thrust its weak arms round his neck, and with that touch all the strength has gone out of him. He gives up the horse and flies away into the night, covering his retreat from this new superior force with obscene curses, and surrendering, dismounting, dazed, and helpless, to the Sheriff when the *posse comitatus* catches him.

Thenceforward two opposing forces rend him, and make life unintelligible and unendurable while they struggle for his soul. Dragged into the Sheriff's court, he is prepared to fight for his neck with the rascals who sit in judgment on him, to lie against them, and to browbeat them. Unjust and filthy as they are, he will be unjust and filthy too. But then there was this apparition of the child. What did it mean? Why has it unmanned him? And here it seems to him that God has at once destroyed and tricked him, for the child is dead, and yet his life is forfeit to these brutes. The situation—this sketch of a sudden, ruthless, unintelligible interference with the lives of men—though apparently unknown to the Censor, will be familiar to readers of the Bible and of religious poetry and prose, and Mr. Shaw's treatment of it could only offend either the non-religious mind or the sincerely, but conventionally, pious man who is so wrapt up in the emotional view of religion that its sterner and deeper moralities escape him.

The literary parallels will at once occur. Browning chooses the subject in *Pippa Passes*, and in the poem in which he describes how the strong man who had hemmed in and surrounded his enemy suddenly found himself stayed by the "arm that came across" and saved the wretch from vengeance. Ibsen dwells on this divine thwarting and staying power in *Peer Gynt*, and it is, of course, the opening theme of the *Pilgrim's Progress*. As it presents itself to a coarse and reckless, but sincere, man he deals with it in coarse but sincere language—the language which the Censor refuses to pass. Here is the offending passage, which occurs in a dialogue between Blanco and his drunken hypocrite of a brother: –

"BLANCO: Take care, Boozy. He hasn't finished with you yet. He always has a trick up his sleeve.

"ELDER DANIELS: Oh, is that the way to speak of the Ruler of the Universe—the great and almighty God?

"BLANCO: He's a sly one. He's a mean one. He lies low for you. He plays cat and mouse with you. He lets you run loose until you think you're shut of Him; and then when you least expect it, He's got you.

"ELDER DANIELS: Speak more respectful, Blanco—more reverent.

"BLANCO: Reverent! Who taught you your reverent cant? Not your Bible. It says, 'He cometh like a thief in the night'—aye, like a thief—a horse-thief. And it's true. That's how He caught me and put my neck into the halter. To spite me because I had no use for Him—because I lived my own life in my own way, and would have no truck with His 'Don't do this,' and 'You mustn't do that,' and 'You'll go to hell if you do the other.' I gave him the go-bye, and did without Him all these years. But He caught me out at the last. The laugh is with Him as far as hanging goes."

Now, let us first note the incapacity of the critic of such an outburst as this to think in terms of the dramatic art—to divine the *état d'âme* of the speaker, and to recognise the method, and, within bounds, the idiosyncracy of the playwright. But having regard to all that the Censor has done and all that he has left undone, let us also mark his resolve to treat as mere blasphemy on Mr. Shaw's part the artist's endeavour to depict a rough man's first consciousness of a Power that, selecting Blanco as it selected Paul and John Bunyan, threatens to drag him through moral shame and physical death, if need be, to life, and not to let him go till He has wrought His uttermost purpose on him. Mr. Shaw naturally makes Blanco talk as an American horse-stealer would talk. But how does Job talk of God, or the Psalmist, or the Author of the Parables? Nearly every one of Blanco Posnet's railings can be paralleled from Job. Listen to this:—

"The tabernacles of robbers prosper, and they that provoke God are secure, into whose hand God bringeth abundantly.

"He removeth away the speech of the trusty, and taketh away the understanding of the aged.

"He taketh the heart of the chief of the people of the earth and causeth them to wander in a wilderness where there is no way.

"They grope in the dark without light, and He maketh them to stagger like a drunken man.

"Know now that God hath overthrown me, and hath compassed me with His net.

"He hath fenced up my way that I cannot pass and He hath set darkness in my paths.

"He hath destroyed me on every side, and I am gone: and mine hope hath He removed like a tree."

Is this blasphemy? Is not Mr. Shaw's theme and its expression a reflection of Job's, save that in the one case a bad man speaks, and in the other a good one? If the answer is that these subjects, these moral and religious relationships, must not be treated on the stage, then we reply first that the Censor is grossly inconsistent, for he did not veto the entire play, but only that passage which most clearly revealed its meaning; secondly, that the licensing of *Everyman*, and of Mr. Jerome's *The Third Floor Back*, where God appears, not merely as an influence on the lives of men, but as a man, sitting at their table and sharing their talk, forbids such an hypothesis; and thirdly, that if Mr. Redford holds this view, he is convicted of opening the drama to horrible mockery of life and sensual trifling with it, and closing it to those close questionings of its purpose which constitutes the main theme of all serious playwrights from Æschylus to Ibsen. That Mr. Shaw could have consented to the omission of the passage we have quoted was out of the question. It is vital. The entire play turns on it. For when the woman comes into court and tells her story, it is seen that the leaven which works in Blanco's mind has leavened the lump; that the prostitute who is for swearing away his life cannot speak, that the ferocious jury will not convict, and the unjust judge will not sentence.

Mr. Shaw had, therefore, to fight for his play, and the Censor has to come into the open and face the music; to reveal his theory of the British drama, and illustrate his continual practice of it; which is to warn off the artist and the preacher, and to clear the path for the scoffer and the clown.

THE SHEWING-UP OF BLANCO POSNET

STATEMENT BY THE DIRECTORS

On Sunday night the following explanation was issued on behalf of the Abbey Theatre Company:

The statement communicated to certain of Saturday's papers makes the following explanation necessary:

During the last week we have been vehemently urged to withdraw Mr. Shaw's play, which had already been advertised and rehearsed, and have refused to do so. We would have listened with attention to any substantial argument; but we found, as we were referred from one well-meaning personage to another, that no one would say the play was hurtful to man, woman or child. Each said that someone else had thought so, or might think so. We were told that Mr. Redford had objected, that the Lord Chamberlain had objected, and that, if produced, it would certainly offend excited officials in London, and might offend officials in Dublin, or the law officers of the Crown, or the Lord Lieutenant, or Dublin society, or Archbishop Walsh, or the Church of Ireland, or "rowdies up for the Horse Show," or newspaper editors, or the King.

In these bewilderments and shadowy opinions there was nothing to change our conviction (which is also that of the leading weekly paper of the Lord Lieutenant's own party), that so far from containing offence for any sincere and honest mind, Mr. Shaw's play is a high and weighty argument upon the working of the Spirit of God in man's heart, or to show that it is not a befitting thing for us to set upon our stage the work of an Irishman, who is also the most famous of living dramatists, after that work had been silenced in London by what we believe an unjust decision.

One thing, however, is plain enough, an issue that swallows up all else, and makes the merit of Mr. Shaw's play a secondary thing. If our patent is in danger, it is because the decisions of the English Censor are being brought into Ireland, and because the Lord Lieutenant is about to revive on what we consider a frivolous pretext, a right not exercised for 150 years, to forbid, at the Lord Chamberlain's pleasure, any play produced in any

Dublin theatre, all these theatres holding their patents from him.

We are not concerned with the question of the English censorship, now being fought out in London, but we are very certain that the conditions of the two countries are different, and that we must not, by accepting the English Censor's ruling, give away anything of the liberty of the Irish theatre of the future. Neither can we accept, without protest, the revival of the Lord Lieutenant's claim at the bidding of the Censor or otherwise. The Lord Lieutenant is definitely a political personage holding office from the party in power, and what would sooner or later grow into a political censorship cannot be lightly accepted.

W. B. YEATS, *Managing Director.*
A. GREGORY, *Director and Patentee.*

ABBEY THEATRE, *August 22nd, 1909.*

The Managing Director of the Abbey Theatre has received a letter from Mr. Bernard Shaw, dated August 22nd, which contains the following passage:

"To-day the papers have arrived . . . You can make a further statement to the Press, that since the last statement Lady Gregory has written to me pointing out that a certain speech was open to misconstruction, and that I immediately re-wrote it much more strongly and clearly; consequently the play will now be given exactly as by the author, without concessions of any kind to the attacks that have been made upon it, except that to oblige the Lord Lieutenant, I have consented to withdraw the word 'immoral' as applied to the relations between a woman of bad character and her accomplices. In doing so I wish it to be stated that I still regard these relations as not only immoral but vicious; nevertheless, as the English Censorship apparently regards them as delightful and exemplary, and the Lord Lieutenant does not wish to be understood as contradicting the English Censorship, I am quite content to leave the relations to the unprompted judgment of the Irish people. Also, I have consented to withdraw the words, 'Dearly beloved brethren,' as the Castle fears that they may shock the nation. For the rest, I can assure the Lord Lieutenant that there is nothing in the other passages objected to by English Censorship that might not have been written by the Catholic Archbishop of Dublin, and that in point of consideration for the religious beliefs of the Irish people, the play compares very favourably indeed with the Coronation Oath."

The Irish Times, Monday, August 23, 1909

MR. SHAW'S PLAY.
PIECE NOT TO BE WITHDRAWN.
LORD LIEUTENANT'S AUTHORITY.

A meeting of the directors of the Abbey Theatre was held on Saturday afternoon last for the purpose of considering what action should be taken with regard to the communication received by them from the Lord Lieutenant touching the production of Mr. G. B. Shaw's play, "The Shewing-up of Blanco Posnet."

The meeting was conducted in private, and at its conclusion a communication was made to the Press, which stated:—

If our patent is in danger it is because the English Censorship is being extended to Ireland, or because the Lord Lieutenant is about to revive, on what we consider frivolous pretext, a right not exercised for 150 years, to forbid at his pleasure any play produced in any Dublin theatre, all these theatres holding their patent from him.

We are not concerned with the question of the English Censorship, but we are very certain that the conditions of the two countries are different, and that we must not by accepting the English Censor's ruling give away anything of the liberty of the Irish Theatre of the future. Neither can we accept without protest the exercise of the Lord Lieutenant's claim at the bidding of the Censor or otherwise. The Lord Lieutenant is definitely a political personage, holding office from the party in power, and what would sooner or later, grow into a political censorship cannot be lightly accepted.

We have ourselves, considered the special circumstances of Ireland, cut out some passages which we thought might give offence at a hasty hearing, but these are not the passages because of which the English Censor refused his licence.

W. B. YEATS, *Managing Director.*
A. GREGORY, *Director and Patentee.*

LETTER FROM W. G. BERNARD SHAW TO LADY GREGORY AFTER THE PRODUCTION OF "BLANCO POSNET"

DEAR LADY GREGORY:

Now that the production of *Blanco Posnet* has revealed the

character of the play to the public, it may be as well to clear up some of the points raised by the action of the Castle in the matter.

By the Castle, I do not mean the Lord Lieutenant. He was in Scotland when the trouble began. Nor do I mean the higher officials and law advisers. I conclude that they also were either in Scotland, or preoccupied by the Horse Show, or taking their August holiday in some form. As a matter of fact the friction ceased when the Lord Lieutenant returned. But in the meantime the deputies left to attend to the business of the Castle found themselves confronted with a matter which required tactful handling and careful going. They did their best; but they broke down rather badly in point of law, in point of diplomatic etiquette, and in point of common knowledge.

First, they commited the indiscretion of practically conspiring with an English official who has no jurisdiction in Ireland in an attempt to intimidate an Irish theatre.

Second, they assumed that this official acts as the agent of the King, whereas, as Sir Harry Poland established in a recent public controversy on the subject, his powers are given him absolutely by Act of Parliament (1843). If the King were to write a play, this official could forbid its performance, and probably would if it were a serious play and were submitted without the author's name, or with mine.

Third, they assumed that the Lord Lieutenant is the servant of the King. He is nothing of the sort. He is the Viceroy: that is, he *is* the King in the absence of Edward VII. To suggest that he is bound to adopt the views of a St. James's Palace official as to what is proper to be performed in an Irish theatre is as gross a solecism as it would be to inform the King that he must not visit Marienbad because some Castle official does not consider Austria a sufficiently Protestant country to be a fit residence for an English monarch.

Fourth, they referred to the Select Committee which is now investigating the Censorship in London whilst neglecting to inform themselves of its purpose. The Committee was appointed because the operation of the Censorship had become so scandalous that the Government could not resist the demand for an inquiry. At its very first sitting it had to turn the public and press out of the room and close its doors to discuss the story of a play licensed by the official who barred *Blanco Posnet*; and after this experience it actually ruled out all particulars of licensed plays as unfit for public discussion. With the significant exception of Mr. George Edwards, no witness yet examined, even among those who have most strongly supported the Censorship as an institution, has defended the way in which it is now exercised. The case which brought the whole matter to a head was the barring of this very play of mine, *The Shewing up of Blanco Posnet*. All this is common knowledge. Yet the Castle, assuming that I, and not the Censorship, am the defendant in the trial now proceeding in London, treated me, until the Lord Lieutenant's return, as if I were a notoriously convicted offender. This, I must say, is not like old times in Ireland. Had I been a Catholic, a Sinn Feiner, a Land Leaguer, a tenant farmer, a labourer, or anything that from the Castle point of view is congenitally wicked and coercible, I should have been prepared for it; but if the Protestant landed gentry, of which I claim to be a perfectly correct member, even to the final grace of absenteeism, is to be treated in this way by the Castle, then English rule must indeed be going to the dogs. Of my position of a representative of literature I am far too modest a man to speak; but it was the business of the Castle to know it and respect it; and the Castle did neither.

Fifth, they reported that my publishers had refused to supply a copy of the play for the use of the Lord Lieutenant, leaving it to be inferred that this was done by my instructions as a deliberate act of discourtesy. Now no doubt my publishers were unable to supply a copy, because, as it happened, the book was not published, and could not be published until the day of the performance without forfeiting my American copyright, which is of considerable value. Private copies only were available; but if the holiday deputies of the Castle think that the Lord Lieutenant found the slightest difficulty in obtaining such copies, I can only pity their total failure to appreciate either his private influence or his public importance.

Sixth, they claimed that Sir Herbert Beerbohm Tree, who highly values good understanding with the Dublin public, had condemned the play. What are the facts? Sir Herbert, being asked by the Select Committee whether he did not think that my play would shock religious feeling, replied point-blank, "No, it would heighten religious feeling." He announced the play for production at his theatre; the Censorship forced him to withdraw it; and the King instantly shewed his opinion of the Censorship by making Sir Herbert a Knight. But it also happened that Sir Herbert, who is a wit, and knows the weight of the Censor's brain to half a scruple, said with a chuckle when he came upon the phrase "immoral relations" in the play, "They won't pass that." And they did not pass it. That the deputy officials should have overlooked Sir Herbert's serious testimony to the religious propriety of the play, and harped on his little jest at the Censor's expense as if it were at my expense, is a fresh proof of the danger of transacting important business at the Castle when all the responsible officials are away bathing.

On one point, however, the Castle followed the established Castle tradition. It interpreted the patent (erroneously) as limiting the theatre to Irish plays. Now the public is at last in possession of the fact that the real protagonist in my play who does not appear in person on the stage at all, is God. In my youth the Castle view was that God is essentially Protestant and English; and as the Castle never changes its views, it is bound to regard the divine protagonist as anti-Irish and consequently outside the terms of the patent. Whether it will succeed in persuading the Lord Lieutenant to withdraw the patent on that ground will probably depend not only on His Excellency's theological views, but on his private opinion of the wisdom with which the Castle behaves in his absence. The Theatre thought the risk worth while taking; and I agreed with them. At all events Miss Horniman will have no difficulty in insuring the patent at an extremely reasonable rate.

In conclusion, may I say that from the moment when the Castle made its first blunder I never had any doubt of the result, and that I kept away from Dublin, in order that our national theatre might have the entire credit of handling and producing a new play without assistance from the author or from any other person trained in the English theatres. Nobody who has not lived, as I have to live, in London, can possibly understand the impression the Irish players made there this year, or appreciate the artistic value of their performances, their spirit, and their methods. It has been suggested that I placed *Blanco Posnet* at their disposal only because it was, as an unlicensed play, the refuse of the English market. As a matter of fact there was no such Hobson's choice in the matter. I offered a licensed play as an alternative, and am all the more indebted to Lady Gregory and Mr. Yeats for not choosing it. Besides, Ireland is really not so negligible from the commercial-theatrical point of view as some of our more despondent patriots seem to suppose. Of the fifteen countries outside Britain in which my plays are performed, my own is by no means the least lucrative; and even if it were, I should not accept its money value as a measure of its importance.

G. BERNARD SHAW.

PARKNASILLA,
27 August, 1909.

APPENDIX IV

"THE PLAYBOY IN AMERICA"

(*Note to page 102*)

From *The Gaelic American,* Oct. 14, 1911

IRISHMEN WILL STAMP OUT THE "PLAYBOY"

October 14, 1911:—"Resolved—That we, the United Irish-American Societies of New York, make every reasonable effort, through a committee, to induce those responsible for the presentation of *The Playboy* to withdraw it, and failing in this we pledge ourselves to drive the vile thing from the stage, as we drove *McFadden's Row of Flats* and the abomination produced by the Russell Brothers, and we ask the aid in this work of every decent Irish man and woman, and of the Catholic Church, whose doctrines and devotional practices are held up to scorn and ridicule in Synge's monstrosity."

From *The Gaelic American*, October 28, 1911

THE "PLAYBOY" MUST BE SUPPRESSED

William Butler Yeats is at it again, this time in the Philadelphia *Record*. The Irish players who are seeking to force the Stage Irishman on us again, in worse form than ever, are to try their fortunes in Philadelphia, and the advance notice of their coming takes the form of "special correspondence" from Boston, but the "fine Italian hand" of Mr. Yeats is visible all through it. He is by long odds the finest press agent who ever struck the United States, and if the plays he puffs were only equal to his gorgeous descriptions they would be all masterpieces.

Of course, he devotes his attention largely to J. M. Synge and his monstrosity, "The Playboy of the Western World," which is the greatest thing since Shakespeare, if, indeed, it does not knock Shakespeare "into a cocked hat." If "The Playboy" were only rewritten by Mr. Yeats it would come up to the expectations created by the reading of his description of it. He reads into it new meanings which the ordinary man cannot find, and attributes to the author motives which no man but Mr. Yeats can discover a trace of. As he expurgated the original text before producing the play in Boston, we may expect later on to find the whole thing revised and amended so as to come up to Mr. Yeats's imaginings. He knew what Synge meant better than Synge himself and he is the only man who can do the job thoroughly.

At his present rate of progress we may expect to find some future Ignatius Donnelly proving from cryptic expressions in "The Playboy" that William Butler Yeats was the real author, as Donnelly proved that Bacon was the master mind that wrote Shakespeare's plays. The same powerfully imaginative style of reasoning which Donnelly brought to bear on his life work characterises all of Yeats's interpretations of Synge. And he also brings his fervid imagination to bear on Synge's critics. He put words in their mouths which they have never used, answers objections they do not make and has no difficulty in knocking down his own men of straw. They are all "ignorant," "stupid," "out of touch with Ireland," and incapable of understanding "art," so Mr. Yeats has to supply them with arguments which he can answer, that he may not be put to the trouble of dealing with the hard, sordid, brutal facts which they cite.

The whole purpose revealed by Mr. Yeats's voluminous disquisitions on "The Playboy" is that it is to be stuffed down the throats of the Irish in America. A brutal misrepresentation of the Irish race, the men all drunken sots of a lower type than can be found in the slums of London, and the women brazen strumpets who would put Indian squaws to shame, is to be put on the American stage, in spite of a universal Irish protest, as a vindication of "the freedom of the theatre." And Lady Gregory joins him in an article in *Collier's*—milder in tone, but still a defence of the vile "Playboy" and repeating the same silly yarn that only "about forty" Dublin people went to the Abbey Theatre to protest against its production.

So that Lady Gregory joins Mr. Yeats in a challenge to the Irish people of the United States and a denial of the right of societies organised for the protection of Irish interests to interfere or to protest. The challenge will be taken up. It is not now a mere question of "The Playboy." The company which insists on presenting that atrocity insults the whole Irish race and should be boycotted by every decent Irish man and woman in the cities where they go. They should remain away from the other plays and take the necessary steps to suppress "The Playboy," no matter what the cost. Mr. Yeats, Lady Gregory and the players themselves must be taught the lesson that the Irish in America cannot be insulted with impunity. We are perfectly able to protect ourselves and to punish our enemies, even when they masquerade as friends. "The Playboy" must be suppressed, and it will be suppressed.

(*Note to page 111*)

From The New York *Times*

November 28, 1911:—When Christopher Mahon said: "I killed my father a week and a half ago for the likes of that," instantly voices began to call from all over the theatre:

"Shame! Shame!"

A potato swept through the air from the gallery and smashed against the wings. Then came a shower of vegetables that rattled against the scenery and made the actors duck their heads and fly behind the stage setting for shelter.

A potato struck Miss Magee, and she, Irish like, drew herself up and glared defiance. Men were rising in the gallery and balcony and crying out to stop the performance. In the orchestra several men stood up and shook their fists.

"Go on with the play," came an order from the stage manager, and the players took their places and began again to speak their lines.

The tumult broke out more violently than before, and more vegetables came sailing through the air and rolled about the stage. Then began the fall of soft cubes that broke as they hit the stage. A first these filled the men and women in the audience and on the stage with fear, for only the disturbers knew what they were.

Soon all knew. They were capsules filled with asafœtida, and their odour were suffocating and most revolting.

One of the theatre employees had run to the street to ask for police protection at the outset of the disturbance, but the response was so slow that the ushers and the doortenders raced up the stairs and threw themselves into a knot of men who were standing and yelling "Shame!"

(*Note to page 113*)

From The New York *Sun*

Wednesday, November 29, 1911:—Col. Theodore Roosevelt, who had been entertained at dinner prior to the play by Lady Gregory, the author-producer of many of the Irish plays, and Chief Magistrate McAdoo sat with Lady Gregory in one of the lower tier boxes. Col. Roosevelt was there representing the *Outlook,* for he said that if he had any ideas on the subject of the morals and merits of Synge's play he would write them in Dr. Abbott's paper, and Magistrate McAdoo was there for Mayor Gaynor to stop the play if he saw anything contrary to the public morals in it. Mr. McAdoo said that his task was a light one and Col. Roosevelt did not have to say anything. He just applauded.

When Col. Roosevelt appeared on a side aisle escorting Lady Gregory to a seat in the box there was a patter of hand clapping and the Colonel gallantly insisted that Lady Gregory should stand and receive the applause.

"He's here because he smells a fight," said some one in a whisper that rebounded from the acoustic board overhead and was audible all over the house.

When Magistrate McAdoo arrived somebody asked him if he were serving in an official capacity, to which he replied that the Mayor had asked him to drop in and see the play which had so roused the wrath of reputed Irishmen on the night before. He had orders, McAdoo said, to squash it the minute that he should see or hear anything that might be considered to have tobogganed over the line of discretion. But Mr. McAdoo said that he thought he would understand in a fair spirit, withal, the satire and irony of the play, if there was such, and he did not intend to be a martinet. The players graciously handed him out the prompt book between acts to see for himself that the line about "shifts" which had raised a storm of protest in Dublin as being indelicate had been deleted.

Nothing happened during the playing of the little curtain-raiser, *The Gaol Gate,* Lady Gregory's grim little tragedy of suffering Ireland, except that near the end of the single act in the playlet people in the gallery began a noisy warming up on their coughs and sneezes. Some of the plain-clothes men there began to amble around back of the aisles, and they laid their eyes on one individual with a thick neck who seemed about to pull something out from under his coat. Him they landed just as a quick curtain fell on the act and without ado they ousted him.

The citizen began to protest loudly that he was wedged in his seat and could not stir, but two of the strong arms persuaded him that he might as well unwedge himself before something happened. The little interlude was not sufficiently stirring even to attract the notice of those in the balcony and orchestra below.

Everybody believed that the trouble was all past with the second act, but the third and last was the noisiest of the three.

It appeared that, failing to find any single line to which they could take exception, those who had come to protest against what they conceived to be the libelling of the Irish race were ready to take it out in one long spell of hissing.

The cue was given when the drunken Michael James, the inn keeper, came on the stage to unite with a maudlin blessing the lovers, Christopher and Margaret.

As in the second act the seat of disturbance was in the balcony and thither six plain-clothes men were hastened. Three heads were together and one man was beating time with his hand while they took relays in hissing. The plain-clothes men descended and the three were yanked from their seats without benefit of explanation.

"But we're Englishmen," said one of them, "and we take exception to the line, 'Khaki clad cut-throats,' meaning of course the English constabulary."

"And don't call me an Irishman," said the third, while he adjusted his neck gingerly in the collar that had been tightened by the cop's grip. "I'm a Jew and I was born in St. Joe, Missoury, and I think this play's rotten, just on general principles. And if I think so I've got a right to show it. The law holds that anybody has got as good a right to show displeasure at a play as pleasure and I saw my lawyer before I came here, and——"

LETTER FROM MR. JOHN QUINN

From *The Irish Times*, January 31, 1912

TO THE EDITOR

DEAR SIR: Now that the Irish players have been to New York and their work seen and judged, the readers of your paper may be interested in the publication of one or two facts in connection with their visit. For some time before the company came to New York there had been threats of an organised attempt by a small coterie of Irishmen to prevent the performance of Synge's *Playboy*. It was difficult for many people in New York who are interested in the drama and art to take these rumours seriously. The attempt to prevent the New York public from hearing the work of these Irish players of course failed. There was an organised attempt by perhaps a hundred or a hundred and fifty Irishmen on the first night *The Playboy* was given here to prevent the performance by hissing and booing, and by throwing potatoes and other objects at the actors, and red pepper and asafœtida among the audience. The disturbers were ejected from the theatre by the police. All the great metropolitan papers, morning and evening, condemned this organised disturbance. The second night, some six or seven disturbers were put out of the theatre by the police, and that was the end of the long-threatened attempt to break up the performance of these plays. The issue was not between the plays and the players and the disturbers, but between the New York public and the disturbers. This fight over Synge was of vast importance for us as a city. One night settled that question and settled it conclusively.

I have seen in some of the daily and one of the weekly Irish papers a statement to the effect that "*The Playboy* was hooted from the stage . . . after the worst riot ever witnessed in a New York playhouse." The statement that it was "hooted from the stage" is of course utterly false. The greatest disorder occurred during the first act. A few minutes after the curtain fell at the end of the first act it was raised again and the statement was made by a member of the company that the act would be given entirely over again. This announcement was greeted with cheers and applause from the great majority of the audience, who indignantly disapproved the attempt of the disturbers to prevent the performance. The play was not "hooted from the stage."

The attempt to prevent by force the hearing of the play having so signally failed, a committee waited upon the Mayor of New York City the next day and demanded the suppression of the plays. The Mayor requested Chief Judge McAdoo of the Court of Special Sessions to attend the play as his representative and report to him. Judge McAdoo is an Irishman, born in Ireland, and has had a distinguished public career as member of Congress, Assistant Secretary of the Navy, and Police Commissioner of New York City, and he is now Chief Judge of the Court of Special Sessions. Judge McAdoo attended the play and made a report to the Mayor completely rejecting the charges that had been made against the morals and ethics of the play.

Both attempts to prevent the performance of the play, the first by force and the second by appeal to the authorities, having completely failed, the work of distorting in the Irish papers what actually took place then began.

Among other things it has been stated that the Abbey Theatre company was not a success in New York. On the contrary the success of the company has been beyond anything in my personal experience. The verdict of critical and artistic New York in favour of the work of the Irish Theatre has been emphatic. The pick of the intellectual and artistic public crowded the theatre during the weeks of the company's performances here and admired and enjoyed their work. In fact intelligent New Yorkers are yet wondering what was the real cause of the attempt to prevent the hearing of the plays. This is one of the mysteries of this winter in New York. I am proud, as a citizen of New York, that New York's verdict of approval was so swift and decisive, and I am proud of New York's quick recognition of the excellence of the new Irish school of drama and acting. As a man of Irish blood, my chief regret is that organised prejudice and prejudgment should have prevented these players from getting that welcome from a section of their own countrymen that I feel sure they will secure in future years. This prejudice was created and the prejudgment was largely caused by the publication of detached sentences and quotations from the plays, while ignoring the art of the actors and the humour and poetry and imaginative beauty of the plays, beauties which, as Sir Philip Sidney would say, "who knoweth not to be flowers of poetry did never walk into Apollo's garden."

Not only have the New York daily papers devoted columns to the work of this company throughout their stay, giving elaborate reviews of their work and long interviews with Lady Gregory and others, but many magazines have had articles on the subject of the plays and writers and on the Irish dramatic movement generally, among others the *Yale Review*, the *Harvard Monthly*, *Collier's Weekly*, the *Nation* (two notices), the *Dramatic Mirror* (five notices), the *Metropolitan Magazine*, *Munsey's Magazine*, the *Craftsman*, *Life*, *Harper's Weekly* (containing repeated notices), the *Outlook*, the *Bookman*, and others. Lady Gregory has contributed articles to the *Yale Review*, the *World of Today* and the *Delineator*, and has lectured at many places upon the Irish dramatic movement. The universities and colleges have shown the liveliest interest in the movement. The professors have lectured upon the plays and the plays have been studied in the college classes and the students have been advised to read them and see the players.

New York, January 8, 1912

"THE PLAYBOY" IN PHILADELPHIA

(*Note to page 119*)

From Philadelphia *North American*

January 17, 1912:—Determined to force their dramatic views on the public despite the arrests at Monday night's demonstration, several Irishmen last night vented their disapproval of *The Playboy of the Western World* which had its second production by Irish Players at the Adelphi Theatre.

They started by coughing, and they caused the player-folk to become slightly nervous. They next essayed hissing, and cries of "shame," and finally one of their number rose to his feet in a formal protest.

Plain-clothes men throughout the house quelled the slight disturbance, but at every opportunity another belligerent broke into unruly behaviour.

The disorder approached the dignity of serious rioting in the second and third acts of the piece, and at the last a man from Connemara rose in the body of the house, whipped a speech from his coat pocket, and proceeded to interrupt the players with a harangue against the morality of the play.

His philippics were short-lived. Sixteen cops in plain clothes reached him at the same time, and the red man from Connemara disappeared, while the play was being brought to a close....

Extra precautions were taken by the police to preserve order at last night's performance. The lights in the back of the house were not turned down at any time except the first few minutes of the one-act play *Kathleen ni Houlihan* which was the curtain-raiser to the longer piece.

Evidence that there would be trouble later in the evening was plain. Nearly the whole rear part of the house downstairs was filled with Irishmen.

As the little poetic vision of the author unrolled itself and the enthusiastic and for the most part cultured audience was steeping itself in the lyric beauty of the lines, two whole rows of the auditors were seized with a desire to cough or clear their throats. That caused a momentary lull in the play.

Up in the top gallery a thin but insistent ventriloquist piped, "This is rotten!" Cries of "Hush!" quieted the interrupter.

In the first act of *The Playboy* where the bulk of the disturbance occurred Monday night, no expression of opinion was made. But just as every one was settling down to enjoy the play, confident no more interruptions would occur, the trouble began.

One of the clan downstairs cried out his disapprobation. The lights were turned on full tilt, and policemen in plain clothes sprang up from every quarter of the house. Women left their seats in fear. A misguided youth near the orchestra threw his programme, doubled into a ball, at Miss Magee. He was promptly arrested.

The play was stopped for fully five minutes until all the men who showed signs of making trouble were evicted. A number of them laid low, however, and bobbed up now and again, whenever they wanted to. It kept the cops busy hustling them out of the doors. Superintendent Taylor and Captain of the Detectives Souder were in charge of the evictions and as each man was taken out two detectives were sent with him to City Hall where all were locked in.

The climax came when near the close of the last act the man from Connaught began his oratorical flights, drowning the speeches of the actors on the stage. All interest then centred upon the little knot of strugglers in the main aisle of the theatre and four more Irishmen were escorted, hatless and without overcoats, to the street.

As the men were arraigned at the City Hall, William A. Gray, counsel for the offenders at Monday night's riot, appeared for them. He said he had been sent by Joseph McLaughlin, a saloon-keeper and vice-president of the A. O. H., and he obtained a copy of the charges, with a view to getting the men out on bail. . . . Mr. Gray said he intended taking the matter before the courts and asking for an injunction to prohibit further productions of the play. He said his backer was Joseph McGarrity, a wholesale liquor dealer, in business at 144 South Third Street, who was one of those ejected from the theatre on Monday night.

Headed by Joseph McLaughlin, a delegation of seven prominent members of the Irish societies of the city waited on Mayor Blankenburg yesterday with a petition asking him to stop the production of John M. Synge's comedy *The Playboy of the Western World* on the ground that it is immoral.

The Mayor heard the comments of the Irishmen, but with

great good humour pointed out that inasmuch as he could find nothing objectionable in the play, he could not promise to stop the production.

He informed the delegation that he had previously made inquiries of the mayors of New York, Boston, and Providence, where the play had been shown, and had received answers which plainly indicated it was not necessary to stop the play.

(*Note to page 122*)

From Philadelphia *North American*

IRISH PLAYERS APPEAR IN A "COURT COMEDY"; NO DECISION

ANSWER CHARGE OF "IMMORALITY" BROUGHT BY A LIQUOR DEALER—"PLAYBOY" DEFENDED AND ATTACKED BY WITNESSES

January 20, 1912:—Second only in point of order, not in worth, was the unadvertised comedy participated in by the Irish Players yesterday afternoon, at a matinee performance held in Judge Carr's room in the quarter sessions court.

The public flocked to see, and stayed to witness, a most complete vindication of Synge's much discussed satirisation of the Irish character. The actors arrested for appearing in *The Playboy of the Western World* kept, however, in the background, while counsel on both sides engaged in lively tilts with two members of the clergy and the judge and other witnesses, furnishing the crowd with entertainment.

Eleven of the Irish Players who were held in $500 bail each by Magistrate Carey, at a hearing in his office earlier in the day, threw themselves upon the mercy of the quarter sessions court, to obtain a legal decision as to whether their play violated the McNichol act of 1911, which makes it a misdemeanor to present "lascivious, sacrilegious, obscene or indecent plays." The hearing before the court was brought about by a habeas corpus proceeding.

Although no decision was handed down after the argument, the attitude of the court was plainly shown, by the line of questions put to various witnesses. The testimony offered by Director of Public Safety Porter, who was called by the commonwealth, indicated that no fault could be found with the play. Judge Carr reserved decision, and adjourned court until Monday.

The defendants were represented by Charles Biddle, William

Redheffer, Jr., Howard H. Yocum, and John Quinn, of New York. Directly back of them, in the courtroom, sat Lady Gregory, Mrs. Henry La Barre Jayne, and W. W. Bradford, the latter representing Liebler & Co., managers of the Irish Players.

SURPRISE FOR PROSECUTOR

William A. Gray represented Joseph McGarrity, the liquor dealer, who has taken principal part in the prosecution of the actors. He was aided at times by Assistant District Attorney Fox on behalf of the commonwealth, although the latter's action in calling Director Porter to give testimony caused Mr. Gray both surprise and embarrassment, inasmuch as Mr. Porter said there was nothing in the piece to offend the most devout and reverent of women. He said he had attended the theatre with his wife and that neither of them was "shocked"; on the contrary, distinctly pleased.

Mr. Gray called Joseph McGarrity to the stand. In all seriousness and sincerity the witness testified that, in his opinion, *The Playboy* was a wicked piece and that he thought he had a perfect right to show his disapproval by protesting. He was questioned by Judge Carr as to the reason why he did not leave the theatre before he was ejected, if he thought the play was bad. He could give no adequate reply.

Mr. Gray then read passages from the book, declaring that it had been expurgated to make it presentable on the American stage. Frederick O'Donovan, one of the company, who takes the part of the Playboy, testified that productions of the play had been made in Dublin, Belfast, Cork, London, Oxford, Cambridge, Harrowgate, Boston, New York, New Haven and Providence without causing any public disturbance except in New York, and without any criminal prosecution being brought anywhere.

It was pointed out to the court by Mr. Gray that Pennsylvania is the only State having a statute preventing immoral or sacrilegious plays and that this was of so recent a date that neither side could argue that other plays of a much more objectionable nature than this had been permitted without hindrance.

Mr. Biddle and Mr. Quinn then summed up their arguments, in which the court concurred, openly. The New York lawyer paid a tribute to Philadelphia concerning the testimony of Director Porter. He said: "Philadelphia ought to be proud of the manhood displayed by such a witness. He stood before this court and testified that he and his wife had witnessed the performancc, and that neither was displeased by any exhibition of immorality.

"I say that any man who takes a lascivious meaning out of any of the lines of the play, or who declares that the piece is in any way improper, must have a depraved and an abnormal mind.

"I am ashamed that such men should come here and insult womanhood with their views. The American people are too good a judge of the Irish race to agree with them."

The court then took the case under advisement, reserving decision, counsel agreeing, under his advice, to allow the company to renew its bail bond of $5000.

(Note to page 130)

"THE PLAYBOY" IN CHICAGO

From Chicago *Daily Tribune*

January 30, 1913:—Mayor Harrison last night was directed by an order passed by the city council to prohibit the presentation in Chicago of *The Playboy of the Western World,* a play which has caused riots and organised protests in New York, Philadelphia, and Washington when presented by the Irish Players.

What action the mayor will take he was not prepared to indicate at the conclusion of the council session. It was stated during the debate on the subject that the mayor holds discretionary powers, and with the backing of the council can prevent the play if he chooses. But there is nothing mandatory in the order of the council, which asked the mayor to co-operate with Chief of Police McWeeny.

The Mayor said he would investigate the legal phases and also look into the character of the play before he decided upon steps to take.

MC INERNEY LEADS FIGHT

Ald. Michael McInerney led the movement for the council order.

"The play is a studied sarcasm on the Irish race," asserted Mr. McInerney, reading from a typewritten sheet; "it points no moral, and it teaches no lesson."

"Press agent!" shouted some one.

Chicago Ill 6

Feb 5th 1912

Lady Gregory — — — — — — ha ha,
Foster mother of the funny play boy,
this is to console you
from the dread that may fill
your grizzly heart after you
have read the contents of this
note. <u>your fate is sealed</u> never
again shall you gaze on the
barren hilltops of Connemara.
<u>your doom is sealed</u>
Irelands make believe friends,
cannot parade in sheeps
clothing under my scrutinising
eye I scent them to the
lair and then 'oi' 'oi' 'oi' DOWN.

P.S. You would be safe had you stayed in Ireland, but now too late. Irelands 10.000 police could not save your head

"No, I'm not the press agent," asserted the alderman. "This play pictures an Irishman a coward, something that never happened, and it attacks the Irishwoman. There are no Irishmen connected with the company in any way."

In reply to a question whether Lady Gregory was Irish, McInerney replied he had not met "the lady," and then added:

"There's a difference in being from Ireland and being Irish. There are lots of people in Ireland that aren't Irish. If you're born in a stable, that doesn't make you a horse."

Mr. Pringle stopped unanimous passage of the resolution.

"While I am not Irish," he said, "I believe Ald. McInerney knows what he is talking about; but I do not know enough about this subject to vote upon it at this time."

"Like Ald. Pringle," said Ald. Thomson, "I am not sufficiently informed, and I shall ask to be excused from voting."

GERMANS STRONG FOR IRISH

"Since some leading Irish organisations have chosen Germans to lead them," said Ald. Henry Utpatel, "I feel that that fact alone makes them a great race, and I shall vote with Ald. McInerney."

"Would you like to hear from the Poles?" asked Ald. Frank P. Danisch.

"That's all right," said McInerney, "if this play is presented there will come along a play insulting the Poles or some other race. It is not right for Chicago to let any race be insulted."

The order was then adopted, Ald. Pringle and Thomson voting in the negative.

(*Note to page 132*)

From Chicago *Record-Herald*

February 1, 1912:—Chicago's City Council erred in passing an order directing the mayor and the chief of police to stop the production *The Playboy of the Western World* according to an opinion sent to Mayor Harrison yesterday by William H. Sexton, the city's corporation counsel.

The brief was prepared by William Dillon, brother of John Dillon, the Irish nationalist leader, one of Mr. Sexton's assistants. It held that the counsel order was of no legal effect, although the mayor could suppress the play if he decided that it was immoral or against public policy. Mr. Dillon further declared that the mayor would not be legally right in prohibiting the production.

"I read three pages of the book," declared Mayor Harrison, "and instead of finding anything immoral I found that the whole thing was wonderfully stupid. I shall abide by the corporation's opinion."

Interview for New York *Evening Sun*

GEORGE BERNARD SHAW ON THE IRISH PLAYERS

"I presume, Mr. Shaw, you have heard the latest news of your *Blanco Posnet* in America with the Irish Players?" he was asked.

"No. Why? Has it failed?" Mr. Shaw answered.

"Quite the contrary," he was assured.

"Oh, in that case why should I hear about it?" he said. "Success is the usual thing with my plays; it is what I write them for. I only hear about them when something goes wrong."

"But are you not interested in the success of the Irish Players? Or was that a matter of course too?"

"By no means," Mr. Shaw answered. "I warned Lady Gregory that America was an extremely dangerous country to take a real Irish company to."

"But why? Surely America, with its immense Irish element ——"

"Rubbish! There are not half a dozen real Irishmen in America outside that company of actors!" he exclaimed. "You don't suppose that all these Murphys and Doolans and Donovans and Farrells and Caseys and O'Connells who call themselves by romantic names like the Clan-na-Gael and the like are Irishmen! You know the sort of people I mean. They call Ireland the Old Country. . . .

"Shall I tell you what they did in Dublin to the Irish Players? There was a very great Irish dramatic poet, who died young, named John Synge—a real Irish name—just the sort of name the Clan-na-Gael never think of.

"Well, John Synge wrote a wonderful play called *The Playboy of the Western World*, which is now a classic. This play was not about an Irish peculiarity, but about a universal weakness of mankind: the habit of admiring bold scoundrels. Most of the heroes of history are bold scoundrels, you will notice. English and American boys read stories about Charles Peace, the burglar, and Ned Kelly, the highwayman, and even about Teddy Roosevelt, the rough-rider. The Playboy is a young man who brags of having killed his father, and is made almost as great a hero as if he were an Italian general who had killed several thousand other people's fathers. Synge satirises this like another Swift, but with a joyousness and a wild wealth of poetic imagery that Swift never achieved. Well, sir, if you please, this silly Dublin Clan-na-Gael, or whatever it called itself, suddenly struck out the brilliant idea that to satirise the follies of humanity is to insult the Irish nation, because the Irish nation is, in fact, the human race and has no follies, and stands there pure and beautiful and saintly to be eternally oppressed by England and collected for by the Clan. There were just enough of them to fill the Abbey Street Theatre for a night or two to the exclusion of the real Irish people, who simply get sick when they hear this sort of balderdash talked about Ireland. Instead of listening to a great play by a great Irishman they bawled and whistled and sang 'God Save Ireland' (not without reason, by the way), and prevented themselves from hearing a word of the performance. . . ."

"Do you think there will be trouble with the Clan in New York?"

"I think there may be trouble anywhere where there are men who have lost touch with Ireland and still keep up the old bragging and posing. You must bear in mind that Ireland is now in full reaction against them. The stage Irishman of the nineteenth century, generous, drunken, thriftless, with a joke always on his lips and a sentimental tear always in his eye, was highly successful as a borrower of money from Englishmen—both in Old and New England—who indulged and despised him because he flattered their sense of superiority. But the real Irishman of to-day is so ashamed of him and so deeply repentant for having ever stooped to countenance and ape him in the darkest days of the Irish Players have been unable to find a single play by a young writer in which Ireland is not lashed for its follies. We no longer brazen out the shame of our subjection by idle boasting. Even in Dublin, that city of tedious and silly derision where men can do nothing but sneer, they no longer sneer at other nations. In a modern Irish play the hero doesn't sing that 'Ould Ireland' is his country and his name it is Molloy; he pours forth all his bitterness on it like the prophets of old.

"The last time I saw an Irish play in Dublin, the line on which the hero made his most effective exit was 'I hate Ireland.' Even in the plays of Lady Gregory, penetrated as they are by that intense love of Ireland which is unintelligible to the many drunken blackguards with Irish names who make their nationality an excuse for their vices and their worthlessness, there is no flattery of the Irish; she writes about the Irish as Molière wrote about the French, having a talent curiously like Molière.

"In the plays of Mr. Yeats you will find many Irish heroes, but nothing like 'the broth of a boy.' Now you can imagine the effect of all this on the American pseudo-Irish, who are still exploiting the old stage Ireland for all it is worth, and defiantly singing: 'Who fears to speak of '98?' under the very nose of the police—that is, the New York police, who are mostly Fenians. Their notion of patriotism is to listen jealously for the slightest hint that Ireland is not the home of every virtue and the martyr of every oppression, and thereupon to brawl and bully or to whine and protest, according to their popularity with the by-standers. When these people hear a little real Irish sentiment from the Irish Players they will not know where they are; they will think that the tour of the Irish company is an Orange conspiracy financed by Mr. Balfour."

"Have you seen what the Central Council of the Irish County Association of Greater Boston says about the Irish Players?"

"Yes; but please do not say I said so; it would make them insufferably conceited to know that their little literary effort had been read right through by me. You will observe that they begin by saying that they know their Ireland as children know their mother. Not a very happy bit of rhetoric that, because children never do know their mothers; they may idolise them or fear them, as the case may be, but they don't know them.

"But can you conceive a body of Englishmen or Frenchmen or Germans publishing such silly stuff about themselves or their country? If they said such a thing in Ireland they would be laughed out of the country. They declare that they are either Irish peasants or the sons of Irish peasants. What on earth does the son of an American emigrant know about Ireland? Fancy the emigrant himself, the man who has left Ireland to stew in its own juice, talking about feeling toward Ireland as children feel toward their mother. Of course a good many children do leave their mothers to starve; but I doubt if that was what they meant. No doubt they are peasants—a name, by the way, which they did not pick up in Ireland, where it is unknown—for they feel toward literature and art exactly as peasants do in all countries; that is, they regard them as departments of vice—of what policemen call gayety. . . .

"Good heavens!" exclaimed Bernard Shaw, waving a cutting

from the *Post* in his hand, "see how they trot out all the old rubbish. 'Noble and impulsive,' 'generous, harum-scarum, lovable characters,' 'generosity, wit, and triumphant true love'; these are the national characteristics they modestly claim as Irishmen who know Ireland as children know their mother. . . ."

"May I ask one more question, Mr. Shaw? Who is the greatest living Irishman?"

"Well, there are such a lot of them. Mr. Yeats could give you off-hand the names of six men, not including himself or myself, who may possibily turn out to be the greatest of us all; for Ireland since she purified her soul from the Clan-na-Gael nonsense, is producing serious men; not merely Irishmen, you understand—for an Irishman is only a parochial man after all—but men in the fullest international as well as national sense—the wide human sense."

"There is an impression in America, Mr. Shaw, that you regard yourself as the greatest man that ever lived."

"I dare say. I sometimes think so myself when the others are doing something exceptionally foolish. But I am only one of the first attempts of the new Ireland. She will do better—probably has done better already—though the product is not yet grown up enough to be interviewed. Good morning."

From *The Gaelic American*

WHAT THE IRISH COUNTY ASSOCIATIONS OF BOSTON SAID OF BERNARD SHAW

January 13, 1912:—The writer of such fool conceptions is as blind as an eight-hour-old puppy to the operation of all spiritual agencies in the life of man. Shaw's writings bear about the same relation to genuine literature as Bryan O'Lynn's extemporised timepiece, a scooped out turnip with a cricket within, does to the Greenwich Observatory. . . .

Shaw stumbles along the bogs, morasses, and sand dunes of literature, without a terminal, leading the benighted and lost wayfarers still farther astray. His unhappy possession of infinite egotism and his utter lack of common sense make of him a *rara avis* indeed, a cross between a peacock and a gander. . . .

In conclusion let us say before we again notice this Barnum of literature he must produce a clean bill of sanity, superscribed by some reputable alienist.

APPENDIX V

IN THE EYES OF OUR ENEMIES

From *America*

THE PLAYS OF THE "IRISH" PLAYERS

November 4, 1911:—The editors, like the patriots of the Boyle O'Reilly Club who fêted him in Boston, took Mr. Yeats at his own none too modest estimation. The United Irish Societies of this city denounced *The Playboy*, and an advanced Gaelic organ exposed its barbarities, but gave a clean bill of health to Mr. Yeats and the rest of his programme. Doubtless they also had not read the plays they approved. Well, we have read them. We found several among them more vile, more false, and far more dangerous than *The Playboy*, the 'bestial depravity' of which carries its own condemnation; and we deliberately pronounce them the most malignant travesty of Irish character and of all that is sacred in Catholic life that has come out of Ireland. The details, which are even more shocking than those of *The Playboy*, are too indecent for citation, but the persistent mendacity of the Yeats press agency's clever conspiracy of puff makes it needful to give our readers some notion of their character.

Of Synge's plays only *Riders to the Sea*, an unIrish adaptation to Connacht fishermen of Loti's *Pêcheurs d'Islande*, is fit for a decent audience. None but the most rabidly anti-Catholic, priest-hating bigots could enjoy *The Tinker's Wedding*.* The plot, which involves an Irish priest in companionship with the most degraded pagans and hinges on his love of gain, may not be even outlined by a self-respecting pen. The open lewdness and foul suggestiveness of the language is so revolting, the picture of the Irish priesthood, drawn by this parson's son, is so vile and insulting, and the mockery of the Mass and sacraments so blasphemous, that it is unthinkable how any man of healthy mind could father it or expect an audience to welcome it. This is the "typical Irish play" which the "Irish Players" have presented to a Boston audience.

* Neither *The Tinker's Wedding* nor *Where there is Nothing* has ever been given by our Company.—A. G.

The twain are kindred spirits; but in vileness of caricature and bitterness of anti-Catholic animus, even Synge must yield to Yeats. He also goes to tinkers for his types; and whereas Synge is content with three, and one priest, Yeats's *Where there is Nothing** glorifies a bevy of unbelieving tinkers and presents in contrast a dozen vulgar-spoken monks, who utter snatches of Latin in peasant brogue, while dancing frantically around the altar of God!

From *The Gaelic American*

YEATS'S ANTI-IRISH CAMPAIGN

November 18, 1911:—The anti-Irish players come to New York on Nov. 20th, and will appear first in some of the other plays. *The Playboy*, it is announced, will be given later, but the date has not yet been given out. The presentation of the monstrosity is a challenge to the Irish people of New York which will be taken up. There will be no parleying with theatre managers, or appeals to Lady Gregory's sense of decency. *The Playboy* much be squelched, as the stage Irishman was squelched, and a lesson taught to Mr. Yeats and his fellow-agents of England that they will remember while they live.

When a woman chooses to put herself in the company of male blackguards she has no right to appeal for respect for her sex.

MRS. MARY F. MC WHORTER, NATIONAL CHAIRMAN, L.A., A.O.H., IRISH HISTORY COMMITTEE, WRITING IN "THE NATIONAL HIBERNIAN," 1913

When it was announced about two months ago that the Abbey players would appear in repertory at the Fine Arts Theatre, in the city of Chicago, I made up my mind to witness all of the Abbey output, if possible, and see if they were as black as some painted them, and now I feel I have earned the right to qualify as a critic.

Having seen them all, I have this to say, that, with one or two exceptions, they are the sloppiest, and in most cases the vilest, and the most character-assassinating things, in the shape of plays it has ever been my misfortune to see. If, as has been often stated, the plays were written with the intention of belittling the Irish

* Neither *The Tinker's Wedding* nor *Where there is Nothing* has ever been given by our Company.—A. G.

race and the ideals and traditions of that race, the playwrights have succeeded as far as they intended, for the majority of the plays leave us nothing to our credit.

Thinking the matter over now, I cannot understand why *The Playboy* was picked out as the one most dangerous to our ideals. True, *The Playboy* is bad and very bad, but it is so glaringly so, it defeats its own ends by causing a revulsion of feeling.

There are other plays in the collection, however, that are apparently harmless; comedies that will cause you to laugh heartily, 't is true, but in the middle of the laugh you stop as if some one slapped you in the face. You begin to see, in place of the harmless joke, an insidious dig at something you hold sacred, or, if it is something you think is inspiring and patriotic, right in the midst of the thing that carries you away for a few moments on the wings of your lofty dreams and inspirations some monster of mockery will intrude his ugly face, and again the doubt, "Is it ridicule?" The certainty follows the doubt quickly, and you know it is ridicule, and immediately you are possessed of an insane desire to seek out Lady Gregory or some one else connected with the plays and then and there commit murder. That is, you will, if you have the welfare of your race at heart. Of course, if you are careless, or in some cases ignorant of the history of Ireland, or unfamiliar with the conditions there, you will accept the teaching of the Abbey school, and say to yourself, "The Irish are a lazy, crafty, miserly, insincere, irreligious lot after all."

In *The Rising of the Moon* our patriotism is attacked, not openly, of course, but by innuendo. We are made to appear everything but what we are. The policy of "Let well enough alone," is the keynote of this play, bringing out the avarice and selfishness that, according to the Abbey school, is a part of our nature.

It has often been said by our enemies that to have a priest in the family is to be considered very respectable by the average Irish Catholic family, and to bring about this desired result we are willing to sell our immortal souls. All this, not from motives of piety, but to be considered respectable.

In the play *Maurice Harte* this is brought out very forcibly. The family sacrifices everything to keep the candidate for the priesthood in college. The candidate has no vocation, but he is not consulted at all. When this poor, spineless creature sees the members of the family have set their hearts upon his becoming a priest he lets matters drift till the day set for his ordination, and then we behold him going mad. All very far-fetched.

We do admit that we like to have a priest in the family—what Irish mother but will cherish this hope in her bosom for at least one of her sons, or that one of the daughters of the house will become the spouse of Christ? Not, however, from such an unworthy motive as to be considered respectable, but from the pure motive of serving Almighty God.

The Workhouse Ward gives you nothing more edifying than the picture of two hateful old men snarling at each other in a truly disgusting manner.

Coats gives the picture of two seedy, down-at-elbows editors, who, while apparently the best of friends still are thinking unutterable things of each other.

The Building Fund is a disgusting display of avarice and insincerity. It strikes at the roots of all we hold sacred, and instead of being sincere, religious Catholics, the family is depicted as grasping, miserly creatures, who have no real love for the Church. There is not a redeeming feature in the whole play.

Family Failing, to my notion, is the worst of the output. *Family Failing*, of course, is idleness and all it carries with it. It is a strong witness in favor of that old fallacy, so often repeated by our enemies, that it was not the cruelty of English laws that sent us forth wanderers, but our lazy, idle, shiftless ways. The curtain goes down after the last act of this play on a disgusting spectacle of a lazy uncle snoring asleep on one side of the stage, and his lazy nephew occupying the other side, snoring also.

Kathleen ni Houlihan is beautiful, but every one knows Yeats wrote this before he became a pagan and went astray. His *Countess Cathleen*, written since then, is a weird thing.[3] One can see he strives after his early ideals, but it is a failure, for who can picture a sincere, devout Catholic lady calmly selling her soul to the devil, even though it is to purchase the souls of her poor dependents. And it is a rather dangerous lesson it teaches to the weak minded, when the angel comes to console the weeping peasantry after the countess dies. Supposedly in damnation, he tells them she is saved, because of the good intention she had in selling her soul to Old Nick.

The Magnanimous Lover presents the nasty problem play. Of course our humiliation would not be complete without the "problem play." And the words that this play puts in the mouth of the Irish peasant girl!

My blood boiled as I listened. What on earth do our Irish peasants know about the nasty problems so much affected by

[3] The first performance of *The Countess Cathleen* was in 1899; *Kathleen ni Houlihan* was written in 1902.

certain writers of to-day? American newspaper correspondents have commented from time to time on the chastity of the Irish peasants, and even the hostile ones have marvelled at the complete absence of immorality among them. But what is that to the Irish National (?) dramatists?

It is plain to be seen the self-styled Irish writers affect the present-day style in vogue among French writers. We have seen the result of all this as far as France is concerned. To-day that once proud nation is in a pitiable condition. And so the Abbey crowd would bring about the same undesirable conditions in Ireland if they could. By clever innuendo they would take all the splendid ideals and noble traditions away from the Irish and leave them with nothing high or holy to cling to. But the Abbey butchers will not succeed. They are reckoning without their host. The Irish character is too strong and too noble to be slain by such unworthy methods.

The plays taken as a whole have no literary merit. The backers of the plays preach about Art with a capital A, but they have no artistic merit, for art is truth, and the plays are not true. The great majority of the plays are made up of nothing more than a lot of "handy gab." You can hear the same any day, in any large city in Ireland, indulged in by a lot of "pot boys," or "corner boys," as they are sometimes called. (May I be permitted to use the American vulgarism, "can-rusher," to illustrate what is meant by "corner boy?") Nor is the conversation much more edifying than would be indulged in by those doubtful denizens. . . .

With this dangerous enemy striking at the very strands of our life and from such a dangerous source, the necessity is greater than ever for men and women of our beloved society to be earnest and honest in their efforts for the revival of Irish ideals. Brothers and Sisters everywhere, place a little history of Ireland in the hand of each little boy and little girl of the ancient race, and all the Lady Gregories in the world will not be able to destroy an atom of our splendid heritage.

APPENDIX VI

IN THE EYES OF OUR FRIENDS

From *The Outlook*, December 16th, 1911

THE IRISH THEATRE

BY THEODORE ROOSEVELT

In the Abbey Theatre Lady Gregory and those associated with her—and Americans should feel proud of the fact that an American was one of the first to give her encouragement and aid—have not only made an extraordinary contribution to the sum of Irish literary and artistic achievement, but have done more for the drama than has been accomplished in any other nation of recent years. England, Australia, South Africa, Hungary, and Germany are all now seeking to profit by this unique achievement. The Abbey Theatre is one of the healthiest signs of the revival of the ancient Irish spirit which has been so marked a feature of the world's progress during the present generation; and, like every healthy movement of the kind, it has been thoroughly national and has developed on its own lines, refusing merely to copy what has been outworn. It is especially noteworthy, and is a proof of the general Irish awakening, that this vigorous expression of Irish life, so honourable to the Irish people, should represent the combined work of so many different persons, and not that of only one person, whose activity might be merely sporadic and fortuitous. Incidentally Lady Gregory teaches a lesson to us Americans, if we only have the wit to learn it. The Irish plays are of such importance because they spring from the soil and deal with Irish things, the familiar home things which the writers really knew. They are not English or French; they are Irish. In exactly the same way, any work of the kind done here which is really worth doing, will be done by Americans who deal with the American life with which they are familiar; and the American who works abroad as a make-believe Englishman or Frenchman or German—or Irishman—will never add to the sum of first-class achievement. This will not lessen the broad human element in the work; it will increase it. These Irish plays appeal now to all mankind as they would never appeal if they had attempted to be flaccidly "cosmopolitan"; they are vital and human, and therefore appeal to all humanity, just because those who wrote them wrote from the heart about their own people and their own feelings, their own good and bad traits, their own vital national interests and traditions and history. Tolstoy wrote for mankind; but he wrote as a Russian about Russians, and if he had not done so he would have accomplished nothing. Our American writers, artists, dramatists, must all learn the same lesson until it becomes instinctive with them, and with the American public. The right feeling can be manifested in big things as well as in little, and it must become part of our inmost National life before we can add materially to the sum of world achievement. When that day comes, we shall understand why a huge ornate Italian villa or French château or make-believe castle, or, in short, any mere inappropriate copy of some building somewhere else, is a ridiculous feature in an American landscape, whereas many American farm-houses, and some American big houses, fit into the landscape and add to it; we shall use statues of such a typical American beast as the bison—which peculiarly lends itself to the purpose—to flank the approach to a building like the New York Library, instead of placing there, in the worst possible taste, a couple of lions which suggest a caricature of Trafalgar Square; we shall understand what a great artist like Saint-Gaudens did for our coinage, and why he gave to the head of the American Liberty the noble and decorative eagle plume head-dress of an American horse-Indian, instead of adopting, in servile style, the conventional and utterly inappropriate Phrygian cap.

AT the time of the Abbey Theatre's second visit to America, that great friend John Quinn wrote two articles in its defence. One appeared in the December 16, 1911 issue of *The Outlook* (which had Theodore Roosevelt as a contributing editor, and which first published Lady Gregory's play *McDonough's Wife*) and the other in the form of a letter to *The Irish Times*, who published it on January 31, 1912, and which is given in Appendix IV.

LADY GREGORY AND THE ABBEY THEATRE

BY JOHN QUINN

I was away from New York when the Abbey Theatre company of Dublin first came here, and I did not see them play until the end of their first week. In writing to a friend to explain who they were and what they had accomplished, I pointed out the perfect naturalness of their acting, the simplicity of their methods, their freedom from all distracting theatricalism and "stage business," their little resort to gesture, the beautiful rhythm of their speech, the absence of extensive and elaborate scenery and stage-settings, and the delightful suggestion of spontaneity given by their apparently deliberate throwing away of technical accomplishments in the strict sense of the word. I said that too many theatres have costly scenery and expensive properties to cover the poverty of art in the play or the players, just as poor paintings are sold by dealers in big glaring gold frames; and that their acting, in comparison with the acting of many theatres, had the same refined quality, not always apparent at the first glance, that old Chinese paintings are seen to have when placed alongside of modern paintings by Western artists.

As I observed the fine craftsmanship of the actors, without a single false note, each seeming to get into the very skin of the part that he impersonated, my thoughts went back some eight or nine years to what were the beginnings of this whole enterprise.

On a Sunday in August in 1902 I travelled with Jack B. Yeats, the artist, from Dublin, through Mullingar to Athenry, and thence by side-car to Killeeneen, in County Galway. On the way from Athenry to Killeeneen we passed little groups of bright-eyed men and women, always with a hearty laugh and a cheery word "for the American" and "a pleasant journey to you." They were on their way to a "Feis" (or festival) that was to be held that afternoon at Killeeneen, where the blind Connacht poet Raftery was buried. The Feis was held on rising ground in a field beside the road. There were perhaps a hundred side-cars and other vehicles and five or six hundred men and women at the meeting. On a raised platform sat Dr. Douglas Hyde, the President of the Gaelic League; Edward Martyn from Tillyra Castle; Lady Gregory from Coole; and others in charge of the Feis. W. B. Yeats, the poet, and his brother, Jack B. Yeats, the artist, and myself stood in the crowd and watched the spectacle.

Yeats told me that Lady Gregory had heard some time before that there was in the neighbourhood a book in Irish with songs of Raftery. She had found it in the possession of an old stone-cutter near Killeeneen. She got a loan of the book and gave it to Dr. Hyde, and he discovered in it seventeen of Raftery's songs. Douglas Hyde has since edited and translated a book of the songs and poems of Raftery, and he gives many interesting stories of the bard. He told me that Sunday that it was to the kindness of Lady Gregory that he owed many of his stories of Raftery. She had got, from a man who, when he was a boy, was present at Raftery's death, a full account of it. The poet was buried in the old churchyard of Killeeneen, among the people whom he knew. In August, 1900, there had been a great gathering there. Lady Gregory was the chief organiser of the gathering. She had raised a high stone over Raftery's grave with the name of the poet in Irish upon it. It was she who had thought of doing it, Dr. Hyde told me that Sunday afternoon, and it was upon her that the cost, or most of the cost, had fallen.

Prizes were given at the Feis for Irish singing, for the recitation of old poems, the telling of old stories all in Irish, and for traditional Irish dancing, flute-playing, and Irish music. A little girl from the Claddagh, the fishermen's quarter of Galway, took two or three of the prizes, and a week or ten days after, in going through the Claddagh, I saw her and spoke to her, and she remembered seeing me at the Feis. There was an old man there, and it took much persuasion to get him to mount the platform and tell his story. He hung back diffidently for a long time, but finally a lane was opened in the crowd and he got his courage up and marched bravely to the platform, and, gesticulating with a big blackthorn stick, made a great speech in Irish. Hyde translated parts of it for Yeats and me, and told us how the old man had boasted that he had been at Raftery's dying and had "held the candle to him."

Over the platform was a big green banner with letters in Irish on it and a picture of Raftery as an old man remembered, painted by a sympathetic artist of the neighbourhood. The Feis continued until some time after nightfall. The guests for Lady Gregory's place at Coole, some sixteen miles away, returned on two side-cars: Lady Gregory, W. B. Yeats, and myself on one; Douglas Hyde, Mrs. Hyde, and Jack Yeats on the other.

It was black night when the lights of Coole welcomed us. Lady Gregory got down from the car first, and, turning to me and extending her hand said, with a pleasant smile, "Welcome to Coole." I wish I could picture something of the charm that hangs around Coole, of its tangled woods, its stately trees, the lake, the winding paths, the two beautiful old gardens, and the view of the distant Burren hills. There seemed to be magic in the air, enchantment in the woods and the beauty of the place, and the best talk and stories I ever found anywhere. The great library was to me a delight, and Jack Yeats told me that Lady Gregory had made a catalogue of it herself. She seemed to me to have a strong sense of property, and took great pride in and had done her share in keeping up the fabled "Seven Woods of Coole," planting every year trees for the coming generation. And I remembered that Arthur Young in his "A Tour in Ireland" had referred to a visit that he made over a hundred years before to the Coole of that period, and had found the Gregory of that time walling and "improving his land with great spirit," and planting the trees which are now among the glories of the place.

Every summer for some years Yeats had spent several months at Coole. He is the best talker I have ever listened to, and he does love to talk. So long as he can amuse himself and interest others with good talk he will not write. Lady Gregory devoted herself to his work. With infinite tact and sympathy she has got the best out of him, and the world of letters owes it chiefly to her that in the last ten years Yeats has done so much creative work and has been able to devote himself so fully to the Irish theatre. At Coole he had leisure and delightful surroundings which in London he could not have. He was able there to dream out and plan out his poems and his plays. She threw herself into his plans for work, worked with him, worked from his dictation, copied out his rough drafts, arranged his manuscripts for him, read out to him in the evenings from the great books of the world at times when his eyesight was poor and he could not read at night, and stimulated his genius by her helpful understanding of all his plans and ideas.

One of the chief charms of my repeated visits to Coole lay in the stores of good talk and anecdotes by Yeats and Hyde, who were there at the time of each of my visits, and in my interest in the genius and personality of Yeats and Lady Gregory. During the whole time of our visit the sparkle and brilliancy of the conversation never failed. Lady Gregory's interest in the people about her was untiring. With a power of work that any man of letters might envy she had the faculty of laying aside her work and making all her guests enjoy to the full the pleasant side of life and the delights of social intercourse. Her enthusiasm was infectious, and those who came in contact with her—Yeats, Hyde, Synge, and the rest—became or were made her helpers and associates.

But with all Yeats's debt to her, she also owes much to him. He is the most disinterested of writers. I have known him to take infinite pains, make long journeys and give hours and days of his time to encouraging other writers, starting them on the right way and giving them unfailing help and assistance. He is incapable of praising bad work even though it be by a friend, and incapable of condemning good work even though it be by an enemy. He was Lady Gregory's severest critic, and she owes to him a big debt for encouragement, criticism, and help in the writing of her books and plays, and because he "taught her her trade." He is, above all things, the man of letters. His mind is one of the most subtle I have ever known. He delights in discussing art and philosophy, and will talk for hours and hours on politics, diplomacy, and international affairs. I remember how interested he became in a volume of Nietzsche that I had with me, and how in reading out from it he quickly pointed out the resemblance of some of Nietzsche's ideas to Blake.

One morning Lady Gregory, Dr. Hyde, and myself wandered through one of the beautiful old gardens. She named over the names of this, that, and the other flower until Hyde said that if she just wrote down the names there was matter for a sonnet ready for Yeats. Yeats was very happy there, and he had just finished a poem on "The Seven Woods of Coole," and he was so pleased with it that he kept murmuring it over and over again, and these lines from it have remained in my memory still:

"I have heard the pigeons of the Seven Woods
Make their faint thunder, and the garden bees
Hum in the lime tree flowers; and put away
The unavailing outcries and the old bitterness
That empty the heart. . . .
I am contented, for I know that Quiet
Wanders laughing and eating her wild heart
Among pigeons and bees."

Yeats, Hyde, and I used to sit up every night until one or two in the morning, talking, it seems to me, about everything and everybody under the sky of Ireland, but chiefly about the theatre of which Yeats's mind was full. These were wonderful nights, long nights filled with good talk, Yeats full of plans for the development of the theatre. The mornings were devoted to work, the afternoons to out-of-doors, and the evenings to the reading of scenarios for plays, the reading of short plays in English by Lady Gregory and in Irish by Hyde. Lady Gregory and Hyde read out to us from time to time their translations of Irish songs and ballads, in the beautiful English of her books and of Hyde's "Love Songs of Connacht." Yeats and Lady Gregory made a scenario of a play and Hyde spent three afternoons "putting the Irish on it." She has written how one morning she went for a long drive to the sea, leaving Hyde with a bundle of blank paper before him. When she returned in the evening, Dr. Hyde had finished the play and was out shooting wild duck. This play was "The Lost Saint." Dr. Hyde put the hymn in the play into Irish Rhyme the next day while he was watching for wild duck beside the marsh. He read out the play to us in the evening, translating it back into English as he went along, and Lady Gregory has written how "we were all left with a feeling as if some beautiful white blossom had suddenly fallen at our feet."

At that time I was more interested in Yeats's writing and lyrical poetry and in Hyde's Gaelic revival than I was in Yeats's plans for an Irish theatre. Yeats was more interested in the poetry that moves masses of people in a theatre and in the drama than in what suffices to make up a book of lyric poetry that might lie on a lady's or gentleman's drawing-room table. I told Hyde and Yeats that that reminded me of Montaigne's saying that he had deliberately put indecencies into his essays because he hated the idea of those essays lying on women's tables.

Lady Gregory was then at work on her two great books, "Cuchulain of Muirthemne" and "Gods and Fighting Men." In these two books she brought together for the first time and retold in the language of the people of the country about her, in the unspoiled Elizabethan English of her own neighbourhood, the great legends of Ireland. She did for the old Irish sagas what Malory did for the Knights of the Round Table, and fairly won the right to be known as the Irish Malory.

Another night I first heard the name of John M. Synge. Yeats told us how he had come upon Synge at a small hotel in Paris and persuaded him to come to Ireland, and of the wonderful book that he had written on the Aran Islands. Yeats and Lady Gregory had tried to have it published. I myself offered to pay the expense of making plates for it, but Yeats said that he wanted the book taken on its merits, even if Synge had to wait some years for a publisher.

Synge's debt to Yeats has not, I think, been fully appreciated. It was Yeats who persuaded him to drop the attempt to rival Arthur Symons as an interpreter of Continental literature to England, and to go back to Ireland and live among the people and write of the life that he knew best.

When Synge was writing his plays, poems, and essays he

came often to Coole. Other guests there were George Russell, the poet and writer, Douglas Hyde, "John Eglington," the brothers Fay, George Moore, and Bernard Shaw, and Lady Gregory's home really became a centre of the literary life of Ireland of the last ten years.

From this great old house, almost covered by creeping vines, with the most beautiful garden I ever saw, the house in which were stored up so many memories of statesmen, soldiers, authors, artists, and other distinguished people, with its great library, its pictures, statues, and souvenirs gathered from many lands, nestling in the soft climate of the west of Ireland, under the grey skies and surrounded by the brilliant greens and rich browns of west of Ireland landscape, or bathed in the purple glow of the air as the sun declined, I carried away two vivid impressions: first, the realisation of a unique literary friendship between the chatelaine and the poet Yeats; and, second, of the gentleness and energy of this woman, the stored-up richness of whose mind in the next eight or nine years was to pour forth essays, stories, farces, historical plays, and tragedies, and translations from Molière and Sudermann; and who has, at the cost of infinite time and pains, proved herself to be, with Yeats, the directing genius of the new Irish drama.

When I would come down to breakfast in the morning, I would be amazed to find that she had already done two hours of writing. Something of her initiative reappeared in her two nephews—the lamented Captain John Shawe Taylor, who brought together the Land Conference that did so much toward the peaceable and friendly settlement of the land question and the changing of land ownership in Ireland; and Sir Hugh Lane, who originated, endowed, and established the Dublin Gallery of Modern Painting, which is, according to the highest authorities, the best European gallery of modern art outside Paris.

The next year in Dublin I saw a rehearsal of "The Shadow of the Glen" and other plays in a little hall. The actors were young men and women who worked in the daytime, none of them at that time drawing any pay from the theatre. I must admit that I then supposed that this venture would go the way of its innumerable predecessors—endure for a few weeks and then vanish. But I was mistaken. I undervalued the tremendous energy, perseverance, and courage of its leaders, Lady Gregory, W. B. Yeats, and John M. Synge; for it has all through required great patience, and not merely courage but audacity in the face of detraction, false friends, discouragement, and croakings of disaster meeting them from all sides. At no time during these years did either Lady Gregory or Yeats receive a penny of profit from their work for this theatre. Douglas Hyde once told me that, apart from his lyric poetry, Yeats's greatest gift to Ireland was the drama. I should add that another gift of Yeats to Ireland was the introduction of the Irish drama of Lady Gregory and John M. Synge.

I first went there—two art centres that all Irishmen may be proud of, the Abbey Theatre and the Municipal Gallery of Modern Painting. Some little time ago Bernard Shaw, writing of Dublin, said that he had returned there and had found it just as sleepy as of old, with the same old flies still crawling over the same old cakes in the windows, except for two things, the Modern Art Gallery and the Abbey Theatre, which were the things showing an influx of new life.

In Dublin that year I spent several long evenings with Synge. He told me of his wanderings in Europe and of his fondness for the people of the west of Ireland and of the Aran Islands. Synge, like Yeats, was much interested in the problem of style, but in a different way. He knew the language of the Wicklow peasant and of the west of Ireland fisherman and of the Aran and Blasket Islanders. Synge came to his style in the same way that Lady Gregory came to hers, by his knowledge of and sympathy with the people who speak Elizabethan English in the west of Ireland, the English of King James's Bible. When Synge's "Playboy" was first produced in Dublin, it was hooted for a few nights by a few organised "patriots" who tried in vain to disprove the reputation that Irishmen are supposed to have of possessing a keen sense of humour. Synge was surprised, but not hurt or even annoyed, at the outburst. He was too much of an artist not to know that some people hate all beauty and that others attack strange beauty that they do not at first sight understand. His chief fear seemed to be lest the outcry against "The Playboy" might hurt the theatre or endanger the cause of his friends.

The first night that "The Playboy of the Western World" was given in New York it was preceded by "The Jail Gate," which is a mournful play; and when the merry row over "The Playboy" was at its height, I recalled the words of the Irish chieftain in Chesterton's "Ballad of the White Horse":

"His harp was carved and cunning,
His sword was prompt and sharp,
And he was gay when he held the sword,
Sad when he held the harp.

For the great Gaels of Ireland
  Are the men that God made mad,
For all their wars are merry,
  And all their songs are sad."

This little company of Irish players and their directors have answered the question that is being so often asked in London and New York—how to make the theatres a success and yet give nothing that is not good art. They have done this, it seems to me, by courage in keeping to the road they have chosen, by nationality in keeping to the narrow limits to which they bound themselves—"Works by Irish writers or on Irish subjects"—and by the deliberate simplicity of staging, by which expense is kept down and they are not driven to put on plays for the sake of profit only.

What lesson can America get from this example?

Mary Boyle O'Reilly in the Boston *Sunday Post*

October 8, 1911;—In two short weeks the Irish Players have done great and lasting service to every lover of Synge's Irish in Boston; a service long to be held in grateful memory, a creative force of other good to come. Very gravely and conscientiously, Lady Gregory and Mr. William Butler Yeats have trained their players to interpret to the children of Irish emigrants the brave and beautiful and touching memories which, through the ignorance of the second generation, have ceased to be cause for gratitude or pride.

Not this alone: by their fine art, the players have dealt a death blow to the coarse and stupid burlesque of the traditional stage Irishman, who has, for years, outraged every man and woman of Celtic ancestry by gorilla-like buffoonery and grotesque attempts at brogue.

. . . Boston owes Lady Gregory and Mr. Yeats and their company not only grateful thanks, but a very humble apology.

From *The Freeman's Journal*

October 26, 1912:—It is time the Dublin public pulled itself together and began to take a pride in its National Theatre, this theatre which has produced in a few years more than a hundred plays and a company of players recognised as true artists, not only by their fellow-countrymen, but by the critics of England and America. The Abbey Theatre has made it possible for a writer living in Ireland and writing on Irish subjects to win a position of equal dignity with his fellow-artist in London or Paris; it has made it possible for an Irish man or woman with acting ability to play in the plays of their fellow-countrymen, and to earn a decent living and win a position of equal respect with any English or Continental actor.

From New York *Journal*

December 18, 1911:—The hysterics and rowdyism that attended the opening of the Irish plays in New York having died away, listen to a few facts concerning the extremely interesting and valuable work of Lady Gregory and her associates, the Irish playwrights and actors.

Some of those entirely ignorant of that which they discussed thought that the Irish players were wilfully irreligious, and others equally ignorant thought that they were weakly lacking in Irish patriotism.

As a matter of fact, the Irish playwrights and actors . . . are thoroughly imbued with the Irish spirit and are trying as well as they can to present certain Irish conditions and characters as they are, utilising literature and the drama as mediums.

. . . It was thought by some good people who had not seen the plays that they were irreligious in character and showed lack of respect especially for the Catholic faith. But this is not true.

In the play called *Mixed Marriage* all the bigotry and religious stupidity is shown by the old Protestant father. The unselfishness, real patriotism, courage, and broad-minded humanity in this play are the possessions of the Catholics—as is, indeed, usually the case in Ireland.

It is interesting to observe how real merit wins and overcomes ignorant prejudice.

Many of the very men that hissed and hooted at the Irish plays on the first night without listening to them now attend the performances regularly.

Those that enjoy most thoroughly the wonderful wit and pathos of the Irish race, as shown in these plays, are those Irish men and women.

Sara Allgood, as the old patient wife and mother in *Mixed Marriage*, is a perfect picture of the womanhood that has created Ireland.

Lady Gregory and her friends have rendered a real service to this country and to Ireland by bringing the plays here.

Anonymous in Chicago *Daily Tribune*,

February, 1912

TO LADY GREGORY

Long be it e'er to its last anchorage
Thy oaken keel, O "Fighting Temeraire,"
Shall forth beyond the busy harbour fare.
Still mayest thou the battle royal wage
To show a people to itself; to gauge
The depth and quality peculiar there;
Of its humanity to catch the air
And croon its plaintiveness upon the stage.

Nay, great and simple seer of Erin's seers,
How we rejoice that thou wouldst not remain
Beside thy hearth, bemoaning useless years,
But hear'st with inner ear the rhythmic strain
Of Ireland's mystic overburdened heart
Nor didst refuse to play thy noble part!

APPENDIX VII

AMONG the items Lady Gregory folded into her copy of *Our Irish Theatre,* was the following letter to her publishers. It is of particular interest in that it shows how she set about writing the book and the difficulties it presented, as well as showing what editors are capable of doing.

Coole Park,
Gort, Co. Galway.
July 17, 1913

Dear Mr. Huntington,

You must think I am keeping the proofs a long time, but I have been working hard at them, and am a good deal worried over them. I have corrected many pages of proofs in my time, but have never had the same trouble. I think it must have been during Mr. Putnam's absence in Europe that they were given to some press corrector who has taken on himself not to make corrections in the ordinary sense, but to revise my style and that of my correspondents. I had found this a difficult book to write, being off my usual lines, and had found when I first started that I was making it too stiff and that it was difficult to avoid running into those journalistic phrases that are so easy to adopt because they are before one every day. Two or three times I tore up all I had written of it. Then I found that by writing it addressed to my grandson for his reading at some future time, and by using as largely as possible letters written to me and by me, I should give it a character of intimacy, I should make it an expression of personality. This it had seemed to be when it left my hands.

When the proofs came I was a little puzzled, I thought I had unconsciously dropped into journalism in the writing. Then I came to the word "evince," That I was sure is a word I have never used. I don't think I have heard it used, or read it except in the poets. I remember PUNCH making fun of a poem long ago written about Prince Alfred, because it said he went to sea "His courage to evince," and pointing out that he didn't go for any such reason but that a rhyme was wanted in every verse to "God bless our Sailor Prince." It is a respectable word enough, but a literary one, and it doesn't belong to my stable. So I looked back at the typed copy and found I hadn't written "evince" I had written "show."

Then I went on and I found it was not only my words that were changed. I found changes made in a letter of Sir Frederic Burton; in letters of Synge's I found such changes as "and contained" for "with"; "members of the day company" for "the day company" "provided" for "if"; besides transpositions; and in Mr. Yeats' letters such corrections as "in a battle like that of Ireland" instead of "in a battle like Ireland's"; "it cannot be improved upon" instead of "it cannot be bettered"; so I have the comfort of finding that I am not alone under this censorship.

In some cases the changes made alter the meaning. In telling of a player having undertaken a rehearsal and thrown it up later I took some trouble not to specify the player, and avoided saying it was a man or woman. Your Corrector assumes it is a man, and has altered the whole sentence to put this in. An anecdote is made lose its whole point by the alteration of "Brooklyn" to "New York." The change "the Fays" to "the players" in another place makes my meaning different from what I intended. And is it not unnecessary when I say I have received an anonymous letter to correct it to "an anonymous letter from an unknown correspondent"?

Now if only my narrative had been altered, I should have certainly been annoyed, but I might have fancied that annoyance came from vanity or the natural dislike to correction. But this is a graver case. A great part of the book contains letters written by me while the events I tell of were taking place; they tell of history in the making; they are fresher and more reliable than any narrative told in retrospect can be. They will be valued by those interested in the building of our theatre on that account. But the moment an impression is given that they have been touched up and doctored, that impression of truthfulness is lost. I felt when I tried to write a history of our troubles in America I was trying to make a case. I found when I collected and read the letters that I had not been making a case, I had simply been writing what took place from day to day, to my fellow worker Mr. Yeats and to my son, and this is the case also with the letters about Blanco Posnet. Now could any human being think that in these intimate letters written without any intention of printing them, or indeed anywhere at all, I should use such expressions as "acquired" for "got," "the role Kerrigan interpreted"; "the sentences he cited"; "he retained his role"; "with such excissions" (this spelled with two s's or perhaps I should say *sic*); "it exceeded this amount"; "he witnessed the entire production"; "I assumed" "located" "the presentation of the play is to be permitted"; "I am the recipient of"; there are many others . . . all changed from simple and familiar words.

Here is an instance. In the letters about Blanco Posnet written home and to Mr. Shaw I gave conversations. In them the words "he said" or "I said" are used too often. That is a sort of thing that is all right in a letter, but irritates by catching the eye too often in a printed page. Therefore it would have been quite right to point this out to me and I should have done what I have done now, dropped the words out altogether often enough to escape too much repetition. But instead of this, and with no query or mark or consultation with me at all, I find myself given as the author, (and much in the style of the novels of Mrs. Henry Wood) of these alternative words: "asserted"; "assumed"; "rejoined"; "added"; "I corrected him"; "made the statement"; "was my rejoinder"; and "he exclaimed" even where there was no "said" at all! "He again cautioned me"—where caution does not give the meaning.

I give the scenario I wrote for the "Workhouse." It interests students to know how a play they have seen came to be written. This shows one's first rough idea. I don't know what is gained and I know something is lost by the change in this of "sent for" to "summoned," of "beds next to each other" to "adjoining beds" or of the sentences of dialect in which the play is to be written into more conventional words, "they who have been" for "and they after being"; "even if he is bedridden" for "if he is bedridden itself"; "bring" for "take" and "replies" for "says."

Well, in whatever other words I ought to put it, that is my case. Of course it is impossible the book should appear with those bantlings in it, and of course the press correction of them does not come into my account. It is lucky the managers of the French picture exhibition at New York did not think of disarming criticism by sending round a paint pot and brush with which cubists and post impressionists could have been brought to one level and one style.

I hope to send with the next proofs my note on our last visit.

I have pinned in the couple of pages that had as it seems wrong numbers. They might as well have been printed in the galleys, as they are a section of a chapter; however, I have corrected the typed copy carefully, and if these corrections are kept to, I shall not require another proof.

Mr. John Quinn, 31 Nassau Street, N.Y., very kindly promised to read in proof the chapter called "The Playboy in America," and I will accept his judgment as final as to the naming of persons, or danger of libel. I don't quite see how libel comes into that paragraph about my having been asked to speak at Washington. I have left the query mark. Will you kindly ask Mr. Putnam to have those Playboy proofs given to Mr. Quinn as soon as convenient.

Yours etc.
A.G.

APPENDIX VIII

SOULS FOR GOLD!

A Pseudo-Celtic Drama in Dublin

"There soon will be no man or woman's soul
Unbargained for in five-score baronies."
Mr. W. B. Yates [sic] *on "Celtic Ireland."*

LONDON MDCCCXCIX

I.—FAITH FOR GOLD

To the Editor of THE FREEMAN'S JOURNAL.

DEAR SIR,

At the same time that I heard of Mr. W. B. Yeats's disparagement of Thomas Davis, I learned also that he was to endow the Celtic Literary Society with "a Celtic drama," called the "Countess Cathleen." Anxious to ascertain if so superior a poetical critic might not be an equally superior dramatic author, I purchased the "Countess Cathleen" in the volume in which it has so long lain unrepresented. In this "Celtic drama" I saw at once many reasons why it continues to lie unrepresented, but not a single reason why it should be called Celtic. Let me as briefly as possible deal with Mr. W. B. Yeats's production.

The general theme or ground-plan shows how the Catholic peasantry of an Irish district, being pressed by famine, hasten to sell their souls to the devil for the means of purchasing food! Out of all the mass of our national traditions it is precisely the baseness which is utterly alien to all our national traditions, the barter of Faith for Gold, which Mr. W. B. Yeats selects as the fundamental idea of his Celtic drama! I could understand such a theme being welcome at a souper meeting at Exeter Hall; but to propose it to the applause of an Irish Literary Association argues an appreciation of the Ireland of to-day as characteristic as the knowledge of Ireland in the past.

Within this general theme develop three particular themes or episodes whose connections or incoherencies are supposed to be dramatic, and, above all things, Celtic. First, there is the story of the eminently Irish and Celtic peasant, Shemus Rhua, who gains the profitable approval of the devil by "kicking the shrine" of the Blessed Virgin to pieces. Then there is the story of the demented female, Countess Cathleen, who exhibits her affection for the soul-selling and soup-buying Irish people by selling her own soul also to supply them with more gold and soup, and who is rewarded for her blasphemous apostacy by Mr. W. B. Yeats, dramatist and theologian, by being straightway transmigrated to the Heaven of Heavens, where, as a special inducement to all good little Irish girls to go and do likewise,

"Mary of the seven times wounded heart
Has kissed her on the lips!"

Thirdly, there is the story of the Minor Poet, Aleel, described as "a young bard," who maunders irrelevantly through the "drama," getting more and more daft with love for the demented heroine, till he finally remarks, on that young lady's final disappearance, that "the proud earth and plumy sea" (*sic*) must now also "fade out," inasmuch as she has departed—to be embraced by the Queen of Heaven for having denied God and gone to the devil!

In order to explain the moral of the whole remarkable composition, Mr. W. B. Yeats most thoughtfully catches—that is, he gets his Minor Poet to catch—"an angel," who most angelically expounds how God warmly approves of sin or crime when done with a good intention; or, as Mr. W. B. Yeats's "angel" puts it:

"The Light of Lights
Looks always on the motive, not the deed."

I remember a song that was popular in London twenty years ago, and related how a flighty Jack Tar, while amiably conforming to the polygamous usages of many strange lands, never really faltered in his virtuous allegiance to his derelict spouse at home; because—as the poetic predecessor of Mr. W. B. Yeats "angelically" added—

"Whatever he might do,
His heart, his heart was always true
To Poll."

Poll's faithless Jack evidently learned in the same school as Mr. W. B. Yeats's "angel" the saving creed of freedom of conduct combined with excellence of intention.

To investigate the countless "Celticisms" of detail which make up a "Celtic drama" of such a unique character would involve much time and space. Let it suffice to say, that Mr. W. B. Yeats's notion of what is Celtic is everywhere illustrated by his harpings on his pet "Celtic idea," that the Gaels of Erin have and had only the thinnest veneer of Christian religion and civilisation, and really reserve their deepest beliefs for demons, fairies, leprachauns, sowlths, thivishes, etc., whom he loves to describe in the stilted occultism of a Mrs. Besant or a Madame Blavatsky, and that "Catholic shrines," "Catholic priests" and Catholic prayers and places are little more than sport for the pranks of the devil's own.

I shall cite but two specimens out of this "Celtic Drama" at present, the one where the Celtic peasant, Shemus Rhua, kicks the shrine of the Blessed Virgin to pieces, and the one where the Demon, disguised as an Irish pig, hunts down and slays "Father John the Priest" while reading his breviary, and sticks his soul into his black bag. I crave the pardon of my readers, Catholic or Protestant, for offending their sight with such grotesque impiety. Just imagine a Dr. Sigerson or a Dr. Douglas Hyde perpetrating such anti-Celtic enormity!

"*The Scene is laid in Ireland in old times.*

ACT I.—*The cabin of* SHEMUS RHUA. *The door is at the back. The window is at the right side of it, and a little shrine of the* VIRGIN MARY *hangs at the other.*

Shemus. Satan pours the famine from his bag.
And I am mindful to go pray to him,
To cover all this table with red gold.
. . . . I would eat my supper
With no less mirth if chaired beside the hearth
Were Pooka, sowlth, or demon of the pit,
Rubbing its hands before the flame o' the pine.
[*The little shrine falls.*

Maire. Look! Look!

Shemus. [*Kicking it to pieces.*] The Mother of God has dropped asleep,
And all her household things have gone to wrack."

The "household things of the Mother of God" have gone to wrack only under the kicks of Mr. W. B. Yeats's fine old Celtic peasant. (Finest *cuvée* reserved.)

"ACT II. SCENE 2.—*Enter the two* DEMONS *disguised as merchants, with empty bags over their shoulders.*

First Merchant. And whence now, brother?
Second Merchant. Tubber-vanach cross roads,
Where I, in image of a nine-monthed bonyeen,
Sat down upon my haunches. Father John
Came, sad and moody, murmuring many prayers.
I seemed as though I came from his own sty.
He saw the one brown ear—the breviary dropped—
He ran—I ran—I ran into the quarry;
He fell a score of yards. The man was dead.
And then I thrust his soul into the bag,
And hurried home."

Good old Father John, in spite of his prayers and his breviary, killed by the devil in the shape of a brown pig! How Irish! How exquisitely Celtic!

In another scene Mr. W. B. Yeats introduces a Celtic peasant woman who is false to her marriage vows. How very Irish that is too. In another scene there are a pair of Celtic peasants who are thieves, and particularly mean thieves. Is that Irish likewise? Nowhere is there a single gleam of manliness, intelligence, or bare civilisation. The Catholic Church only appears in Shrines of the Virgin that are "kicked to pieces" by Celtic peasants, and in priests who are killed by devils in the shape of pigs. We are told that the land is full of famine, and that it is the Ireland of old days. Where was the aid of friendly and generous chiefs and clansmen to the suffering district? Where was the charitable hospitality of a hundred monastic foundations, which were afterwards to be "kicked to pieces," not by Celtic peasants, but by the reformed chivalry of England? Mr. W. B. Yeats seems to see nothing in the Ireland of old days but an unmanly, an impious and renegade people, crouched in degraded awe before demons, and goblins, and sprites, and sowlths, and thivishes,—just like a sordid tribe of black devil-worshippers and fetish-worshippers on the Congo or the Niger.

Of course Mr. W. B. Yeats is entitled to construct any "drama" he pleases, and to people it with as many abject thieves and devil-worshippers as he may please, and to preach to his heart's content the loathsome doctrine that faith and conscience can be bartered for a full belly and a full purse. Only he has no right to lay the scene in Ireland, whether of to-day or in the golden days when "Dark Rosaleen was a Sceptred Queen." He has no right to outrage reason and conscience alike by bringing his degraded idiots to receive the kiss of the Mother of God before the whole host of Heaven as reward for having preferred the gold of the devil to the providence of the All-Father.

I remain, dear Sir,

Yours faithfully,

F. HUGH O'DONNELL.

IRISH NATIONAL CLUB,
LONDON.

II.[1]*—BLASPHEMY AND DEGRADATION.*

To the Editor of THE FREEMAN'S JOURNAL.

DEAR SIR,

From some of the comments on my former letter in reference to Mr. W. B. Yeats's pseudo-Celtic drama, it would appear that my protests are held in some quarters to be specially directed against the share taken by the author in its proposed production upon an Irish stage. Quite the reverse is the case.

Mr. W. B. Yeats is a literary artist. He has found for his English readers what is described as a new vein of literary emotion. The transfusion of what is alleged to be the spirit of the Celtic Past into modern English is hailed as quite an agreeable diversification of the Stage Irishman dear to the London playwright, and the Political Irishman dear to the London caricaturist. Instead of Donnybrook and Ballyhooley, or rather by the side of these types, and, as it were, suggesting their development, the genial Anglo-Saxon is asked to regard the fine old Celtic peasant of Ireland's Golden Age, sunk in animal savagery, destitute of animal courage, mixing up in loathsome promiscuity the holiest names of the Christian Sanctuary with the gibbering ghoul-and-fetish worship of a Congo negro, selling his soul for a bellyful, yelling alternate invocations to the Prince of Darkness and the Virgin Mary. Surely this is a dainty dish to set before our sister England!

But I repeat I am only concerned in a comparatively remote degree with these achievements of literary art from the point of view of the literary artist who is their author. What infinitely more concerns all Irishmen is the sort of ratification or consecration which is obtained for such hideous travesties of Ancient or Modern Ireland by their being presented to the admiration, or followed by the bare toleration, of Irish audiences.

Even without coming to the spectators, let it be considered who or what sort can be the Irish men and women who stoop to play the actors in so unclean a medley? Take the part of Shemus Rhua, the eminently Celtic peasant, whose burst of blasphemous blackguardism welcomes the evil spirits on the scene, as he triumphantly "kicks to pieces" the Shrine of the Mother of God.

[1] This second letter was refused publication by *The Freeman's Journal.*

Who will be Shemus Rhua? And as he kicks to pieces the Holy Virgin's image in Catholic Dublin, has he secured beforehand an escort of Cromwellians and a life insurance policy?

The character of the so-called "Countess Cathleen"—there never was such a dame or damsel in baron's hall or prince's palace in all Celtic Ireland—were a tempting theme for the student of wild incoherencies. Imagine that, according to the drama, there has been wasting famine in the land for weeks and months, and the people have been feeding on docks and nettles. And all the time this "Countess" has tons of gold in her treasuries, and flocks tended by a hundred shepherds; and there are oxen to be bought by the hundred in Meath, and all the ports are open to fleets of grain ships, but not a ducat does the "Countess" spend until it is too late, when, having no alternative but the mercy of God or the gold of the devil, she, according to Mr. W. B. Yeats, hurries off to bargain her soul for the latter, and to be kissed by the Blessed Virgin in heaven for denying God and Christ the Lord. Why, why has Mr. W. B. Yeats called this thing a "Drama of Ancient Ireland"? If he had called it a "Drama of Colney Hatch" no man living would have protested.

But, as I have already intimated, it is not the wild incoherencies but the revolting blasphemies and idiotic impieties which sicken and astonish. Who can be the actors, who can be the spectators, while such repulsive lines as these are declaimed as a chapter of Celtic literature?—

"The Mother of God
Has dropped in a doze, and cannot hear the poor."

"*God and the Mother of God have dropped asleep,*
For they are weary of the prayers and the candles."

"No curses injure the immortal demons."

"Wherefore should you sadden
For wrongs you cannot hinder? *The great God,*
Smiling, condemns the lost."

What actors—what amateurs—impersonate before Dublin people the two Demon Merchants, the buyers of souls, whose cynical impieties drivel on in wearying monotony? Take these neo-Celtic lines spoken by one merchant as he watches the heroine, and thus blithely mocks at the Christian God as deaf to prayer and supplication:

"*First Merchant*. She lies worn out upon the altar steps:
A labourer tired of ploughing *His hard fields,*
And deafening *His closed ears* with cries on cries,
Hoping to draw His hands down from the stars
To take the people from us."

The second demon is so struck with the fantastic "Cathleen," that he declares that nothing more than the possession of such a precious person is wanting in order to make the crown of Satan *equal to the Glory of God!*

"*Second Merchant*. How may we gain this woman for our lord?
This pearl, this turquoise, fastened in his crown
Would make it shine *like His we dare not name*."

What hideous silliness, and what hideous profanity! The perdition of one lost woman is to make the devil's majesty resplendent as. . . . But the utter idiotcy of it all puts even the impiety in the shade. I will not ask if Mr. W. B. Yeats has any sense of reverence. But has he any good taste, any sense of the becoming and the decent? The veriest spirit-rapper or table-turner might shrink from impropriety so vile.

But if Irish amateurs and Irish spectators may be somewhat embarrassed with the major personages of Mr. W. B. Yeats's heroines and demons, will there be much improvement for the players of the minor parts of common Celtic peasants and common Celtic people? Is this the picture which Irishmen would have drawn of their Celtic Ireland, with its miserable, spiritless slaves crowding "noisy as seagulls tearing a dead fish" to bargain away their Faith for Gold?—

"*First Peasant*. I fell on Shemus Rhua and his son,
And they led me where *two great gentlemen*
Buy souls for money, and they bought my soul.
I told my friend here—my friend also trafficked.
Second Peasant. His words are true.
First Peasant. Now people throng to sell,
Noisy as seagulls tearing a dead fish.
There soon will be no man or woman's soul
Unbargained for in five-score baronies."

What a contemptible Ireland is the Ireland of Mr. W. B. Yeats's neo-Celtic fantastications! Not an Irish man or woman in "five-score baronies" to prefer Faith and Honour to a full belly in the Devil's Kitchen.

But the mud-slinging at Faith and Fatherland and Manhood would be incomplete without some up-to-date appreciations of Irish Womanhood as well. What contempt, what suggestiveness of foulness comes out of this sketch of a poor "Celtic" wretch bargaining for her soul's price with the Fiend:

"*A Woman*. What price, now, will you give for mine?
First Merchant. Ay, ay,
Soft, handsome, and still young,—not much, I think.
[*Reading in a parchment*.
'She has love-letters in a little jar
On a high shelf behind the pepper-pot
And wood-cased hour-glass."
The Woman. O, the scandalous parchment!
First Merchant. [*Reading*.] '*She hides them from her husband, who buys horses,*
And is not much at home.' You are almost safe.
I give you fifty crowns. [*She turns to go*.
A hundred, then?
[*She takes them, and goes into the crowd*."

Going, going, gone! An Irish wife—an unchaste Irish wife—secured for hell for a hundred crowns! The Celtic Muse of W. B. Yeats is tireless in its flattering appreciations of the Irish nation. Its men, apostate cowards; its women—such as this; its priests, the prey of demon swine; its shrines, kicked to pieces by its Celtic peasantry; the awful majesty of the Christian God flouted and mocked by spirits from the pit! What is the meaning of this rubbish? How is it to help the national cause? How is it to help any cause at all? Mysticism? Nonsense! This is not Mysticism. The great mystics are intellectual and moral glories of Christian civilisation. This is only silly stuff, and sillier, unutterable profanity.

Where can you find actors, amateur or professional, for such offensiveness? Where can you get an audience? Not among Catholics. Not among Protestants. Not among Nationalists of any manly race or nation. There is rich material, there is a noble mission, for a Celtic Theatre in Ireland. The story of our race is full of themes the most tender, the most tragic, the most heroic, the most divine. From the waters that heard the lament of the Swan Children, to the legend-haunted Glens of Kerry;—from the mead where fell the Dane, to the shore whence the Wild Geese flew away;—our land is full of memories such as were never outrivalled in the dramatic poetry of any country of the world. If the mind has not arisen which could be the Æschylus or

Sophocles of such a history, at least there is no reason for tolerating the preposterous absurdity—"made in Germany," it is now explained[2]—which would degrade Ancient Ireland into this sort of witch's cavern of ghouls and vampires, and abject men and women, and blaspheming shapes from hell. I am sorry to have to say this, but it must be said.

F. HUGH O'DONNELL.

Yours faithfully,

IRISH NATIONAL CLUB
LONDON.

[2] The precious "Celtic Legend of Countess Cathleen" is a nightmare yarn found in some German magazine.

INDEX

NOTE

Newspaper references can be found under their country of origin, as "American Journals and Papers" and "English and Irish Papers and Journals"